jean hureau

syria today

**92 pages of colour photographs
15 maps and plans**

éditions j.a.

syria today

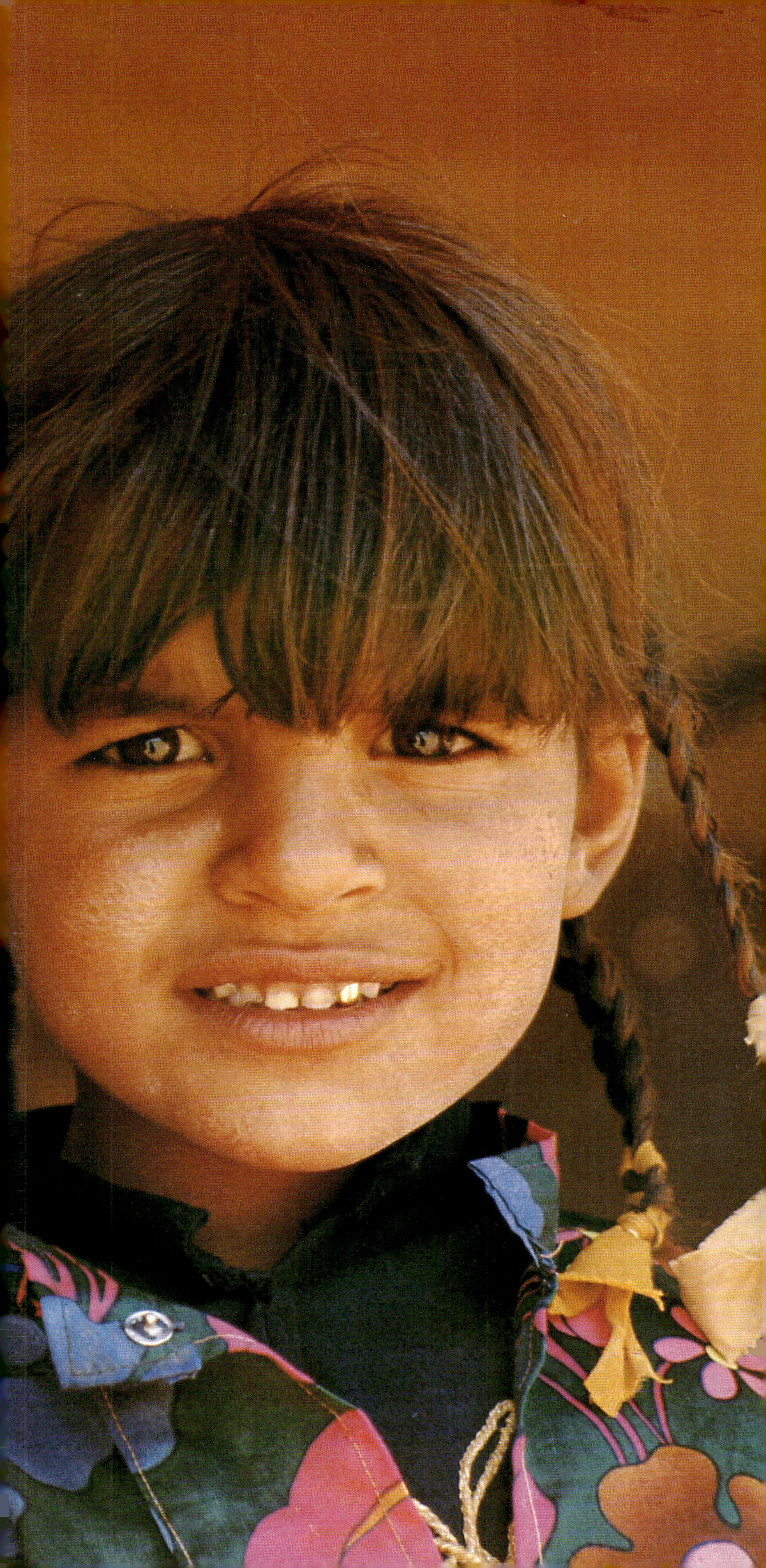

contents

Cover: *Syria, a land of history where monuments of many periods stand side by side. Here in Damascus the Roman Temple of Jupiter and the Islamic Umayyad Mosque (photo J. Prevost, Explorer). Unless specified otherwise all photographs are by Jean Hureau*

Previous page: *All the determination and the kindness, so typical of Syria today, can be read on the face of this Syrian citizen of tomorrow. (Photo Jacques Guillard)*

Following page: *This panoramic view of Palmyra has all the essential hall-marks of Syria: mountains, desert, a lush oasis and the presence of an age-old past in a modern setting. (Photo Bruno Barbey, Magnum)*

panorama

8	**the land and its people**
8	little known and misundestood
13	a proud nation
13	the heart of the Arab people
17	a wedge thrust into Asia
17	the apex of a fertile crown
17	regions and natural divisions
21	a coast dominated by mountains
21	the Orontes, or nahr al-Asi
21	the Zaouiye and the hills of the dead
25	the Sharqi and the Damascus region
25	the desert and the steppes
29	the Euphrates, river of life
32	**Syria for the tourist**
32	A crossroads of climates, commerce and ideas
35	humanity and culture
35	things particularly Syrian
39	five years for development tourism pact
47	**the syrian economy**
51	industry: scope for development
52	duty free zones and Damascus Fair
54	**human Syria**
55	a living folklore
59	education
59	women in Syria
59	the Syrian Arab Republic
62	**An immensely long history**
62	one November...
65	the human melting pot
66	a very present past
67	an Arab presence in Syria for the past 50 centuries
67	allies with Egypt
68	Assyria, Babylon and Persia
68	a subtle game with Rome
69	Zenobia or avenging pride
69	three centuries of uneasy christianity
70	the spread of Islam
72	damascus the Umayyad capital
72	the revenge of the Alids
73	a war of liberation lasting two hundred years
76	Nur ad-Din
76	Salah ad-Din the liberator
78	the mamluk builders
80	Faisal and colonialist intrigues
81	resistance and independence

town by town site by site

84	aleppo (halab)
96	apamea (qalaat al-mudiq)
101	baniyas
102	bara (al-)
104	bosra
108	crac des chevaliers (qalaat al-hosn)
115	damascus (dimashq ash sham)
130	deir ez-zor
132	doura europos
133	ezraa
134	hama (hamaa)
142	homs
145	idlib
147	jable
148	jisr ash-shugur
150	latakia (al-ladhiqiya)
153	maalula
156	maarat ann-numan
157	mari (tell hariri)
158	marquab (qalaat marqab)
160	masyaf
162	palmyra (tadmor)
173	qalaat najm
175	qalaat salah ad-din
177	qalaat samaan (saint siméon)
180	qalb loza
182	qamashli
183	qanawat
184	qnaytra
185	raqqa
188	ras al-basit
189	rasafa
191	safita
192	shahba
193	shaizar (qalaat shaizar)
194	suwayda
196	tartus (tartous)
201	thaura (al-) (tabqa)
202	ugarit (ras shamra)
208	zabadani-bludan

Many other sites are are described under the main headings above. They are all listed in the alphabetical index at the end of the book.

syrian journey

212	**getting to syria**
212	by air, road, rail and sea
213	information and formalities
213	police
213	customs
214	health
214	syria by road, rail and air
216	**essential information:**
216	currency and exchange facilities
216	days and times
216	freedom and communication
216	climate and health
217	festivals and fairs
217	restaurants in damascus
218	**a thousand souvenirs**
219	cooking and food
220	drinks
220	accommodation
220	younger visitors
220	camping
221	**the hotels of syria**
226	**syria fifteen maps**
226	getting to syria
228	syria: administration and communications
230	syria: natural and tourist regions
232	history and archaeology
234	syria in 8, 15, 30 days
238	palmyra
241	crac des chevaliers
242	damascus
245	syrian national museum
246	environs damascus
248	aleppo
251	the coast and the orontes valley
252	environs of aleppo
254	**general index**

Spellings of place names in this guide are usually those used on the road and tourist map prepared by the Ministry of Communications and published by the Ministry of Tourism.
The main variant forms and some phonetic renderings as well as old forms, are given in the text and repeated in the general index.

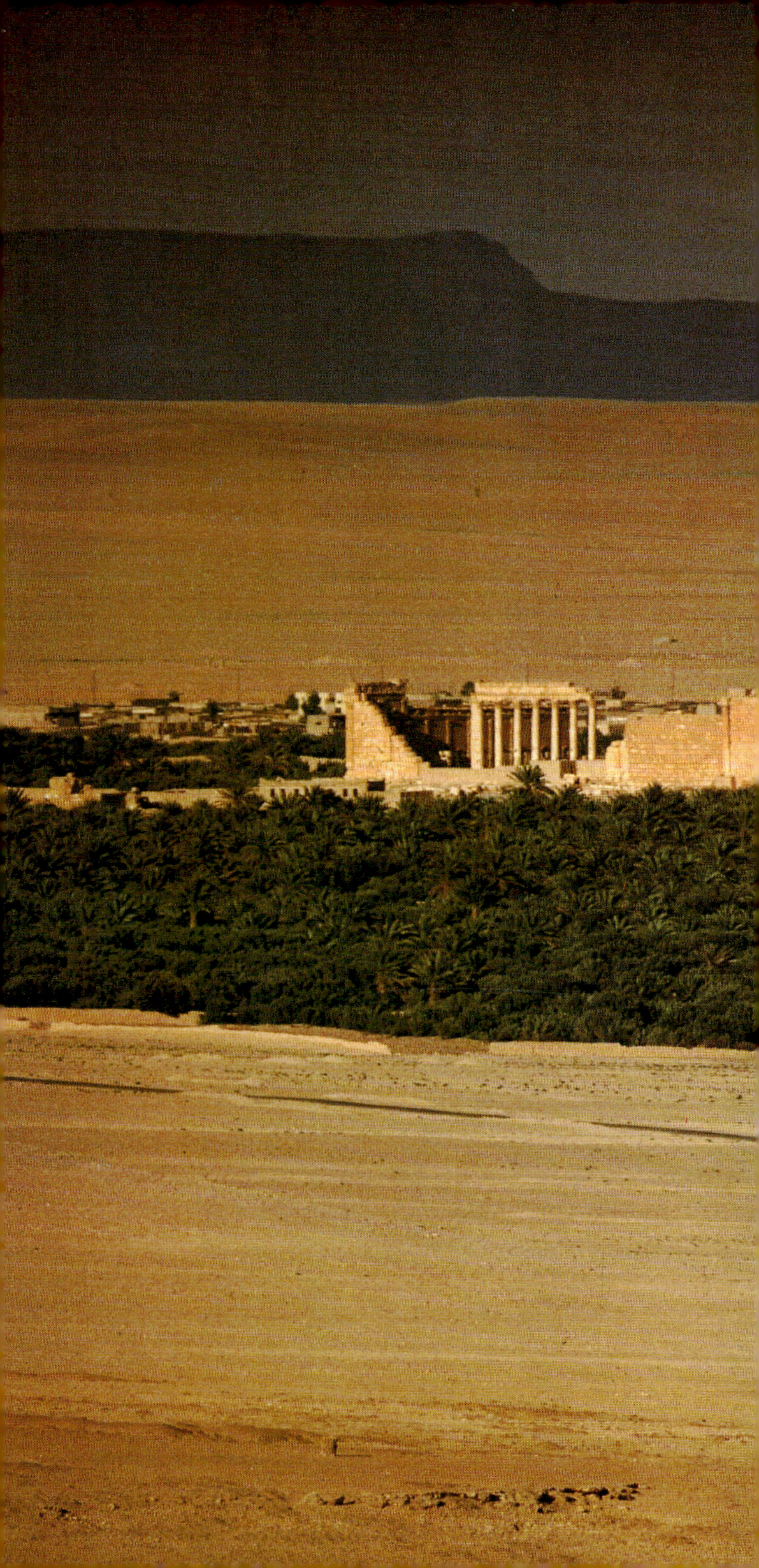

panorama

the land and its people

■ Syria is a remarkable country. It is both little known and misunderstood. Even its official name—The Syrian Arab Republic—is unfamiliar to many foreigners. The Syrian flag, composed of red, white, and black horizontal bands, with three green five-pointed stars on the central white band, is sometimes confused with other flags. And these are only some examples.

Little-known; misunderstood

Clichés and stereotypes, to use a sociological term, abound concerning Syria.

Syria?—"A desert country"... We all remember "The Great Syrian Desert"—from the chapter on Mesopotamia in our school textbooks. Yet less than twenty per cent is waste land and even this proportion is decreasing year by year thanks to the gradual improvement of the arid zones.

"A land of nomads"... Western minds seem still bemused by nineteenth-century travellers' tales and pictures of the Romantic Orient. Yet the briefest excursion into any part of the country reveals a tough, peasant people; hard-working, going early to bed and rising early; men and women working the fields by hand or with machines to wrest as much as possible from an often reluctant soil.

"A turbulent and warlike country"... After all aren't we always reading about its involvement in some crisis that's hit the headlines? There is a grain of truth in this. Yet it is to his credit if the Syrian is prepared to proudly fight and die defending his country—as the Parthians, the Romans and the Crusaders all learned to their cost. But it is hard to foist dreams of hegemony and conquest on a country which is undertaking—when times are far from settled—an enterprise on the scale of the Euphrates Dam. Nor do the young people of Syria look particularly warlike as they wander through field and orchard, books in hand, attentively studying mathemat-

*Syrians like good workmanship.
Despite modernization old crafts,
such as silk-spinning, are still practised
and esteemed.*

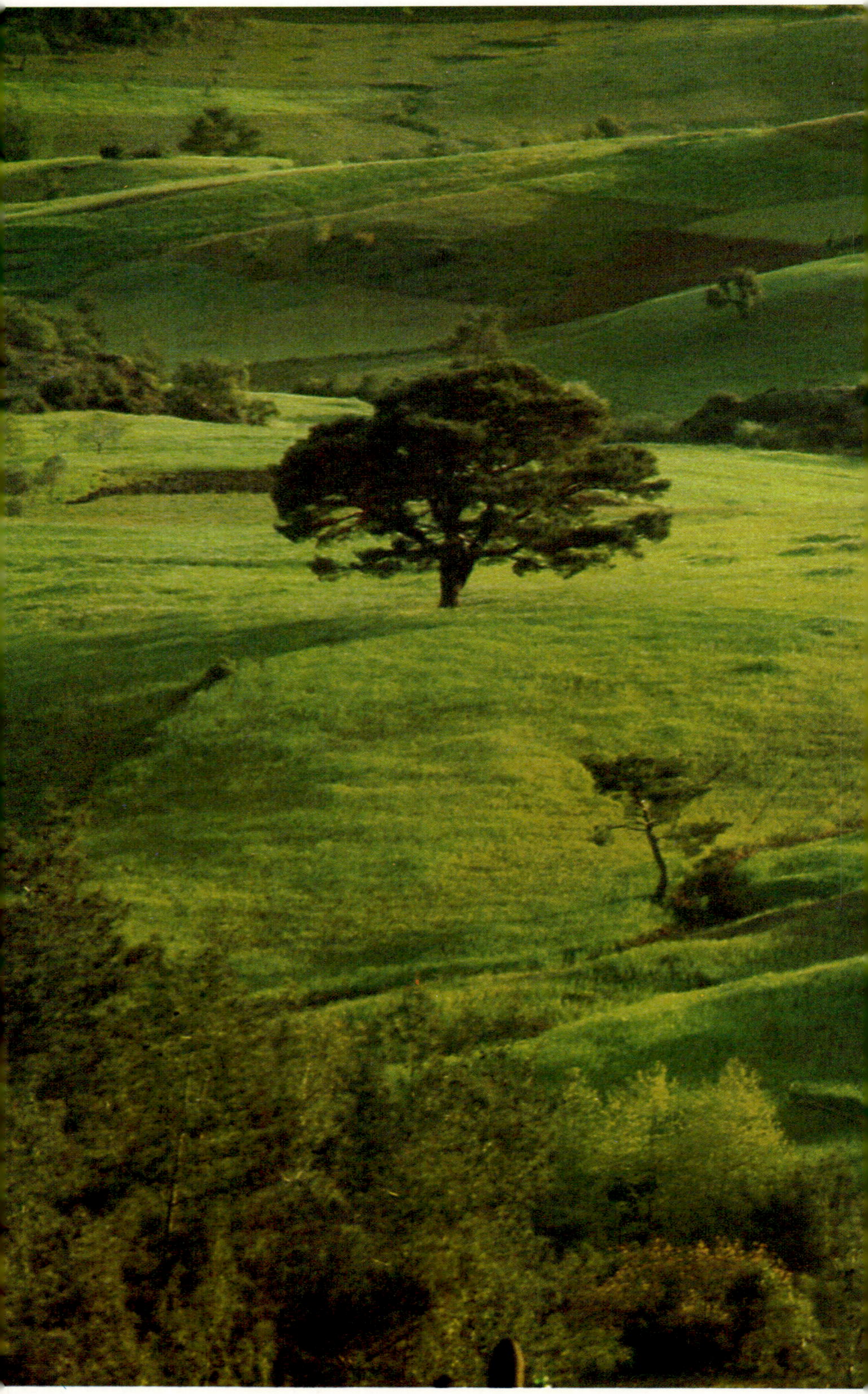

*Verdant Syria—this is no paradox.
An are of green encircles the central steppes.
Here at Slenfe, above Latakia, the Mediterranean slopes
of the Coastal Chain, are covered with
orchards and cornfields.
(photo Bruno Barbey, Magnum).*

From the earliest times Syrians have been master builders. The Citadel of Aleppo, defying wind and time, is a fine example; its multicoloured stones and decoration are extremely beautiful.
(photo Bruno Barbey, Magnum).

ics, languages or philosophy. Both in bearing and in speech the Syrian is calm, composed and reflective. He does not raise his voice and there is often just a faint smile on his face.

The fact that such stereotypes —and others just as false—are so often bandied about, stems in fact from traits noticeable in the individual Syrian and in the people as a whole. They are timid, modest, somewhat reticent. Such attitudes explain to some degree their violent reactions when their pride is hurt.

This undoubted reticence could, on the administrative level, be interpreted as a deliberate neglect of "public relations". Other countries make much of achievements, inundating us with photographs of blossoming deserts, gigantic dams, model farms, motorways, national airlines, five star hotels; or perhaps they ostentatiously display their artistic treasures, the work of their craftsmen or their great cultural achievements. Syria too could show herself off like this. She does not do so. Fortunately the birth of a tourist industry is gradually allowing her to overcome her scruples and reveal her great charm and interest to a growing number of visitors from abroad.

A proud and self-confident nation

Syria is a peaceable nation and is directing her main effort to systematic development, often in the face of many difficulties. Agriculture, energy, civil engineering, chemicals and metallurgy—all are being developed according to carefully thought-out programmes. The Constitution of 12 March 1973 defines the Syrian Arab Republic as a "popular socialist democracy" with a "planned economy"; but these principles are not applied in a rigid or restrictive way; investment of foreign capital is warmly encouraged, for example, and large sectors of the economy remain free for private enterprise.

The Syrian is not a boaster and prefers to make an impression by his tenacity, competence, and his taste for study, rather than by putting on a show. Syrian doctors, teachers and engineers are rated highly throughout the Middle East.

This inclination on the part of the Syrian state to play a background role, together with the calm self-assurance of its citizens, has its roots deep in history. It may be summed up in a phrase—often repeated as a slogan—to the effect that "Syria is the beating heart of the Arab nation."

The heart of the Arab people

Syria was an Arab kingdom long before the Arabs achieved glory with the coming of Islam, and has long been the home of Arab nationalism. Before becoming, under the Umayyads, the capital of the Muslim world Damascus had for fifteen centuries spoken and written a language which was the direct ancestor of modern Arabic. Today Damascus prides herself, together with Aleppo, on being the oldest continuously inhabited city in the world. Aleppo now has a population of 700,000 while Damascus is approaching the two million mark.

Such roots give the country stability. Moreover they lend her two important qualities: a certain wisdom in the face of current events—no matter how dramatic, and a tolerance of minorities and of differing creeds. Many Christians of various denominations, full citizens of Syria, can bear witness to the latter.

The visitor from abroad, struck by the wholly Arab context of Syrian life, baffled by its novelty perhaps, at first, is soon entranced both by the evident signs of a rich and deeply rooted culture and by the hospitality, kindliness and friendliness of a people both masters in their own house and masters of themselves as well.

Syria, so much a unity linguistically, historically and politically, is a country of great natural diversity.

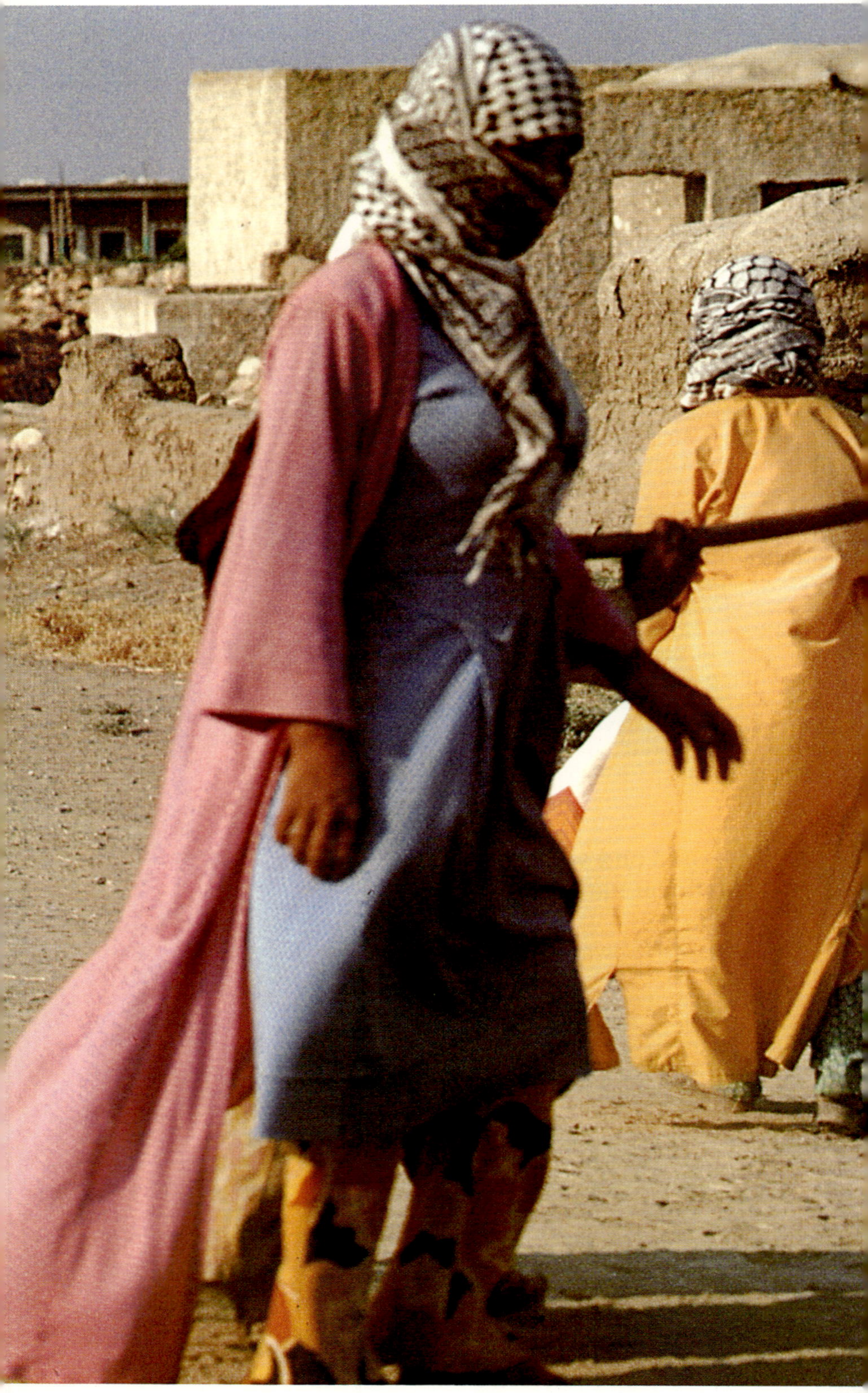

*The peasant women from the uplands
are warmly wrapped up against the winter cold
and the winds that blow relentlessly
across the central steppes.*

*The capital, Damascus, has grown up around
the splendid Umayyad Mosque.
It stands on the foundations of earlier temples,
of which occasional columns still rise amid
the urban sprawl.
(photo Robert Azzi, Magnum).*

This contrast between cultural unity and varied landscape is ideal for tourism. The visitor to Syria can follow an unbroken thread on the human level, in the arts and in folklore, while at the same time enjoying a constant change of scene which makes even the longest journey interesting.

A wedge thrust into Asia

From its regular, almost geometric, outline one might conclude that the country's frontiers had been determined quite arbitrarily in the absence of outstanding natural features. Yet this vast triangular wedge, thrust into the flank of Western Asia, has the river Tigris at its apex and the Mediterranean as its base. The high, rugged mountains of the eastern Taurus dominate the northern frontier, whilst those between Syria, Jordan and Iraq run in straight lines, across steppe and desert. These few names alone conjure up a variety of colour, vegetation and habitat.

Syria has an area of 185,180 square kilometres (cf. Britain's 244,000) and 2,413 kilometres of frontiers.

But more than distances and differences of longitude, two factors determine the variety of the landscape. In the west there are two mountain ranges—the Sharqi, which forms Syria's frontier with Lebanon, and whose highest peak is the Jebel Al-Shaikh (2,814 metres):—and the Jebal Ansariya, or coastal range, which rises without a break from the Mediterranean shore. In the centre there is the mighty furrow of the Euphrates, the first third of its course now widened by the blue waters of Lake Al-Assad, some fifty kilometres long.

The great green arc of fertile Syria begins in the south-west, follows the coastline, takes in the valley of the Orontes, then Aleppo, widens as it crosses the Euphrates, and finally peters out in the Khabur valley.

The apex of a fertile crown

According to soil, altitude, the caprices of nature and the often considerable works of man, this is a land of cornfields, orchards and sometimes of cotton plantations—heralds of future industry—stretching away to the horizon.

Throughout this vast sweep every possible square inch of land is under cultivation. The peasants plough right up to the edge of the great desert, snatching the last few square yards of poor soil from the goats who would otherwise graze there. And right to the top of the arid jabals every possible sheltered terrace is meticulously cultivated; the peasants scouring the very crevices of the karstic uplands for a few shovelfuls of red earth that the storms have not yet washed away.

The yields of course vary greatly. The rich harvests of the Ghab contrast with some very meagre ones indeed. The combine-harvester gives way to the scythe—or even the sickle where the crop is very sparse. The cherry trees of Idlib, the apricots of Blondau and the figs of Al-Bara offer a lush contrast to the pathetic vines that cling to the volcanic rocks of the jabal al-Arab and the the scrawny almond and stunted olive trees struggling for life an the eroded northern hills near the ruins of abandoned towns.

Regions and natural divisions

Syria is divided, for administrative purposes, into fourteen "mouhafazats", which are governorships rather than provinces. These official divisions, each with its headquarters in a large town, do not always coincide with a distinct geographical area, let alone a tourist one.

Yet there are several large natural divisions—defined by climate or ter-

18 PANORAMA

*An essential stopping-place between the Indian Ocean
and the Mediterranean, Tadmor-Palmyra brought
luxury to the desert. A view (by courtesy
of the telephoto lens)
of the Great Colonnade and the Arab Castle.
(photo Bruno Barbey, Magnum).*

*The creaking of the norias pervades.
The town of Hama on the Orontes is alive
with the sound of the norias—
reminiscent of the harsh and plangent cry of the muezzin...*

rain—which the traveller can easily identify both on the map and on the ground. The contrasts between them are often striking.

A coast dominated by mountains

The seaboard: 183 kilometres of coastline, lowlying (except in the extreme north, between Ras al-Basit and the frontier) often dead-straight, bounded by a narrow plain where early vegetables and fruit are grown in vast quantities. Latakia, Syria's largest port, has been joined recently by two oil outlets, at Baniyas and Tartous, which are still being developed.

Dominating the Mediterranean shore, and only a few kilometres inland as the crow flies, is a jagged but continous mountain ridge; it runs north-south at an altitude of 1,200 to 1,600 metres. This coastal chain, known as the jabal Ansariya, is a high limestone barrier and it dominates the whole Syrian coast. Historically it has been an obstacle to communications between the coast and the hinterland (there is virtually only one road across it) and it effectively prevents the Mediterranean rainclouds from moving inland. Its seaward slopes are split by steep, tortuous ravines; between them the terraced hillsides, with villages and fortresses perched on rocky outcrops, form a highly picturesque landscape.

The western side, by contrast, falls away abruptly in a series of almost sheer cliffs, beneath which the nahr al-Assi, the river Orontes, flows northwards.

There are now two roads across the coastal mountains: the one in the south leads through the historic Homs gap; the northern one follows the valleys of the Khabir and its tributaries and is much more dramatic. The northern road has recently been paralleled by a railway, whose construction was quite a feat of engineering.

The Orontes, the nahr al-Assi or Rebel

Rising near Baalbeck (see "Lebanon Today" in this series) the Orontes (Arabic nahr al-Assi, "the rebel river") flows into Syria south of Homs; here a dam, said to date from the times of the Pharaohs, holds back its fertilizing waters. Thence, until very recently, it flowed unimpeded except by the ancient waterwheels or "norias" at Hama, along the foot of the coastal chain. Then the mighty Orontes, of which the poets sang, simply drained away in the fever-infested marshes of the plain of Ghab.

To tame the Orontes and make its valley healthy was one of the first tasks of independent Syria. This aim has now been fulfilled. The surrounding countryside has been transformed; harvests there are the richest in all Syria, and industry is being developed around the dams at Homs and Hama.

The Zaouiye and the hills of the dead

A series of jabals on the right bank of the Orontes runs parallel to the coastal chain, so that the Ghab is a long deep corridor only a few kilometres wide. This can be clearly seen from the heights of Qalaat el-Muiq, Apamea in ancient times.

The most important mountain mass here is the al-Zaouiye. This chain is lower and gentler than the coastal range and it gives way to fertile uplands of which those of the Idlib region are the most beautiful. These green and populous parts contrast with the ridges above, with their outcrops of sheer grey rocks; they are now almost deserted. This is a dramatic landscape born of a dramatic history.

In the seventh and eighth centuries a series of disasters struck the region. Earthquakes shook the towns and the peaks were swept by violent storms which washed the soil down

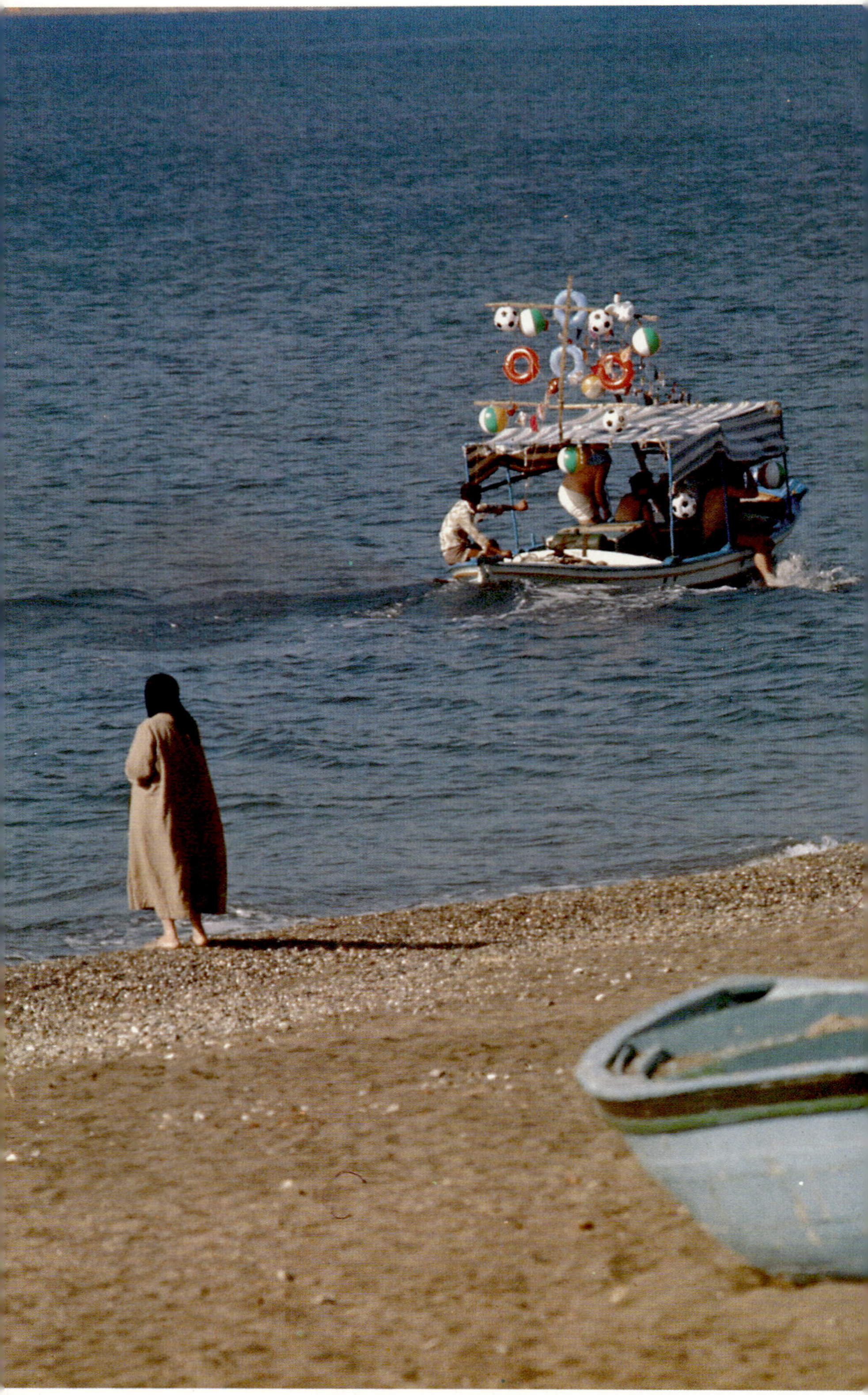

*Syria has a sea coast too. Her window
on the Mediterranean has many sites which could become
attractive resorts.—Here is Ras al-Basit,
where various developments are planned.
(photo Jacques Guillard).*

Maalula is one of the most picturesque villages in Syria. Its houses cling to the cliffs like some gigantic honeycomb in which every cell is painted white or yellow, violet or blue. (photo Jacques Guillard).

to the bottoms of the valleys and scoured the limestone rocks leaving them bare and deeply fissured. At the same time economic changes and political upheaval, following the spread of Islam and the ascendancy of Damascus over Aleppo, speeded the departure of the inhabitants and the ruin of towns that had flourished until then. Today the "ghost towns" of the north—one of the sights of Syria—are mere shadows of their former selves.

The Sharqi and the Damascus region

The jabal ash Sharqi range is the Anti-Lebanon to the Lebanese. The Syrian-Lebanese frontier follows its ridge, which rises to peaks where the snows linger until the middle of Spring. The highest points are, in the north, the Talat Musa, 2,659 metres, and in the south, the majestic jabal ash Sheikh (the Mount Hermon of the Bible), 2, 814 metres. —The latter takes its name from its cap of snow which looks an immaculate turban on the head of some venerable tribal, chief, a "sheikh".

Many watercourses rise in this range, frequently gushing down in torrents at first—only to slacken and divide many times before finally disappearing, on the very edge of the desert, into ill-defined lakes. The most famous of them is the river Barada, whose upper valley is a veritable Garden of Eden, and whose middle reaches have enabled Damascus to blossom—for the past two thousand years—in the midst of its lush oasis, the Ghouta.

Remnants of past grandeur

To the north and south of Damascus there are limestone uplands where cereal crops are grown. Villages are rare here, huddled around a waterhole, strung out along a drainage channel, or clinging—as at Maalula—to a hollow in the cliffs, taking advantage of a nearby spring. In the stoniest parts the vines refresh the eye with a splash of green.

As you approach the Jordanian frontier the landscape changes colour. Limestone gives way to basalt and lava. The soil is black; the villages are black. Remnants of past grandeur seem to defy the passage of time but the ruins—sometimes impressive, as at Bosra, Qanawat and in a dozen half-deserted villages—are sober, solid, almost primitive, and display no useless decoration.

The hills are extinct volcanoes. Here, to the west, lie the Golan heights, while to the east is the jabal al-Arab (formerly known as the jabal Druzze) where the inhabitants proudly keep themselves to themselves.

The deserts and the steppes

The Aleppo-Damascus highway and its continuation towards Suweida marks a clear limit to the cultivated and cultivable lands. To the east, extending as far as the Euphrates, is a high plateau between 800 and 1,200 metres above sea level from whose bare expanses ranges of hills rise here there.

This vast area has an annual average rainfall of only 200 millimetres a year—which means that in some years parts of it never get the slightest drop of water.

A distinction may be drawn between the fairly wide peripheral zone of steppe, where there is some vegetation and even scanty cereal crops are grown, and the desert proper which extends south of Palmyra, on both sides of the Damascus-Bagdad road, and far beyond the frontiers, into Jordan and Iraq.

In the steppe zone there are many flocks of sheep and goats, which move slowly across the sun-drenched landscape in search of what passes there for pasture. In the villages around the fringe the houses cluster together like cells in a bee-hive, their walls made of mud and their roofs

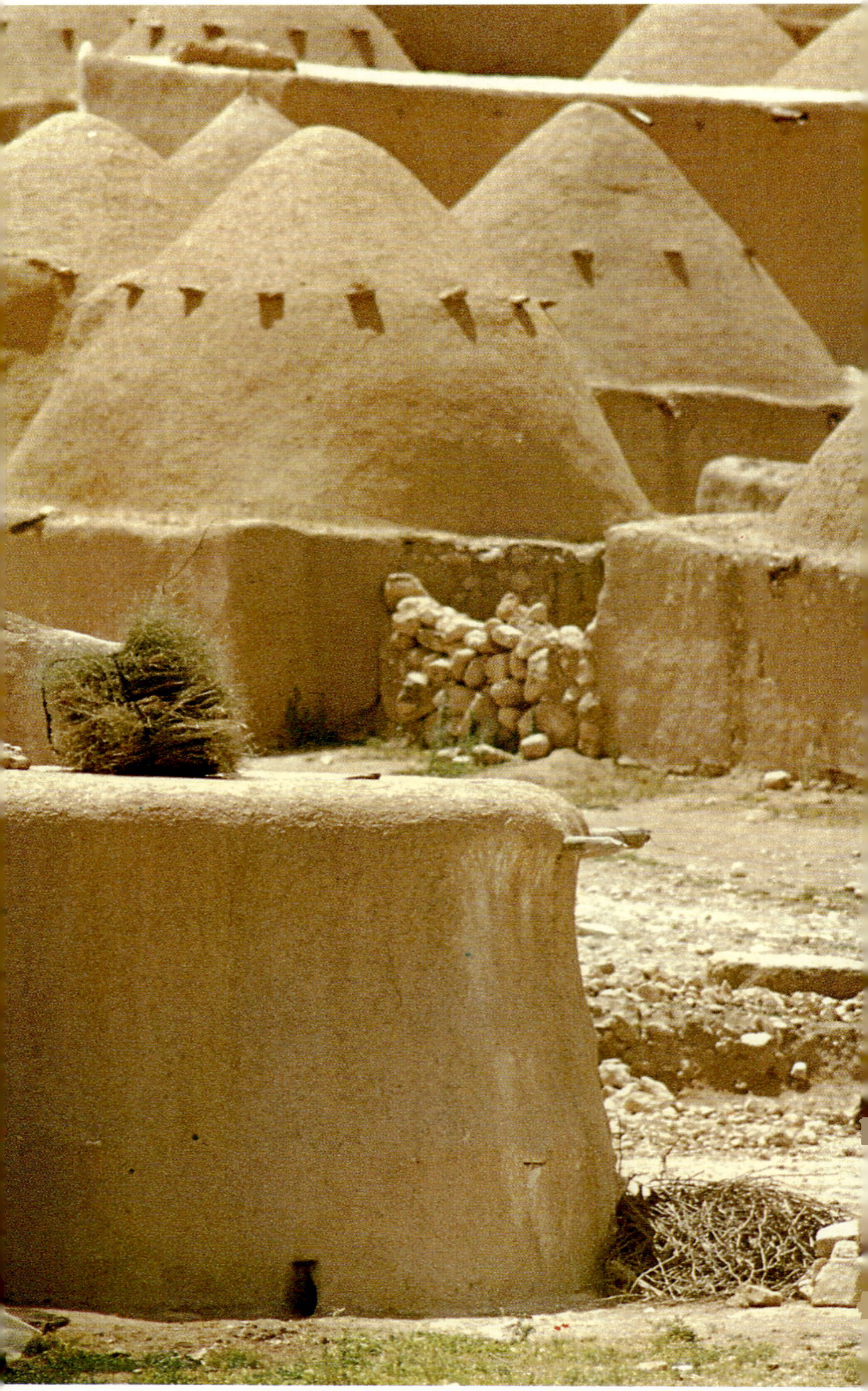

*Excursions to little-known parts of Syria enable the visitor
to see typical unspoiled villages where the inhabitants,
shy at first, will soon give him a warm welcome.
Above: one of the villages on Lake Al-Assad (near Al-Thaura)
where traditional architectural styles, well adapted
to the climate, have been used.*

*History is no mere abstraction in Syria.
The events of a glorious past rise to greet us everywhere.
A view of the great fortified entrance to the Citadel
of Aleppo. (Photo Jacques Guillard.)*

like sugar-loaves—ideal protection against the rigours of the climate. Here too, to the north of Palmyra, a few waterholes have given birth to small oases such as Arak, Sukne, and Qariatein.

Palmyra, in the very centre of this arid zone, offers a pleasant contrast. This ancient capital, with abundant water from a generous spring, has wealth of many kinds to show—olives, fruit and palm trees, and, more recently, phosphates and iron ore. The inhabitants no longer bother to gather the resin from the turpentine trees which grow on the desert hills; they are preparing to replace the caravans with which they used to trade with more lucrative caravans of tourists, attracted here by the marvellous remains of Palmyra's days of glory.

The Euphrates, river of life

The Euphrates, a river both mythical and historic, a corridor through which civilisations and migrations have passed, a frontier for which the blood of Empires has been shed. The Euphrates is the great good fortune of present-day Syria.

After having cut its way through steep gorges on entering the country, the Euphrates, heavy with mud from the Taurus mountains, used to meander sluggishly along. Today, as the result of a Herculean effort, these same waters feed an immense reservoir from which 640,000 hectares of previously unproductive land are now irrigated. Lake Al-Assad, several kilometres wide, stretches like a blue mirror under the white cliffs for more than 50 kilometres. Harnassed at Al-Thaura (see entry under this name) by eight groups of giant turbines the waters of the Euphrates will first of all make Syria self-sufficent in energy. Soon the will enable her to develop heavy industry and become an exporter of electric power.

Downstream from Al-Thaura (literally "city of the Revolution") the Euphrates continues to wind its way peacefully along its verdant valley, between trees and gardens, surveyed here and there by an ancient fortress on a spur round which the river flows.

The right bank, which is followed closely by the Aleppo-Baghdad highway, is the same tawny colour as the central uplands: steppe and desert are not far away. The few depressions that lead down to the river are merely the beds of permanently dried up wadis. On the other side two respectable tributaries flow into the Euphrates. These are the Balikh and the Khabur, swollen in their turn by the torrents that gush down from the mountains of Turkey. Vast works are planned to regulate the flow of these rivers in the same way as the Euphrates. Already the lower areas are planted with cotton as far as the eye can see; the uplands will become the principal granary of Syria. If we add that it is around Qaratchok (not far from the valley of the Tigris) that oil deposits have been exploited since 1968 it becomes quite clear just how important, for Syria as a whole, are the Euphrates and these distant regions of the north west. □

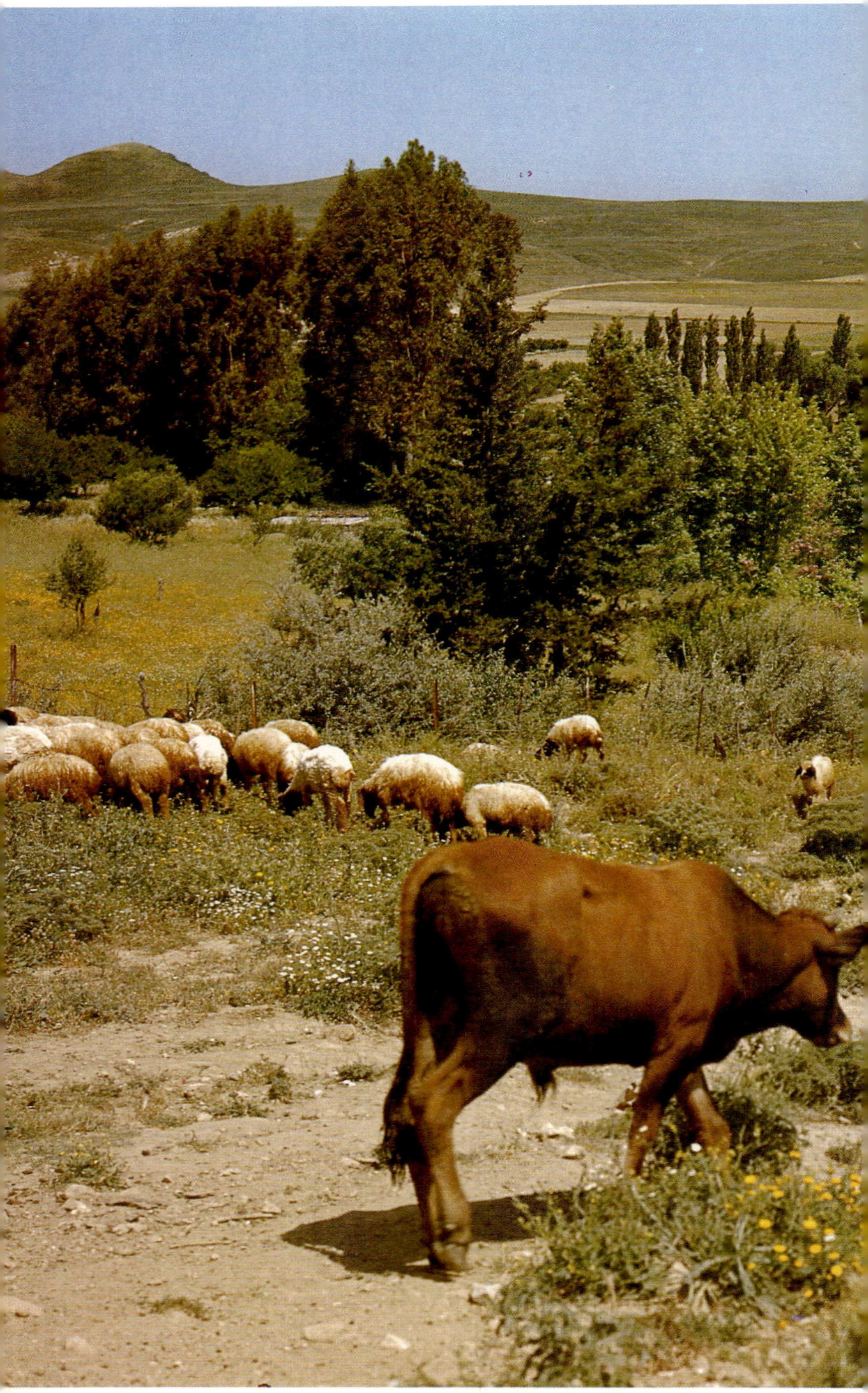

Syria has lovely countryside too. The nahr al-Khabir, which joins the sea near Latakia, is typical of the coastal rivers which flow —sometimes very swiftly—down to the Mediterranean creating gardens as they pass.

syria for the tourist

■ Syria's geography, political structures, and economic realities and aspirations are little known and misunderstood abroad. Her wealth of interest for the visitor is all too often quite unknown to outsiders, particularly to Europeans. They are missing so much!

A crossroads of climates, commerce, and ideas

By virtue of its very position on the globe Syria has been, from time immemorial both a crossroads and a centre.

A passage between the Mediterranean and the Indian Ocean, between the Black Sea and the Nile, Syria has always been—and still remains—a meeting place and a home of civilisation. The oil piplines of today follow the ancient "Silk Road"... and the craftsmen of Damascus are still the most skilled in all the Middle East.

Different peoples have made their way up the age-old Euphrates, have descended from the fastnesses of Anatolia or from distant Altai, have energed from the sands of Arabia, galloped down from Macedonia or from Vézelay... All have left a part of themselves behind in Syria—their crafts, their stories, their gods. But the natives of the place, the men of Ugarit and Mari, of Aradus and Tadmor, Halap (Aleppo) and Ash-Sham (Damascus), the ancient Amorrites and Arameans and their present-day Arab descendants, have always displayed an originality of some kind. From the unknown inventor of the alphabet to the engineers of the Ministry for the Euphrates—not forgetting the architects of Queen Zenobia or the scholars of the Umayyads—the line remains unbroken. The Syrian personality has a recognizable face.

How then could this country fail to attract the visitor? How could it fail to capture the interest of anyone interested in "finding out about the world"—if we can thus describe, perhaps flattering him somewhat, the "true" tourist?

Bosra, an interesting town bypassed by today's highways, has an astonishing Roman theatre in the middle of its Arab citadel. Performances are given here during the summer. (Photo Kromli, Ministry of Tourism.)

*The cool drinks seller who goes
from shop to shop through the souks of Damascus
and Aleppo may look picturesque—
but he is certainly no anachronism.*

Humanity and culture

Syria cannot claim to rival those privileged countries whom Nature and circumstances have endowed with all the most sophisticated attractions and amusements.

Syrians have only recently begun to turn their attention to planning for leisure. This is scarcely surprising when one considers the years of tension and difficulty through which their country has passed. Understandably there are still gaps to be made up—in the provision of hotels, car hire, and the facilities available at some sites. But recent achievements, in hotel building, legal provisions, and in the training of specialized staff, give great hope for the future. The keenness and goodwill of the Ministry of Tourism is manifest. Syria's occasional shortcomings in this field are merely the result of a late start.

Moreover it must be admitted that, with certain exceptions, (e.g. the Zaouiye mountains mentioned earlier) Nature has not blessed Syria with dramatic and impressive scenery—although it always has character and interest.

In short a journey to Syria is above all a voyage of discovery in which the main elements are art, history, culture and human contact. It is the towns that hold the main interest for the visitor, as well as the spectacle of a country undergoing rapid and fundamental social change. What strikes one most is the essentially different and Syrian quality of all these things. A visit to Syria offers a complete, and delightful, change.

A complete change

Syria is Islamic soil. It is moreover where the Orient begins. Syria is a Mediterranean bridge-head into Asia, but it is also the home of the Arab people. These factors alone are a guarantee of its unique character.

Comparisons with other Muslim countries—those of the Maghreb for example—are not very useful. Syria, mercifully, never having been a colony with a foreign, land-owning population, her people have no extraneous barrier between them and their history. Their habits, traditions and language have suffered no painful hiatus.

One senses the differentness of Syria at every street-corner, at every bend in a country road...

What a different world it is when you plunge into the souks of Aleppo or Damascus, seething pedestrian labyrinths right at the heart of cities buzzing with traffic. Here there are thousands of skilful craftsmen, plying trades almost unchanged for centuries, still at work in cities where modernity is all the rage!

What different world it is where a kindly peasant offers a cucumber, a pomegranate or a handful of cherries to the stranger he meets by the roadside; where a student goes out of his way—quite unasked—to put a visitor back on the right road; where the smiling waiter in a simple café places a rose beside your glass...

How different too are the splendid museums where the treasures of forgotten civilisations are displayed—or others, no less interesting, where you can learn of the folk arts and traditions of a more recent past.

Things particularly Syrian

Cultural values and the human aspect inevitably dominate any survey of what Syria has to offer the tourist.

The Syrian soil is rich with archaeological remains and history is with us at every step.

This becomes even more interesting as we realize than these are not just any old remains and that the history in question is that of the peoples and fortunes of a little triangle bounded by the Tigris, the Yarmuk and the Mediterranean.

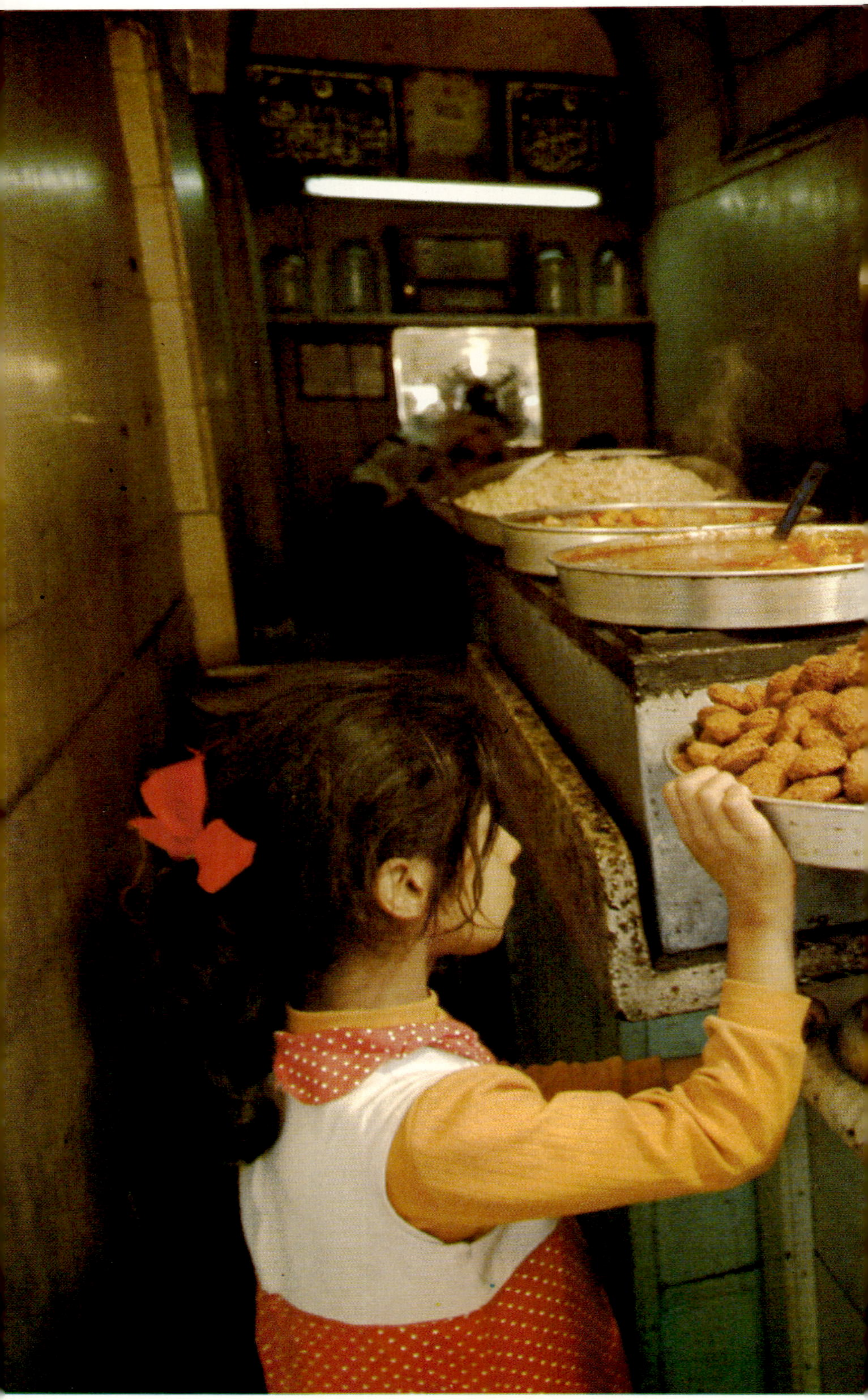

*Syrian cooking is essentially based
on country foods—cereals, salads, and fruit.
In the towns there are many restaurants offering
a wide variety of appetizing dishes.
(photo Robert Azzi, Magnum).*

*A commercial crossroad, but also a battlefield
throughout its thousands of years of history,
Syria has many ancient citadels
and medieval castles; Qalaat al-Hosn, better known
as Crac des Chevaliers, is surely the finest.
(Photo Bruno Barbey, Magnum.)*

Syrian antiquities illustrate original civilisations. Mari, the highly urbanized metropolis on the banks of the Euphrates, with its little men with bulging eyes and smiling faces; Mari is on Syrian soil. Ugarit, where the alphabet was invented, was the predecessor of Latakia, and Ebla (Tell Mardikh), where a library of ten thousand clay tablets was dug up, is on the north-south highway. "Younger" by a thousand years or so, Palmyra, a Syrian and an Arab capital, was rated highly by the great powers of the time for her contributions to art, town-planning, economics and even politics.

"The ghost towns of the North", with their fine churches standing up against the winds and decked with deep-yellow stone lace, illustrate five centuries of Syrian history.

The mosques and fortified towns built by the Umayyid caliphs in the early years after the call of the Prophet, are essentially Syrian too. Damascus was after all the first capital of Islam.

And for a final example of Syria's cultural wealth there is the great series of castles built by Arabs and Crusaders. They witnessed two centuries of warfare—a war of religion for one side, a war of liberation for the other—during which East and West dealt each other cruel blows, but also, for the first time for centuries, got to know, and perhaps respect, each other.

All the schoolchildren in Europe have a picture of the great Crusader castle, Crac des Chevaliers, in their history books. They know that those fairytale walls and towers stand on Syrian soil. They will be the tourists of tomorrow.

Five years for development

At the end of 1975 a National Plan for Tourism was adopted by the Syrian Government. The effort it envisages should quickly place Syria amongst the best equipped countries in this part of the world.

Some of the schemes and some of the achievements to date are most impressive. Three schools of hotel management and tourism (in Damascus, Latakia and Aleppo) are now receiving five hundred students for specialized courses lasting three years. At the same time training and re-training courses have been set up for existing personnel. This is a sound beginning.

The Plan for Tourism envisages the expansion of hotel accomodation by 150,000 beds over the next fifteen years. This will be achieved at the rate of 10,000 new beds a year—half of them on the Mediterranean coast.

Large international-class hotels are to be opened at regular intervals. In 1976-1977 there are first of all the four "Méridien" hotels (Damascus, Palmyra, Aleppo, Latakia); the "Sheraton-Damascus" will follow in 1977; in Damascus, Homs and Tartûs there wille be: a "Novotel", a "Mercure" (300) in 1978, and in 1979 a "Holiday Inn" will open. They will be followed by the "Intercontinental", the "Mariût" and the "Hilton". International tourism having been launched, the next economic Plan (1981-1985) will give priority to "two star" hotels in all the provincial towns. Starting in 1981, "Tourist Villages" catering for large numbers (5,000-10,000 beds) will be built on the coast, at Ras al-Basit, Latakia, and to the south of Tartous. The Isle of Arwad will become a boating centre. Finally the E5 international highway will have ten motels in Syria and Jordon, strung out between Aleppo and Akaba. There is also to be a motel at Crac des Chevaliers, and a "bedouin camp" at Palmyra. Camp sites are also planned.

A cure centre at Palmyra will make use of the sulphur springs which were known in ancient times.

The road network, already impressive in quality, is being expanded steadily; priority is being given to the Aleppo-Akaba motorway. More two-language road-signs are being provided. The airports at Aleppo, Latakia, Deirez-Zor and Qamischli are to be enlarged and equipped for international traffic.

40 PANORAMA

*The growing importance of the port of Latakia
involves the development of many different kinds
of facilities and services.
Many are administered from this new centre
which illustrates the expansion of
the great Syrian port.*

*The Azem Palace, in Hama, typifies a delicate
and refined way of living and evokes
an "Oriental atmosphere" both subtle and stifling
—such as the Romantics delighted to portray.
(Photo Azad, Ministry of Tourism.)*

Finally—and this is characteristic of those responsible—there is a "Tourism Pact" between Syria and Jordon. (Before the unhappy recent events Lebanon was also a party to this agreement.) It is hoped in Damascus that Turkey will join in. The first tangible result of the pact is that a single visa for any member country permits the visitor to travel freely in the others also.

It is much to be welcomed that a country such as Syria, which is playing an increasingly active role internationally, should also be paying such careful attention to the development of tourism.

economy

The Euphrates Dam is the cornerstone of Syria's future. Energy, industry, agriculture and social development all depend on it.
(Photo Jacques Guillard.)

The economic foundations of Syria's renewal:
oil, from Qaratchok; dams on the Euphrates,
the Khabur, and the Orontes;
development of the arid lands; extension and
mechanization of cotton growing—among other crops.
(Photos Azad, Ministry of Tourism, Ministry for the Euphrates.)

■ The fact that a plan for tourism is being worked out is a sign that economic prosperity is not far away and that the first priorities have been achieved.

For resurgent Syria the number one priority was a dam—the Euphrates Dam (see under Al-Thaura). Even before the attainment of the full 320 metre water-level in the lake nearly 100,000 hectares of arid land had been improved. The Fourth Plan (1976-80) provides for the irrigation of 240,000 hectares. Ricefields where the yield never rose above 1.5 tons per hectare are now producing 5 tons, and, in some places, 8 tons. Half of the 640,000 hectares which it is planned to improve, belong to the Syrian state, the remainder is worked by cooperatives and by individual farmers.

With regard to energy the Dam guarantees Syria's independence and development. Electricity production, of the order of a billion kilowatts in 1976, is expected to rise to two billion—double the country's present consumption.

Oil is the second area in which Syria has recently become self-sufficient. Exploration and research began in 1971 in the north-west and in the Aleppo region; since then 160,000 metres of bores have been drilled. Some 360 wells had been sunk in the Rumayan, Qaratcok, Suwaydiye, and Jbaisse fields: there are now 334 wells in production which yield more than 10 million tons of crude oil. Some of it is exported through the port of Tartous (Tartus) which is linked by a pipeline from the north-western fields via the modern refinery at Homs. Despite the bombings of 1973 this refinery achieved a capacity of 4.45 million tonnes in 1976. A new refinery at Baniyas, with a capacity of 6 million tons, will begin production in 1978, in conjuction with the nearby oil port facilities. There are 520 kilometres of pipeline, in addition, which bring refined petroleum products to Damascus, Hama, Aleppo, and Latakia.

The third area of Syria's economic emancipation is that of agriculture. Quite independently of the area

PANORAMA 47

48 PANORAMA

*Lake Al-Assad, a veritable inland sea 50 kilometres long, has definite tourist potential.
With the aid of Unesco ancient monuments have been moved to other sites. Sporting and cultural facilities are now being planned.
(Photo Ministry for the Euphrates.)*

*Great schemes have been completed recently to drain
the marshy Orontes valley and make it healthy and fertile.
The Ghab now symbolizes Syrian renewal.
The cotton growing areas have been extended
and agricultural mechanization is proceeding apace.
(Photos p. 51: Ministry of Tourism/Ministry of Economy)*

served by the Euphrates Dam there has been extensive work done to irrigate the Orontes valley and make it a healthy place in which to live and work. The building of dams and canals has made the Ghab plain into one of the most fertile areas in Syria. (see entry under Apamea, for example). Effort is now being concentrated on the improvement of the basin of the river Khabour—the main tributary of the Euphrates. A million hectares of good land will be reclaimed there, for the production of mainly cotton, rice, cereals and fruit. Cotton accounts for almost half of the country's exports at the moment.

An "Agrarian Reform", promulgated in 1963, encourages the formation of cooperatives. It also limits the extent of private agriculture in terms of the fertility, location, and yield of the land in question—thus private holdings are limited to 8 hectares in irrigated areas, to 30 hectares in non-irrigated areas having a rainfall higher than 350 millimetres per annum, and to 45 hectares elsewhere.

Industry: much scope for development

Syria's resources of electricity have permitted her to plan extensive industrial expansion. A large cement works is already in production at Homs; phosphates are being produced from the deposits at Palmyra and Hafe, near Latakia; iron and steel will follow the exploitation of deposits (estimated at approximately 100 million tons) at Rajo, near Palmyra, at Aafrine, near Aleppo, at Masiaf, near Homs, and at Zabadani, near Damascus. A plant for the production of reinforcing steel was opened at Hama in 1971. Also near Hama an iron and steel works is being built for the manufacture of sheet-metal and iron and steel pipes; it will be producing some 300,000 tons by 1980 and and when this capacity is doubled, as planned, it will meet two thirds of the country's requirements.

The development of a chemical and pharmaceutical industry will follow naturally in the wake of oil production, whilst the increase in the cotton crop has led to the expansion of the textile industry. Among food manufactures the production of beet sugar has almost doubled over the past ten years.

Syria has recently begun to manufacture tractors and agricultural machinery, refrigerators, batteries, washing machines, and television sets...among other things. Industrial refrigeration plant is being produced at Latakia, Aleppo and Homs.

Duty-free zones and the Damascus Fair

Since 1973 measures to facilitate trade and economic development have encouraged foreign investment in Syria. These include tax concessions, State guarantees, freedom for private importation of capital without declaration of source and freedom to open foreign-currency accounts with Syrian banks. (All banks in Syria have been nationalized.)

Another incentive to international trade has been the creation of "Duty-free zones", within which all commercial transactions are authorized and facilitated by a bank operating outside Syrian customs regulations. These duty-free zones, in Damascus, at Damascus International Airport, Adra (where the Damascus, Homs and Baghdad motorways intersect), Aleppo, Latakia and Tartous, cover a total area of 176 hectares.

The growth of Syria's foreign trade is the best index of progress so far: imports rose by 335 per cent between 1970 and 1974, exports by 376 per cent. The Common Market countries have supplanted the Eastern Bloc as Syria's most important trading partners.

However, the Syrian State bears a considerable financial burden—due to heavy defence expenditure and to its debt to the Soviet Union, on which repayments for 1976 alone came to 328 million U.S. dollars.

Nevertheless, Syria's overall economic growth during 1975 was estimated by World Bank experts to have been 14 per cent!

The annual Damascus International Fair is a graphic illustration of Syria's economic progress. It takes place in the centre of the capital, during the last fortnight of July. In 1976, 51 countries (including 15 Arab ones) took part; there were two thousand exhibitors and more than a million visitors. The Fair is the occasion for various other activities such as a scientific and technological symposium, an international crafts festival and a major arts festival.

One of the most remarkable things about Syria today is that her technological achievements and the beginnings of real economic progress—under a system in which the State plays the dominant role—do not cause her people to neglect human values and the art of living. Culture is by no means forgotten. The Fair is not allowed to blot out the Floralies. □

The busy port of Latakia on the Mediterranean.
Cargo vessels from all over the world wait to unload.
A duty-free zone has given
a boost to Syria's overseas trade.

syria on the human level

■ No, the Damascus Fair does not blot out the Floralies (see under Damascus) the dams do not drown the fine arts...

No less than forty towns (and the term embraces some very small places indeed) possess a Cultural Centre. These Centres, usually housed in buildings specially designed for them, are open to all, boys and girls, young and old. A wide range of activities and artistic pursuits is available—from painting and modelling to carpentry, drama and singing, to name but a few. Their libraries frequently contain several thousand volumes.

Regional and national competitions stimulate a friendly rivalry between the Centres. Archaeology is frequently taught in them. But they are also centres of social development where such things as civics and family planning are often discussed. The fight against illiteracy is also carried on there.

The Ministry of Culture has established four National Theatre Companies: The National Theatre performs plays by foreign authors in Arabic translation, as well as others by local or Arab dramatists; the Omayya Company specialises in folk art (costume, dance and music); the Travelling Theatre performs in factories, barracks and in even the poorest villages; the Marionette Theatre gives an average of two shows a day, for six months of the year, mainly in Damascus. A theatrical festival and a folk art festival take place each year.

Two Arab Institutes of Music have also been set up, one in Damascus the other in Aleppo. Many art exhibitions occur throughout the year, either organized or assisted by the Ministry of Culture, which is also involved with the publication of new literary works as well as of Arabic manuscripts and documents dispersed in libraries abroad or lying forgotten in distant archives.

Syria's museums (at Damascus, Aleppo, Hama, Tartous, Borsa, and Palmyra) can rival the most famous in their displays. They are worthy repositories of their fabulous collections which have been assembled from all over the country by archaeological teams—both Syrian and foreign—under the aegis of the Department of National Antiquities and Museums. These collections are growing year by year.

A living folklore

The Syrian's taste for the traditional arts continues undiminished. It is expressed in dances such as the famous al-Samah, the Dabkes in all their variations and the sword dance, to name but a few. Marriage ceremonies and even the breaking in of horses are occasions for the lively demonstration of folkcustoms. Folk art of another, and very impressive kind is demonstrated by the nimble fingers of craftsmen—and women—as they weave and embroider in gold and silver to make lovely silk brocades and fine cotton and woollen cloth.

Glasswork, "damascened" steel, coppersmithing, brightly-painted woodwork—all demonstrate skills going back a thousand years (see the chapter "*Syrian Journey: a thousand souvenirs*").

And as for dying or changing traditions—for example with the disappearance of the nomads—they can still be seen, with extensive commentaries, in the main folk art museums in Damascus (in the remarkable Azem Palace), Palmyra, Bosra Aleppo and Hama.

As a land of ancient culture Syria has always been the champion of the Arabic language. This feeling, still strong among the Syrian élite, is

*Tradition and economic development
need not clash. They still dance
in the streets of Aleppo during the Cotton Festival.
(Photo Azad, Ministry of Tourism.)*

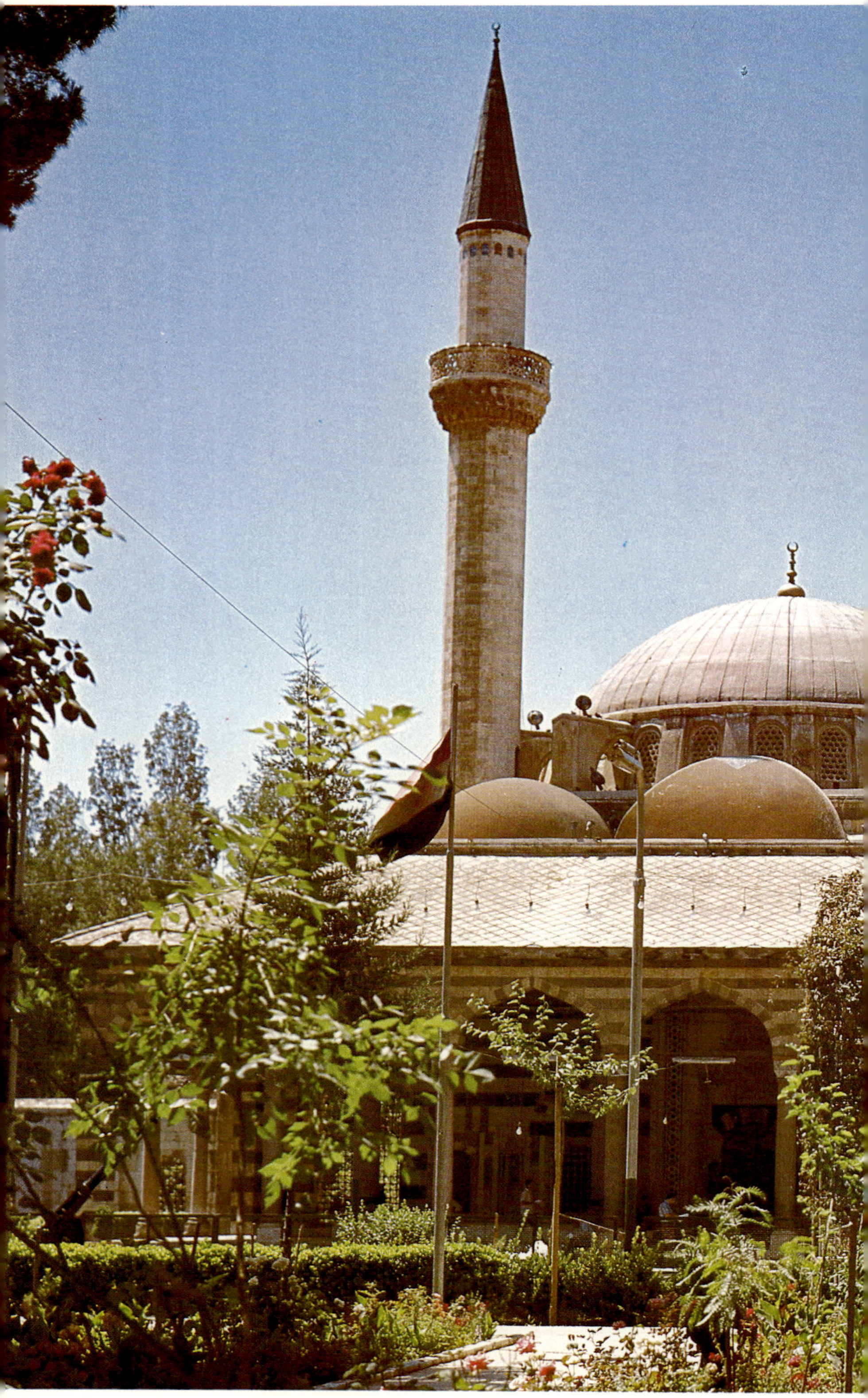

*The Suleimaniye, in Damascus, a former Dervish hospice
has become a promenade and a meeting place
for lovers. It shows the Syrians' love
of balance and harmony...and of roses,
"the Damask rose" their symbolic flower.*

*Sixty-three thousand students,
a third of them women, attend three universities,
at Damascus, Latakia and—the most recent—Aleppo
(above).*

enough to explain the vigour with which President Assad's government is fighting illiteracy and striving to raise the general standard of culture.

80 per cent of Syrian children attend school

According to reliable estimates there was still 55 per cent illiteracy in Syria in 1970; amongst the peasants the proportion was 80 per cent. 73 per cent of all illiterates were women.

In 1971 compulsory schooling was introduced and education at all levels was made free. In 1975, 80 per cent of all children of primary school age were in fact attending school, some 1,160,090 according to the official figures. 412,000 were attending secondary schools, and 15,600 were attending the fifty eight technical schools.

The three universities: Damascus, Aleppo and Latakia, have a total of 63,000 students, of which a third are women—a laudably high figure.

Indeed Syrian women have recently begun to play a significant role in the social, economic and political life of their country. Organised in the "General Federation of Women" the most active of them are taking full advantage of their legal rights and of the reputation some have earned in the armed forces and the resistance, and are devoting themselves to the fight against illiteracy, to infant welfare, and to training for the professions.

The young women of Syria are making their way everywhere—even into the world of sport. This was clearly demonstrated at the opening of the Arab Games in October 1976, for which occasion Damascus built an impressive series of stadiums, gymnasia, and swimming pools. (See photograph p.   )

Such rapid progress in so many varied areas, as our examples show, is not possible except in a stable and well-ordered State.

The Constitution of 1973 defines the Syrian Arab Republic as a "democratic, popular, socialist State"

PANORAMA 59

and makes it clear that Syria is a "*part of the Arab homeland*" and that her people are a "*part of the Arab nation*".

Sovereignty resides with the people

The legislative power is exercised by the Council of the People, elected for four years by universal suffrage (men and women) by direct and secret ballot. The executive power is vested in the President of the Republic, elected for a seven-year term by popular vote. He is assisted by a council of Ministers who are appointed, like the Prime Minister, by the President himself.

The judicial power is independent and the High Court pronounces on the constitutionality of laws.

Syria is divided for administrative purposes into "mohafazats". Each mohafazat is divided into several "mantika" which, in turn, are divided into "nahié". Each nahié contains a certain number of villages; the village constitutes the smallest administrative unit. There are 14 mohafzats (Damascus City, Damascus, Aleppo, Homs, Hama, Latakia, Deirez-Zor, Idlib, Hassakah, Al-Raqqa, Sûwayda, Deraâ, Tartous, Qnaytra), 48 mantika, 127 nahié, 56 towns, 6,319 villages and 7,729 farms.

And all this is the end-product of an immensely long history... □

THE CAMEL OF THE SYRIAN DESERT

■ *The came was indispensable to the Bedouin who used them not only as beasts of burden and a means of transport but ate their flesh and drank their milk. For the transhumant peoples the camel was a sure guide and an indefatigable "ship of the desert". There are many different species of camel. The "massh", "al ba'r" and "al khouare" are raised for their milk and as mounts. The banat woudaihan" with an almost white stomach and hooves, are famous for their fleetness. The "banat abjali", the "bajjanyyat" and the "dhouloul" are also ridden, the "tihyyat" were reserved for razzias. The "harrah" were also good racers, rivalling horses for speed.*
Camels live on straw and spiny desert plants—"shih" and "qaissoum".
From its hair the men of the desert made rope and wove material for tents, rugs, bags and clothes. From its skin they made water-bottles, footwear and saddles. From its bones they made combs. Thus the whole life of the nomad was closely linked with that of his faithful companion, the camel.

The melting-pot of humanity.
Syria has many mementos of civilisations that have
completely disappeared. These stone beasts guard
the Museum at Aleppo as they used to guard the temple-palace
at Tall Halaf, twenty-eight centuries ago.

an immensely long history

■ Their very long history has made the Syrian people into a mature, highly politicised nation, well able to look after itself.

However, political independence did not come overnight. Promised in 1919, in 1930, in 1936 and again in 1941, it only became effective in 1946 after the departure of the last French and British forces. Moreover, it was only achieved at the cost of popular uprisings, notably in 1925 and 1945, and with the loss of the province of Alexandretta, ceded to Turkey by France in 1939 without consulting Syrian opinion.

One November...

Free at last the young State fell prey to conflicting clans and ambitions. From the very first months there was a series of coups. Dictatorial regimes established themselves only to fall in the face of armed rebellion. The tentative scheme for an organic union with Colonel Nasser's Egypt, begun in 1958, far from bringing stability caused only more troubles and the union was dissolved in 1961. There was a change of regime in 1963, and another in 1966.

Syria's friends were sad to see her establish an unenviable record for coups d'état, all the more so as there was an enemy at the gates...

But then on 16 November 1970, everything changed.

That was the day when General Hafez El-Assad, a former pilot and the then Minister of War, a man known to be firm, disinterested and thoughtful, decided to launch what was called a "recovery movement". A Western observer noted: "It was a gentle coup d'état, designed to replace draconian rigour by the most reasoned moderation." (Thierry Desjardins, Cent Millions d'Arabes, pub. Elsevier).

That day marked the beginning of a major Syrian renewal. Fundamental reforms were soon initiated in the economic as well as the political and constitutional spheres. These were some of the stages.

*Syria offers her visitors glimpses of history
that they cannot find elsewhere... of ancient times,
of the Crusades, or of the early period of Christianity.
Here the church at Qalb Loza exemplifies the grace and
elegance of Syrian art in the early Christian period.*

*The five thousand year history of Mari
comes to life again in these figurines.
This is "Nani the Pious"—his story is recounted
on thousands of clay tablets.*

On 12 March 1971 the Syrians, for the first time, elected their President by universal suffrage. General Hafez El-Assad was elected with a large majority.

In March 1972 the National Progressive Front was formed, grouping all nationalist and progressive elements together and operating under the aegis of the Arab Ba'th Socialist Party.

On the 31 January 1973, the People's Council composed of representatives of the Arab Ba'th Socialist Party, popular organizations and progressive elements, approved a permanent Constitution, on which it had been working for many months. Syria, which had been governed for so long by legislative expedients with no constitutional backing, now had a written charter guaranteeing the basic liberties of her citizens.

Next, the "Local Administrative Law" was promulgated, establishing regional government through fourteen mohafazats or provinces, each with a representative council.

At the same time President Assad's government was preparing to launch a major programme of economic development—despite the extra financial burden due to the threat of war.

Under the Third Plan (1971-75) total investment amounted to 8 billion Syrian pounds (2.1 billion dollars approx.) and the rate of growth was nearly 8% annually. Agriculture, oil, and the Euphrates Dam were the top priorities at this time—as we have algready seen in the chapter "The Syrian Economy".

The Fourth Five Year Plan, which covers the years up till 1980, will see the emergence of Syria as an industrial power and should make possible further significant economic progress.

Tourism is by no means neglected in these plans, for after all it is a highly contemporary phenomenon, although drawing deeply on the riches of the past.

The Arabs have always called Syria "the land of Shem". Damascus is Dimishq ash-Sham—the town of Shem—the second son of Noah according to the Bible, from whom the Canaanites descended. They have lived in this land from time immemorial—this corner of earth and sand, mountains and great rivers, which men have imagined—especially around Damascus—to be the site of the Garden of Eden. The Prophet Muhammad himself was of this opinion.

It is to this Eastern land, a land of men and a land of faith, that the thoughts and prayers of so many people turn. Although they may scarcely know of it, though they may never have even opened an atlas, they are dimly aware that here somewhere, between a desert and a valley, their religion was born.

Taking this thought further the Muslim writer Habib Boulares says: "As a believer one cannot deny the evident fact that this land has been chosen by God both to test men and to bring out their true qualities—both for better and for worse. If one has no faith one reverses the problem and concludes that such a land could do no other than engender exaltation, mysticism, fanaticism, proselytism and messianism... »

The entire Middle East was the melting-pot of mankind.

The human melting-pot

When history is mixed with legend, when historians—for convenience or because they await precise evidence from the archaeologists —name peoples after towns and regions, and when certain cities achieve domination over others, we end up with a mosaic of nations the colours of which are heightened by religious differences. Yet, apart from the Hittites who came from Asia Minor (and whose origins are still hotly disputed), the Greeks and Romans from the west, and the Medes and Persians who came down from the Iranian plateau, everything tends to prove that all these peoples: Babylonians, Amorrites, Assyrians, Arabs,

Arameans, Canaanites... were one single nation, branches of the same basic race.

In the lands between the Iranian plateau and the Mediterranean, between the Taurus Mountains, the Gulf of Oman and the Valley of the Nile, history has hesitated for centuries to designate one single metropolis. Ourouk, Babylon, Assur, Palmyra, Niniveh, Ur, Jerusalem, Memphis, Thebes, Mecca, Damascus, Baghdad, Persepolis and Sousse—all of them by turns, with varying degrees of success, have played the part of unifier.

The succession of desert and valley, and the scattered pattern of oases and waterholes have determined the shape of an extremely eventful history. This sense of history at every step is one of the particular delights that awaits the visitor to Syria.

A very present past

History is no abstraction in Syria. It is not confined to some dusty tome. It lives in every river, hill, colonnade, mosaic, fortress and museum...

The tens of thousands of clay tablets, engraved with cuneiform script, which have been discovered, neatly classified, in libraries and archives, at Mari, Ugarit, Ebla and in a dozen other "tells", enable scholars, in front of the astonished eyes of the layman, to re-create the beginnings of a civilisation which has influenced the whole Western World. From these account books, police reports, diplomatic treaties, medical prescriptions and cookery recipes—there is little we do not know about life as it was lived in this corner of the world some three, four, even five thousand years ago.

It would almost seem that, pleased with themselves for having invented writing, the peoples of the Euphrates, Syria and the Levant had insisted on talking across the centuries to their present-day descendants.

Even more evocative are the objects that have been recovered by the archaeologists, who continue patiently to scratch and sift the sand and mud. Beautifully displayed in museum showcases in Damascus, Aleppo, Tartous, and Palmyra, we can see children's toys, women's jewellery, the gems that belonged to priests and kings, funerary sculptures and ornaments, and, of course, weapons of many kinds. They bring to life in an almost poignant yet realistic way the daily life of that distant world. What would Mari mean to us if we had not seen this little circular, five-roomed house, modelled in clay by an architect who lived four thousand years ago? And in the same room in the Damascus Museum we can see the very inhabitants of Mari—a singer, a bailiff, a miller, a shepherd carrying a kid, all of them wearing cloaks of "kaunake" (sheepskin with the wool left on).

Thus every period in Syria's history is brought to life. Should the visitor be interested in the great periods of city building and of Syrian sculpture he can see them in Palmyra. If it is the early history of Islam, the Umayyad period when the Arab nation attained self-consciousness, that interests him—then he has Damascus. If he is fascinated by that early Christian period in the country where St. Paul preached after his inspiration on the Damascus Road, then he must visit the monasteries, the churches, the "ghost towns" of the North. If it is the conflict of Cross and Crescent during the two centuries of the Crusades that he wants to trace, then he has Crac des Chevaliers, Qalaat Salah-ed-Din, Marqab and a dozen more. If he wants to learn more of the Ottoman period with its luxury, and the commercial intrigues and ambitions of the sultans, then he can do so, in peaceful Hama and in bustling Aleppo. Even the most recent history (not at all the least dramatic either!) is there to be seen—in the very interesting Army Museum in Damascus and there on the ground at Qnaitra.

To make even more sense of all that he sees it is useful for the visitor to know certain historical landmarks. Here are some of the main ones.

An Arab presence for the past 50 centuries

It is estimated that there have been Arabs in Syria for five thousand years: since 3000 B.C.

Five thousand years ago the first slow migration of Arameans from the Arabian desert began. It was at this time that great palaces were built at Mari and that writing made its appearance at Uruk.

About the middle of the century between 2500 and 2400 B.C. (some specialists believe it was a century later, around 2350) a mighty leader arose: Sargon, Sargon of Akkad (or Agade). He reigned for fifty years. His empire extended from Babylon to Anatolia. His reign marks such and important stage in our knowledge of antiquity that historians and archeologists speak the "pre-" and "post-Sargonid" periods. After his time nations took shape and international relations began. Sargon's third successor, Naram Sin, King of Akkad, turned back the Anatolian invaders and extended the Syro-Mesopotamian empire as far as Cyprus and Asia Minor. He had himself proclaimed "King of the Four Nations"—Akkad, Sumer, Elam, and Assyria. Weapons were still made of bronze at this time but the bow and the war chariot had already been invented.

The second wave of Arabs to establish themselves is Syria, the Canaanites began to arrive at the beginning of the second millennium. The Canaanites, soon known as Phoenicians (dealers in purple) turned their attention towards the Mediterranean. Their many trading stations along its shores, as far as the Atlantic, (see "Morocco Today" and "Tunisia Today" in this series) constituted a veritable maritime empire. To defend it the Canaanites fortified their cities, notably (in present-day Syria) Aradus (the Isle of Arwad) and Ugarit (Ras Shamra), which also raised their own armies and fleets. The Phoenician triremes, vessels of commerce or war, with their skilled crews, brought wealth to the coastal kingdoms; whilst their workers in metal, exploiting the mines of the Syrian coast, perfected weapons for the capture of new trade routes.

Allies with Egypt against the northern invaders

Relations with nearby Egypt were close. This was the time of the great Pharaohs of the Twelfth Dynasty (the period known as the Middle Kingdom: see "Egypt Today" in this series). They took the form of loosely-formulated alliances. In the seventeenth century B.C. a dual danger arose, from the turbulent Hyksos and Hittites. These raiders from the Anatolian plateau were much to be feared as their weapons of iron were more than a match for the bronze weapons of their opponents.

It was not until the great expeditions of Thutmose III and Amenhotep II (1505-1425 New Kingdom, 18th Dynasty) that the Hittites were contained; although even then the Syrians were not entirely safe from invasion. In 1285 another battle—indecisive but bloody, judging from the sculptured panels of the Ramesseum at Thebes—took place on Syrian soil, at Qadesh (near present-day Homs).

It was only around 1200 that the Hittite empire collapsed under the repeated attacks of the "Sea Peoples", invaders whose origins are uncertain (Cyprus, Crete, the Aegean Sea?) and whose history is still obscure. The ports of the Syrian coast suffered from raids by these mysterious Sea Peoples, but the inland population, reinforced by another migration of Arabs from Arabia (the Arameans) established small kingdoms at Damascus, Hama, Aleppo, and at Tadmor (the future Palmyra). The towns were strongly fortified. The Aramaic tongue, which made use of the alphabet, spread everywhere. Commerce developed continuously, from north to south and from east to west. The valley of the Euphrates became an busy corridor.

Assyrians, Babylonians and Persians

From now on danger came from the east: from the kings of Assur (the Assyrians) who, leaving their capital on the banks of the Tigris, launched regular raids to plunder the prosperous towns and wealthy ports to the west. But at the end of the seventh century Babylon threw off the Assyrian yoke. In 612 B.C. Nineveh (which had replaced Assur as the capital of Assyria) was destroyed and Nabolpolassar proclaimed himself king of Babylon and founded a dynasty. His son, the famous Nebuchadnezzar II, led the neo-Babylonian empire to its height. The Upper Euphrates and Syria fell under his sway.

Before a century had passed, proud and luxurious Babylon had to bow in its turn to the new great power that had arisen in the unstable Middle East. The city fell in 539 B.C. to Cyrus, the Achaemenian king, founder of the Persian empire and famous for clemency and justice (see "Iran Today" in this series). Under Darius, the second successor of Cyrus, Syria and the Mediterranean coast were ruled by Persia, despite repeated revolts which were harshly put down.

When Alexander of Macedonia, avenger of the honour of Greece, set out to conquer Asia, Syria again (in 333 B.C.) became a battlefield. Some of the coastal cities fought valiantly. At Gaza there was the spectacle of single combat between the Arab prince defending the town, Barthes, and the young conqueror—who was severly wounded; the town fought to the last man.

After the death of Alexander his generals divided his conquests. Syria was torn limb from limb: the north went to Seleucus (founder of the Seleucid dynasty) who made Babylon his capital; the south was joined to the Graeco-Egyptian empire of the Ptolemys, governed from Alexandria, the city which had been the Macedonian's own creation.

At the end of the second century B.C. the Seleucids reconquered Damascus and the south from Egypt, before being themselves defeated by the new thrusting power from the West.

When the Romans, on the pretext of settling some troubles in Palestine, established themselves in the Near East, Syria ceased to be a Seleucid kingdom and became a Roman province. These changes of sovereignty meant little to her... Independence was still a very long way off.

A subtle game between Rome and Syria

In fact the situation was not quite so clear-cut. More skilful or more shrewd that its predecessors the Roman authority, despotic though it was, knew how to dispense honours and riches. Playing upon local rivalries it knew when to be harsh and when to protect. The Romans rewarded loyal allies but knew also just when to apply pressure. They were surprised to find the Arabs of Syria were subtle politicians too... all the more awkward for them when they were on the defensive against the Parthians (whom the Sassanids succeeded in Iran) who were dreaming of rebuilding the empire of Cyrus. The Syrians were well placed to help the Romans who, in return treated them with flattery and tact.

In 106 A.D. the Emperor Trajan incorporated the Nabatean kingdom into the Empire. Splendid monuments were built at Bosra, Suwayda, Damascus and in many other places, all of which enjoyed unparalleled prosperity. But it is not easy to be a subject state... The pacific and reforming Emperor Hadrian (117-138), the learned and literary successor of the warlike Trajan, decided to withdraw his legions to the Orontes, entrusting the defence of the frontier on the Euphrates to his Syrian allies. Relations between Rome and Syria grew more cordial, The Emperor Septimus Severus (193-211), married to a Syrian, favoured his wife's country. The year 232 actually saw Syrian: Philip the Arab (from present-day Shahba, south of Damascus) assume the Imperial Purple—for only four years to be sure. This was the time when the Sasanians were dreaming once more of an opening to the Mediterranean...

The situation encouraged the Syrians to think of their freedom.

In the heart of the country a city, proudly isolated amid the surrounding desert, illustrated this regained sense of Syrian identity. This was Tadmor (the "town of dates"), which the Romans named Palmyra, the "town of palm trees." (for detailed history of Palmyra see the article under its name.)

Palmyrene archers and lancers recruited into the Roman legions had the reputation of being doughty warriors. The merchants of Palmyra had come to dominate trade between the Mediterranean and the empires of Asia. The city had quickly become one of the luxurious cities of the age. Its architects, town planners and artists were obviously men of genius; their works were copied even in Rome itself.

Zenobia or avenging pride

Odenathus, ruler of Palmyra, brought off a political masterstroke by rescuing the Emperor Valerian (262) who had been taken prisoner by the Sasanian, Shahpur, during the battle of Edessa (near Homs) where a Roman army had been defeated (260). On the strength this exploit he awarded himself the title of "King of Kings". As for Valerian he could do no less than grant his liberator the title of Governor (literally corrector) of all the East.

Zenobia, the wife and successor (in rather dubious circumstances) of Odenathus, gave free rein to her ambition and her pride. Dreaming of a Syrian empire she soon held sway over Asia Minor and the Near East, conquered Lower Egypt and brazenly defied the Romans... She was just half a century too soon. The Empire was not yet on its knees. The reaction was brutal and remorseless. Diocletian sent troops which soon captured and humiliated proud Palmyra and Zenobia died in relative obscurity in Rome.

Three centuries of uneasy Christianity

The days of the Roman Empire were numbered. In 313 Constantine made Byzantium the imperial capital. Christianity, which had been gradually making individual converts for many years, now became the official religion. The statues of the household gods and the symbols of paganism were destroyed. Some temples were adapted for Christian worship and new churches were built in the towns and villages.

Monasteries too were built quite soon, often in the arid hills and burning desert, to shelter the first hermits. The fame of some of these, often keen to demonstrate their faith in a striking manner, has come down to us often embroidered by legend. The remains of the pillar of Simon Stylites for example, on which is said to have spent forty two years, can still be seen on a hill near Aleppo. (See under Qalaat Samaân.)

This was where the early Church took shape. It can't be positively proved that it was in a basket (even though such details don't invent themselves) and through a window, at a spot still pointed out today, that a certain Saul (Paul), a tentmaker by trade, fled from his hostile and incredulous brothers to follow in the steps of the Master... the "Damascus Road" is no vain symbol.

The depopulation of the mountain settlements in the north-west during the 7th and 8th centuries, as a result of extraordinary climatic and economic events (see p. 25), has enabled the present-day visitor to find there examples of genuine Syrian art. Churches, in a remarkable state of preservation, have survived unaltered, having been suddenly abandoned, in all their original purity of style and with characteristic local decoration.

Unfortunately doctrinal unity was less perfect than artistic unity. How could it have been otherwise in this country exposed to all the cross-currents of civilisation flowing between East and West? Centuries of cultural exchange and confrontation had prepared the Syrians for the tortuous theological controversies from which Eastern Christianity emerged disunited in both doctrine and organization. Even today in all the villages of Syria there are lively Christian minorities who are the direct heirs of those distant rivalries and parochialisms.

It seems appropriate to wonder whether this "*Byzantinism*" (in both senses of the term), which had become so burdensome by the 7th century, did not predispose the Syrians (as it did the Spaniards for similar reasons) to accept and assimilate so quickly the simple purity of the message of Islam?

Syria: the first stage in the spread of Islam

The revolution that sprang from the sands of Arabia in the middle of the 7th century was to be one of the greatest, and the most rapid, the world has ever known. The inspired vision of the humble son of a merchant of Mecca was to change the map of the world, transform relations between empires, and affect the most intimate thoughts and feelings of millions of men. The behaviour of nations today is still influenced by it. Syria, the first to be conquered and won over, has remained an unflinching and valiant standard-bearer of Islam.

Thirteen years after Muhammad had established himself at Medina (622 in the Christian calendar, Year 1 in the Muslim), only three years after the death of the Prophet (632), and with the tribes of Arabia—so often at odds—united behind the red and green banner, two Arab armies converged on Damascus. After a few weeks' seige, the "oldest city in the world" was conquered.

Byzantium, having been busy for decades with its ancient struggle against the Persians, quickly reacted to this new danger. The Emperor Heraclius despatched his own brother Theodore to Syria, at the head of an army of fifty thousand men. They encountered the Arab army, under Kaled ibn Al-Walid—the man whom Muhammad had called the "Sword of Islam"—on the banks of the Yarmuk (100 km south of Damascus) on 30 August 636. The day was very hot, a strong wind blinded both armies with dust, but the Arab horsemen, accustomed to desert warfare, were too much for the Byzantine troops hampered by their armour. Theodore was killed. The whole of Syria rapidly fell to the "*caliphs*", "Commanders of the Faithful" and temporal successors of the Prophet.

By 636 the first Caliph, the wise and pious Abu Bakr, had been succeeded by Omar. He combined, it was said, both energy and modesty, courage and a strict obedience to the laws of Islam. His skill and the respect he showed towards conquered peoples still faithful to their old beliefs, did much to propagate the new Revelation.

During the reign of Omar, which lasted ten years, Islam advanced rapidly. In 639 the conquest of Egypt opened the way to North Africa; in 644 that of Persia served as a springboard into Asia. Damascus became the most important political and military base in the new empire.

There was however a dark and dramatic side to all this. Islam in its early days, triumphant and purifying, could also show a bloody, tragic and almost sordid aspect.

Muhammad left no instructions as to who was to succeed him as head of the Islamic community and so the way was left open to personal ambition, clan rivalry and fanaticism as well as the clash of genuinely-held beliefs among the faithful.

A painful family quarrel

Three of the first four Caliphs were assassinated and the Empire was for decades the scene of revolts and civil wars.

Without going into the details of this gigantic family quarrel it is perhaps useful to note the protagnonists and the main events.

Abu Bakr and Omar, the first to be designated by the assembly of wise men, had both been early colleagues and counsellors of the Prophet himself. When Omar fell to the dagger of a Christian slave, the Caliphate passed to Othman, a descendant of Umayya a great-great uncle of Muhammed, Othman spent most of his most of his time working on a definitive edition of the Koran and was frequently manipulated politically by his numerous and powerful family. Discontent erupted in various places (notably in Egypt) and Othman, like his predecessor, died at the hand of an assassin. However this time the assassin was a Muslim. It was said that Othman's blood bespattered the Koran which he was reading when he was struck. It was an all too accurate omen of the fraternal strife and bloodshed to come.

As Othman's successor the elders and wise men elected Ali, cousin and son-in-law of the Prophet—whom many Muslims said should have been immediately chosen to succeed him.

A pacific man, without ambition and without political flair. Ali found himself straight away at odds with the Umayya clan and with the officials whom Othman had appointed.

FIVE THOUSAND YEARS OF HISTORY

■ *Recent, very recent discoveries—particularly those at Mari and Alalakh'have completely upset our knowledge of the East since the 3rd millenium and have given a history to civilisations which were formerly only names, allusions or documentary fragments.*

...Taking all present evidence into account it is now possible to describe in general terms a remarkable phenomenon within this vast period. It concerns Aleppo where an extremely important urban civilisation has existed without a break for the past 5,000 years. This is all the more striking in a land where so many great civilisations have collapsed leaving little more than a few buried ruins.

A powerful kingdom during the 3rd millenium and at the beginning of the 2nd, Aleppo today is the second largest city in Syria and one of the most important in the Middle East in terms of commerce and culture. It can now be shown that it has had a continous existence since the first Sumero-Akkadian dynasties.

Soubhi Saouaf
(adapted)
"Alep dans sa plus ancienne histoire"
(Aleppo 1972)

His clumsy acceptance of an attempted arbitration caused him to lose ground with his own ardent supports. Muawiya, Governor of Syria and a member of the Umayyad family, publicly displayed Othman's bloodstained galabieh in the Mosque at Damascus, and openly accused Ali of complicity in his murder!

Shortly afterwards Ali was killed by one of his own disappointed supporters, one of the Kharijis or secessionists, sometimes known as "heretics" or "protestants" (see "Tunisia Today" in this series).

After Ali's death Muawiya, who had been governing Syria as if it were an independent country, had no difficulty in securing the Caliphate for himself. Damascus became the capital of the Islamic Empire.

One of the first acts of the new ruler was to replace the elective principle by the dynastic. Without more ado he designated his son Yazid as his successor.

From 661 until 750, when the last descendant of Muawiya was overthrown, fourteen Umayyad Caliphs in succession held the supreme political, military and religious authority over Islam.

Damascus the Umayyad capital

It was a glorious period. The Koran held sway from the Atlantic to the China Sea. A specifically Islamic culture—though influenced by its Arab heritage—gave rise to many new developments in both science and the arts.

Arabic soon took the place of Greek, Latin and Persian, for official purposes at least, throughout the conquered lands. The first Islamic coinage—gold dinars and silver dirhems, bearing Koranic inscriptions—replaced the Byzantine and Persian ones. An extensive communications system facilitated the movements of official messengers, merchants and armies. Great public works were undertaken, particularly in hydraulics and irrigation.

In the arts both grandeur and refinement were characteristic of this new civilisation—the Great Mosque at Damascus is a prime example. It was to Damascus that commercial routes now turned, bringing wealth and a new taste for luxury. Damascus was now the great crossroads for pilgrims on their way to Mecca. It was on Damascus that men of science and letters now converged—to be received like princes at the Ummayyad court.

In the north the rulers of Byzantium—who had seen Arab troops encamped around Constantinople—were kept at a respectful distance. To the east Persia was gradually becoming Islamified.

The revenge of the Alids

Yet at the centre the Umayyad Empire was less secure. The theologico-political differences had not really been resolved and the divergent interests of the various parties were all too clear.

The supporters of the descendents of Ali and Fatima his wife (daughter of the Prophet) had not given up. In their various groups—Kharijis, Shi'ites, Fatimids, Abbasids (after Abbas, uncle of Muhammed)—they fomented murders and revolts, which were brutally suppressed. Yet they continued to exploit the regime's economic difficulties and the discontents provoked by its oppressive administration.

In 747 the Abbasids seized power in Persia and declared open war against Damascus. In 750 a decisive battle was fought on the banks of the Tigris.

The Umayyad army, under the personal command of the Caliph, Morwan II, was put to flight. Morwan escaped to Egypt where he was killed. His whole family was hunted down and put to death—with one exception: Abd al-Rahman fled to Spain where he founded a new Umayyad dynasty at Cordoba (see "Spain Today" in this series).

Abbas had already proclaimed himself Caliph in 749.

His brother, Mansur, who succeeded him in 754, made Baghdad his capital in preference to Damascus.

The Abbasid reached its greatest glory shortly afterwards under Haroun al-Rachid (786-809), but disintegrated later into a multitude of kingdoms, princedoms and emirates which were often at odds.

The sovereignty of the Caliph of Baghdad soon becme merely nominal. Power fell into the hands of able usurpers, the Seljuks.

Former Turkish slaves, converts to Islam, mercenaries in the Caliph's guard, the Seljuks gained control first of Baghdad, then, in the mid-eleventh century, of Syria and Asia Minor.

The fragmentation of the Islamic Empire provided the opportunity for Christians in the West to launch the first of their rash Crusades.

A war of liberation lasting two hundred years

Two centuries!

1099: Crusader knights, their heavy armour emblazoned with a red cross symbolising their vow to "recover the Holy Sepulchre from the Infidel", landed in Asia, took the coastal route through Syria, invaded the plain of Judea, and surprising its local defenders, captured Jerusalem...

1302: the last occupiers of the Isle of Arwad, off Tartous, the final bastion of the Westerners, managed to put to sea, with no thought of returning.

Two centuries and three years. Two centuries of invasion. Two centuries of a strange sort of warfare—battles and massacres, marked by valour and base betrayals, redeemed occasionally by sudden gestures of mutual respect, even friendship, between adversaries, and producing

KHALED IBN AL-WALID

■ *As they were on their way to Persia, Khaled's troops were ordered to rejoin the forces fighting in bsyria. Tradition has it that they covered 350 kilometres across the desert with-out a single major stop. Camels which had drunk their fill before they set out were killed whenever they paused, to let their horses drink the water that flowed from their stomachs.*

When Damascus surrendered the Muslim chief proclaimed capitulation conditions both remarkable for their fairness and for their political skill: "In the name of Allah the Merciful, these are the terms of Khaled ibn al-Walid. ... He promises the citizens of Damascus that their lives and churches will be spared. The walls of their city will not be destroyed and no Muslims will be lodged in their houses. We accordingly grant them a pact with Allah and the protection of His Prophet, the Caliphs and the faithful. As long as they pay their taxes, nothing but good will befall them.."

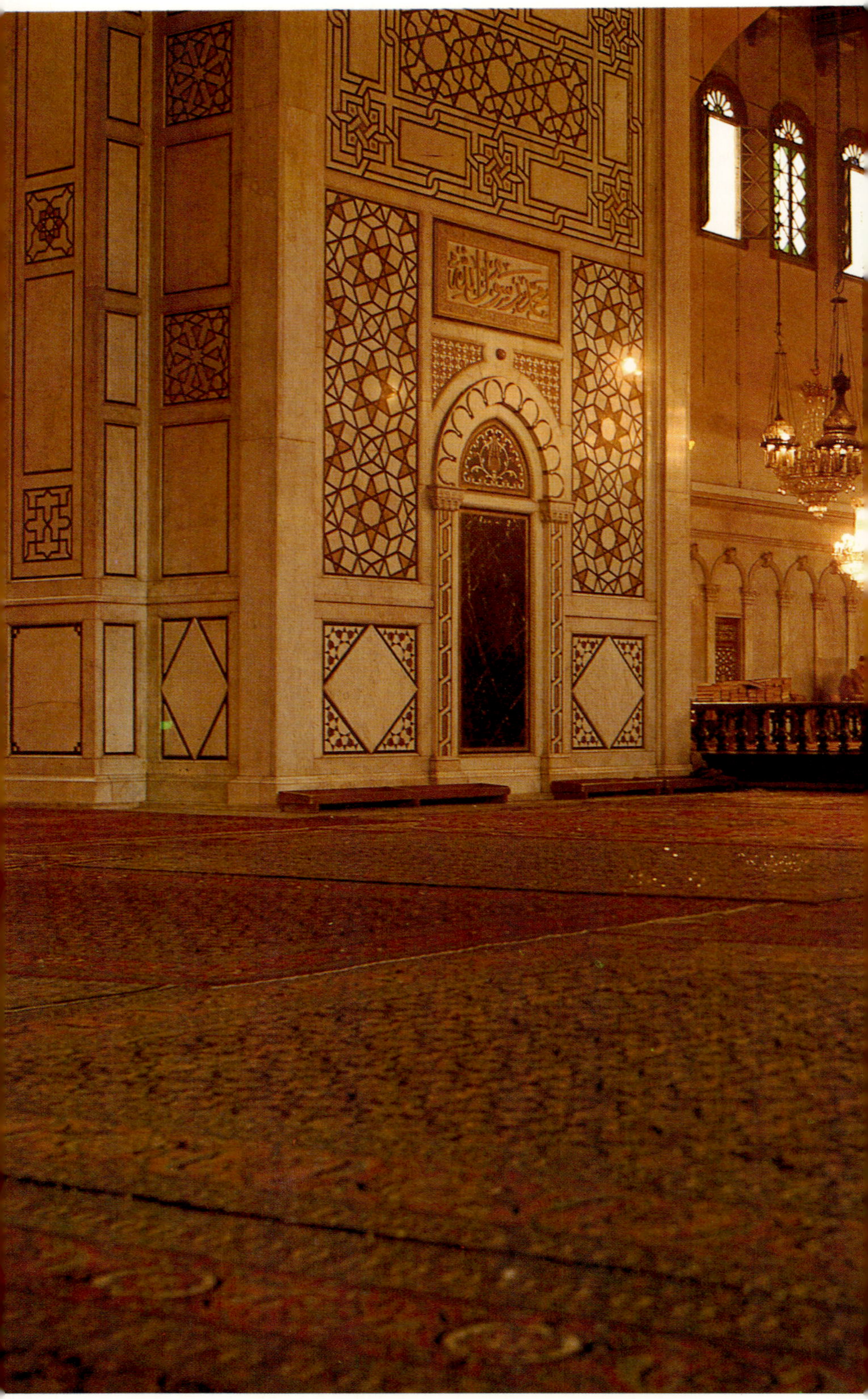

*Purity of form, richness of materials,
and fluid and geometrical mural decoration
characterise the Great Umayyad Mosque at Damascus.
These elements blend harmoniously in its vast carpeted halls
to provide an ideal atmosphere for recollection.
(Photo Bousquet, Explorer.)*

knightly heroes of the quality of Baldwin IV, the leper king, and Saladin himself...

Although certainly begun, by the Franks, as a holy "crusade", the invasion soon degenerated into a war of occupation, and appropriation—a colonial war in fact. Whilst on the one hand popes and saints preached, distributed indulgences and promised divine grace as the reward, on the other doughty warriors were carving out territories for themselves.

Syrian lands were involved from the outset. Aleppo and Damascus were threatened by the very first Frankish incursion. The Crusaders reached the Euphrates. The whole of the western side of the country was occupied. A chain of marvellous castles was built all along the coast. Ancient Byzantine and Arab strongholds were taken over and their defences doubled or trebled. They are still there today, proud and useless sentinels bearing silent witness to the grand and futile drama which ran its course here in one of the loveliest lands on earth. (See entries under Latakia, Qalaat Salah ad-Din, Masiaf, Crac des Chevaliers, etc.)

Nur ad-Din

With Frankish counts governing Tripoli and Edessa, a Frankish prince at Antioch and a Christian King in Jerusalem, it was clear, by the beginning of the twelfth century, that Seljuk power was disintegrating and that the Abbasid Caliph was losing his authority.

Power in the Muslim lands fell into the hands of a host of local emirs who were entirely taken up with family quarrels and tribal rivalries. Immured in their little capitals they trusted to the deserts to protect them and simply watched the Crusaders pass by—or even cashed in on their neutrality.

However, the capture of Jerusalem stirred many Muslim consciences. From 1110 onwards there were signs of vigorous reaction. Syrian deputations demonstrated in front of the Caliph's palace in Baghdad. A holy war or "jihad" was proclaimed in all the mosques. Armies were organized. On 25 December (a black Christmas for the Crusaders) the County of Edessa was recaptured. Four years later Damascus beat off an attack by the combined forces of the Second Crusade. At the same time the Aleppo region was liberated by a man of great valour and authority, Sultan Nur ad-Din.

Throughout the twenty-eight years of his reign, from 1146 to 1174, Nur ad-Din bent his efforts to unifying Syria and harassing the Crusaders. He destroyed the castle of the Count of Tripoli, put the outskirts of Harim to the sword and set fire to them, crushed the knights of Antioch in a bloody affray, forced the defenders of Apamea to capitulate... In less than two years he captured nearly all the Crusader strongholds in northern Syria.

Anxious to assure his rear by shattering Frankish schemes for Egypt and also to settle an old score with the Fatimids who reigned in Cairo, Nur ad-Din, who governed from Damascus, mounted an expedition and gave the command to Shirkuh a leader of Kurdish origin. On 8 January 1169 Cairo was taken and the Sunni Muslims of the city welcomed the Syrians as liberators.

Shirkuh died shortly afterwards and his nephew, a clever if modest and rather austere young man, was named Vizier and Commander of the Syrian forces in Egypt. His real name was Youssef, but he was not long in justifying the name by which he is known in history: Salah ad-Din, "the good order of religion". We in the West know him as Saladin.

Salah ad-Din the liberator

Islam had found a leader. The high-minded young man showed himself to be a statesman and a courageous general. Deeply religious he acted without weakness but without cruelty. His integrity was acknowledged by his opponents and History endorses their verdict.

Conscious of his responsbiilities and ambitious less for himself than for Islam, Salah ad-Din, as Governor of Egypt, gradually shook off the tutelage of Nur ad-Din. He re-established the Sunni faith, had himself recognised by the Abbasid Caliph of Baghdad and, at the age of thirty-five, founded his own dynasty, the Ayyubid.

On the death Nur ad-Din, Salah ad-Din left Cairo and established himself in Damascus where, at the head of a reunified empire he was able to lead an unrelenting fight against the western invaders.

It was a fight characterized by swift attack and tedious waiting. Days of glory followed days of mourning. Treaties and truces—for a day or a whole winter—gave some respite between battles and sieges. They were fighting not only the armies and their constant reinforcements, but against treachery, slackness, climate and disease.

The Muslims avenged their defeat at Ramla, near Ascalon, in 1177, by their great victory at Hattin, ten years later. Salah ad-Din was everywhere, giving no thought to danger. On 20 September 1187, ten weeks after Hattin, the 16 of the Redjeb moon in the year 583 of the Hegira, Saladin appeared before Jerusalem and laid siege to the holy city. It fell ten days later.

The Christians still held the coast and several powerful fortresses. Reinforcements brought by the Third Crusade rekindled hope in their ranks.

In 1188 another great campaign was needed. Saladin failed to capture Crac des Chevaliers but soon took the castle of Saône (Sayoun) which had been reputed impregnable (see under Qalaat Salah ad-Din, as the site is known today, in commemoration of its liberator).

THE ALPHABET: SINAI, BYBLOS, UGARIT...

■ *Many stone inscriptions have been found in Southern Sinaï, dating from the 15th century B.C. They are written in pictograms, signs representing the initial consonants of words whose meaning had been previously conveyed by a picture—a crucial stage between pictorial representation and phonetic writing. Pictograms are generally hieroglyphics but these read as Canaanite not Egyptian. So the Canaanite alphabet was the result of a conscious creative act. Canaanite was the language spoken at Ugarit in the 14th century B.C. Out of the thirty alphabetical signs found on the site, twenty-two are consonants in the Byblos alphabet (a development of the Sinaï pictograms) and are arranged in the same order. The proto-Canaanite alphabet thus represents the same signs as the Ugaritic one—the first in linear form, the second in cuneiform, in imitation of the Akkadian signs which were well known to the Ugaritic scribes. Since the name of the letter.*

JEAN STARCKY and PIERRE BORDREUIL
(adapted)
"L' Invention de l'alphabet"
Dossier de l'Archeologie n° 12, sept. 1975

The ghastly seige of Acre marked the culmination of the conflict. The Muslims defending the town held out for nearly two years, from October 1189 until 12 July 1191 when death and famine finally defeated them. Three hundred thousand Christians under the banners of the German Emperor and the Kings of France and England were involved in the seige and were attacked from outside by Saladin's Muslim forces.

Victors at Acre but exhausted, the Christians failed in their attempt to re-take Jerusalem at the beginning of following year. So 1192 was a year of precarious peace, enabling the Muslims to regain their breath. Richard Cœur de Lion, who had briefly flirted with the notion of linking his family by marriage with the Ayyubids, returning to England worn out by fighting and by fever. Salah ad-Din returned to Damascus after four years' absence and was rapturously welcomed. He too was exhausted and a few wekks later, on 4 March 1193, he died at the age of fifty-six.

The greatest of Islam's heroes died in extreme poverty, his fortune consisting of forty-seven dinars and one Tyrian gold piece. His friends had to borrow in order to pay for his funeral and the cadi Al-Fadel gave the splendid grave clothes and a shroud.

The total liberation of the Islamic homeland did come about until after another century of fighting, intrigue and diplomatic action. The antagonists were exhausted. The almost traditional rivalry between Cairo and Damascus was exploited by the Christian occupiers.

The Mamluk builders

The situation became more complex after devastating Mongol invasions. The Christians attempted to ally themselves with these hordes who swept down from the Altai to pillage the cities of Asia. Syria was attacked by them in 1260. But in September of that same year salvation came from Egypt where a new dynasty the Mamluks, mercenaries who had revolted against the Ayyubids, had raised a considerable army. Under the command of Sultan Zaher Beybars the Mamluks crushed the Mongols led by Holaku (or Holago) a grandson of Gengis Khan, at Ayn Jalut, and thus liberated Syria. For more than two and a half centuries Syria was to be united under a common sceptre with Egypt.

Beybars established himself at Damascus in order to deal with the Frankish enclaves; one by one the proud fortresses fell. In 1303 one of his successors saw the last Crusader ship leave Arwad, their final stronghold.

In 1401 the Mamluks had to withstand a new whirlwind from central Asia—the raid led by the Turk Timur (Tamerlane).

This trial over, the Mamluks resumed their wise rule, giving considerable autonomy to their provincial governors, and raising tangible monuments to their religious zeal in the mosques, tombs, and madrassas (schools) with which they covered the country. The Mamluks were above all great builders.

A mere province of the Ottoman Empire

After so many troubled centuries Syria was at last regaining her equilibrium when a new danger erupted in the north, in Asia Minor, where the Ottoman Turks (named after Othman who had founded the dynasty in 1299) were dreaming of hegemony.

On 24 August 1516 the troops of Sultan Salim I invaded Syria and, a few weeks later, entered Damascus. His successor Suleiman, called "the Magnificent" (also "the Legislator"), who reigned from 1520 to 1566, organized his vast Empire which stretched from the Danube to the Nile. Syria was divided into three provinces: Damascus, Tripoli and Aleppo. Arts and literature were encouraged. Splendid buildings were constructed in the style of Constant-

The "Old Houses' of the Jadeide quarter enclose courtyards whose style, from and decoration all express the epicurean taste of the bourgeoisie of Aleppo in the 16th and 17th centuries.

inople—palaces, mosques, madrassas, "*takiyeh*" (resting places for pilgrims), khans, and hammams.

But gradually Egypt, Palestine, Iraq, Syria and the rest—all countries with a great past but which were now only provinces of a vast empire whose interests were elsewhere and whose capital was a long way away—all began to feel the yoke becoming increasingly oppressive. The representatives of the Sultan of Constantinople—his emirs, walis and pashas—made their impact not merely by their luxurious style of life but all too often by their ferocity.

In 1831 the Russo-Turkish war considerably weakened the Ottoman Empire. Mehemet Ali, the innovating Sultan of Egypt, seized the opportunity to occupy Syria to which he despatched Ibrahim Pasha as Governor; he remained until only 1840 however.

During the First World War the Ottoman Empire fought on the German side and Syria was involved as a matter of course. On 1 October 1918 Allied troops entered Damascus and in November the last Turkish soldiers left Syria.

Faisal and colonialist intrigues

The British staged a military occupation of Syria and French forces established themselves on the coasts.

In fact Britain and France were intending to apply their secret understanding of 1916 (commonly known as the "Sykes-Picot" Agreement) in which Syria was to be divided, the French taking the coast.

At the same time Britain had made it known to King Hussein Ibn Ali, Sharif of Mecca and Sovereign of the Hijaz that he would become ruler of inland Syria. His son, Faisal I, entered Damascus at the end of

---

TOURIST APHORIMS

■ *They told her "You are so old" Yet she felt so young. Independence had not long ago opened the gates of freedom to her. In her joy she identified freedom vith birth. Set free in this new morning, like a bird from a cage, she thought she would henceforward look only ahead, and now they were demanding that she looked back again.*

Busy with her present, concerned about her future, Syria for a while forgot her past. But tourism is obliging her to list all her palaces, her temples, her churches, her mosques and her fortresses.

In Salzburg, it's Mozart they come to see; in Stratford it's Shakespeare. In Greece people come to see the cradle of Hellenism. But in Syria one can literally learn the history of the world! All the gods have lived in our skies and all the great civilisations of the Mediterrean basin have flourished on our soil.

The day when her visitors spoke of the mists in their own home countries Syria learned the importance of her sunshine.

GABRIEL SAADE

1918 and formed a government. On 7 March 1920 he was proclaimed King of Syria. But the Allied supreme Council, meeting in San Remo, decided that Syria was to become a French mandate. On 22 July 1920 French forces defeated the Arab army after a hard-fought battle at Maysalun 40 kilometres west of Damascus—which they entered three days later.

Under the Treaty of Sevres (10 August 1920) Syria was officially placed under French tutelage.

The French and British, victors and rivals, divided the East between them. Nationalist risings were forcibly put down.

Resistance and independence

The French divided Syria into six "States": Damascus, Aleppo, Jabal Druze, Alouite, Greater Lebanon, and the Sanjak of Alexandretta. In 1922 the States of Damascus, Aleppo and Alouite were grouped to form a "Syrian Federation". The experiment failed and so a "Syrian State" was proclaimed, uniting Damascus and Aleppo.

After the repression of the 1925-1927 revolution the only change in the administration of Syria was the replacement of military by civilian high commissioners.

In 1930 a Constitution was drawn up and a parliamentary system was introduced.

Early in 1936 negotiations were begun with Syrian nationalists which eventually led, fifty days later, to a Franco-Syrian treaty granting internal automomy and guaranteeing the unity of the country. But by the end of the year elections had produced an assembly and a government in which nationalists predominated. In 1939 the French government reversed its policy; it denounced the treaty, suspended the Constitution and took power into its own hands. It even went so far as to dispose of part of Syrian territory—against the wishes of the inhabitants—by ceding the Sanjak of Alexandretta to Turkey whom the Western Powers were cultivating on the eve of the Second World War. Syria to this day refuses to recognise this cession.

In 1943 a nationalist parliamentary regime was instituted, after much equivocation, but the British and French still continued their military occupation—after some regrettable conflict between themselves in 1941.

It was not until the general upheaval at the end of the War that a sovereign and independent Syria was born. In 1944 France handed over power to the first Syrian government and, on 17 April 1946, the last foreign forces left the country.

The newly-independent state was to undergo many vicissitudes before it finally found its way on that March day in 1963 which was described at the beginning of this brief summary of an immensely long but equally fascinating history.

(1) In connection with this rapid survey of a dramatic and confusing period in Syria's history, our thanks are due to Mr. Gabriel Saade. We have frequently drawn on his erudition and kindness and he has provided information on many aspects of Syrian life both past and present.

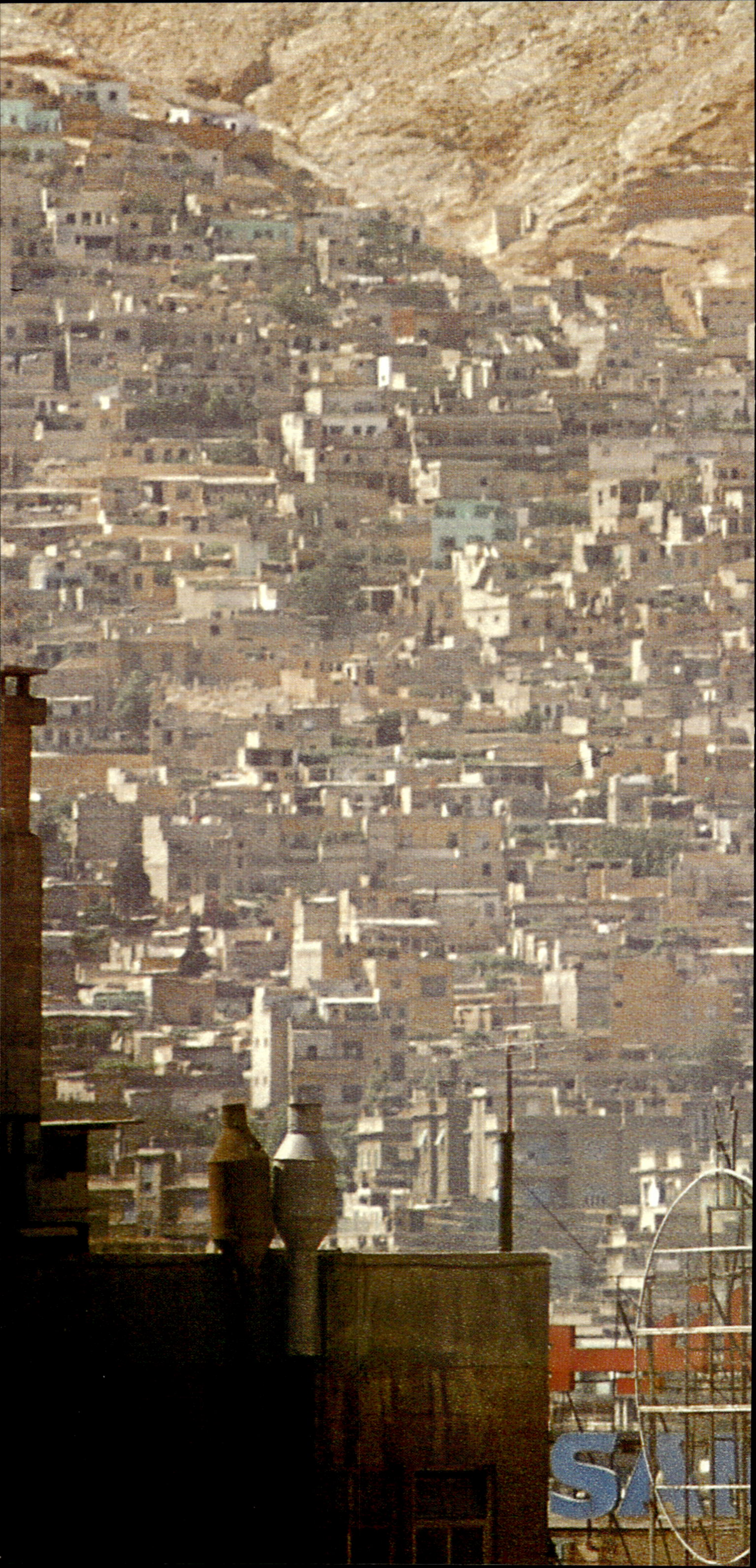

town by town
site by site
from aleppo to zabadani

aleppo

■ "Of all the towns of Syria it is Aleppo that leaves the profoundest impression upon the visitor.

In order to reach it one has to spend many hours crossing extremely monotonous red-earth uplands which stretch to the horizon, almost flat, treeless and without a trace of water. There is no sign of human presence apart from some sullen mud-domed villages and a few wandering flocks and herds. Occasionally a slight undulation arouses hope in the traveller than he is about to see something new, but beyond it the plain stretches ahead monotonous and empty. Then, suddenly, Aleppo appears. Without any warning a slight rise reveals a wide valley, dusty green, in which lies a jumble of houses of the subtlest pastel colours with here and there a slender minaret and, dominating it all, the great mass of the Citadel. It is a striking sight with an austere grandeur of its own; the suddenness of its appearance makes it seem almost unreal. After such a tedious journey one is overjoyed to have reached Aleppo at last. Fortunately, and this is rare in the East, closer acqaintance confirms this delightful first impression..."

These lines written nearly fifty years ago by the the historian and archaeologist J. Sauvaget are still true today—although the landscape around is no longer quite so arid and monotonous. He captures admirably the impression one has arriving late in the afternoon on the road from Damascus and seeing the city lying down there clustered around its central mound crowned with towers and ramparts. With its domes and minarets rising above the houses Aleppo is a poem in stone—grey by day and golden in the evening it looks at first glance uncannily like a romantic print.

On closer inspection, however, as one goes down into the city, modern quarters, fine buildings, fountains, stadiums, public gardens and a large hotel all show that Aleppo is a twentieth-century city too. Modern factories on its outskirts, a bus station in the centre, a university quarter on the slope to the west, together with noise of traffic and motor horns day and night—all serve to remind us that Aleppo is indeed the oldest continuously inhabited city in the world, as all the local publications remind us. (This palm is also claimed by Damascus—just one of many ways in which they show their rivalry.)

Aleppo in outline

(See plan of Aleppo p. 248)

The Damascus road ends in a wide esplanade leading up to the ramparts of the old city—the first houses rise above their towers. Beneath them are little shops and stalls. To the right is the bus station and a a vast open market always thronged with people. To the left, behind the flowerbeds is the *Tourist Information Office*. Its staff are friendly and speak many languages. Opposite a large low simple building houses the rich collections of the archaeolical museum—some mythological animals on the lawns outside serve to identify it.

Between the Tourist Office and the museum lies the beginning of the *rue Baron*, soon crossed by the *rue al-Kouatly*. In this part of town there are hotels, travel agencies, transport company offices, as well as small restaurants and food shops and cool fruit-juice bars decorated with garlands of oranges and multi-coloured jars.

A left turn from the rue Baron into the rue al-Kouatly brings us to a wide esplanade recently planted out as public gardens, dominated by the *General Post Office* and bordered on the north by a shady *public park*. The river Quweiq flows through it and it is famous for its floral displays and its zoo.

In the other direction the rue al-Kouatly crosses the *rue al-Gassaniynn* (sometimes called the rue Tilel), one of the busiest streets in Aleppo. On the right it widens to form a square, the Bab al-Faraj, whose clock-tower has serves at least as a landmark and from here one can

Previous page: Damascus. The city has grown up between an oasis and the Jabal Quassiun whose slopes are now covered with houses. A has been built to the top, from which there is a magnificent view.

easily reach either the old city or the museum. The al-Gassaniynn to the left skirts the *Jedeide*, "old houses", quarter, with its marvellously decorated courtyards; it is largely inhabited by Armenians. St. Georges Cathedral stands behind a labyrinth of narrow streets on a tiny square where there are several antique shops.

There are many interesting routes through the *old city* to the Citadel.

The simplest, and by no means the least picturesque, begins by passing through the postern gate in the middle of the ramparts, known as the *Bab Antakia*, the Antioch Gate. This leads directly into the central axis through the *souks*; it is covered by a vaulted roof for most of its 800 metres and brings us out as the foot of the mound on which the *Citadel* stands. Bab Antakia can be reached by going through an archway on the north-west corner of the ramparts and taking the first narrow street to the right. This leads up to the rampart walk, lined today with houses; there is a good view down onto the crowded esplanade.

Starting again from the north-west corner of the ramparts, the wide *rue al-Moutanabi* leads to a square with a fountain; from there a wide street lined with large modern buildings takes us to the *Great Mosque* and the interesting buildings in its vicinity.

There is a circular road around the foot of the Citadel. To the south wide avenues give access to some interesting madrasas and mosques on the way to *Bab al-Makkam*, a working district where there are many warehouses. To the north of the Citadel the rue *al Kawakbi* crosses the eastern end of the rue al-Kouatly near the picturesque Souk of the Coppersmiths.

The southern ramparts, partly cleared of houses, lead to the most impressive of all the fortified gates: *Bab Qinesrin*. From here a long narrow street brings us back to the central part of the covered souks and to the Great Mosque. South of Bab Qinesrin, half-hidden by an expanse of cemeteries, lies the beautiful *medersa al-Fardos*.

The outskirts to the north and east, expanding residential and industrial areas, have nothing to tempt the tourist. To the west some attractive suburbs are being built around the new *University* and the Hotel Méridien—from the hillsides they have a fine view of the old city.

A three-day tour of Aleppo

This tour outline is only a suggestion. It is designed to offer a varied programme for each day and to alleviate as far as possible the fact that Aleppo can only really be seen on foot. (See plan on p. 248).

First day: The ramparts, Bab Antakia, the Al-Bharamyah Mosque, the covered souks, the Great Mosque and neighbouring buildings, the Citadel.

Second day: the Jedeide district ("Old Houses", St. George's Cathedral, antique shops), the souk of the coppersmiths, the al-Mahmandar Mosque, the Armenian churches, the Archaeological Museum, the Public Gardens and Zoo, the University quarter (look-out point at sunset).

Third day: the al-Firdows Madrasa, Bab Qinesrin, the bimarstan (asylum) al-Kamily, the Cotton Souq (caravansarays and neighbouring buildings), the Al-Atroush Mosque (and other buildings nearby) the Museum of Popular Art and Traditions (in the al-Adjami Palace).

These different sights will now be briefly described in the above order.

Of course this minimum stay in Aleppo should be extended by another three days or more to see some of the sights further afield: Qalaat Semaan, Al-Bara, Cirrhus, Al Thaura, Rasafa, etc., which are described in the relevant entries but where hotel facilities are either non-existent or rudimentary.

Aleppo was a key town on the trade routes for thousands of years and still uses, for local and regional trade, a considerable proportion of the facilities that were developed in the time of the caravans: khans,

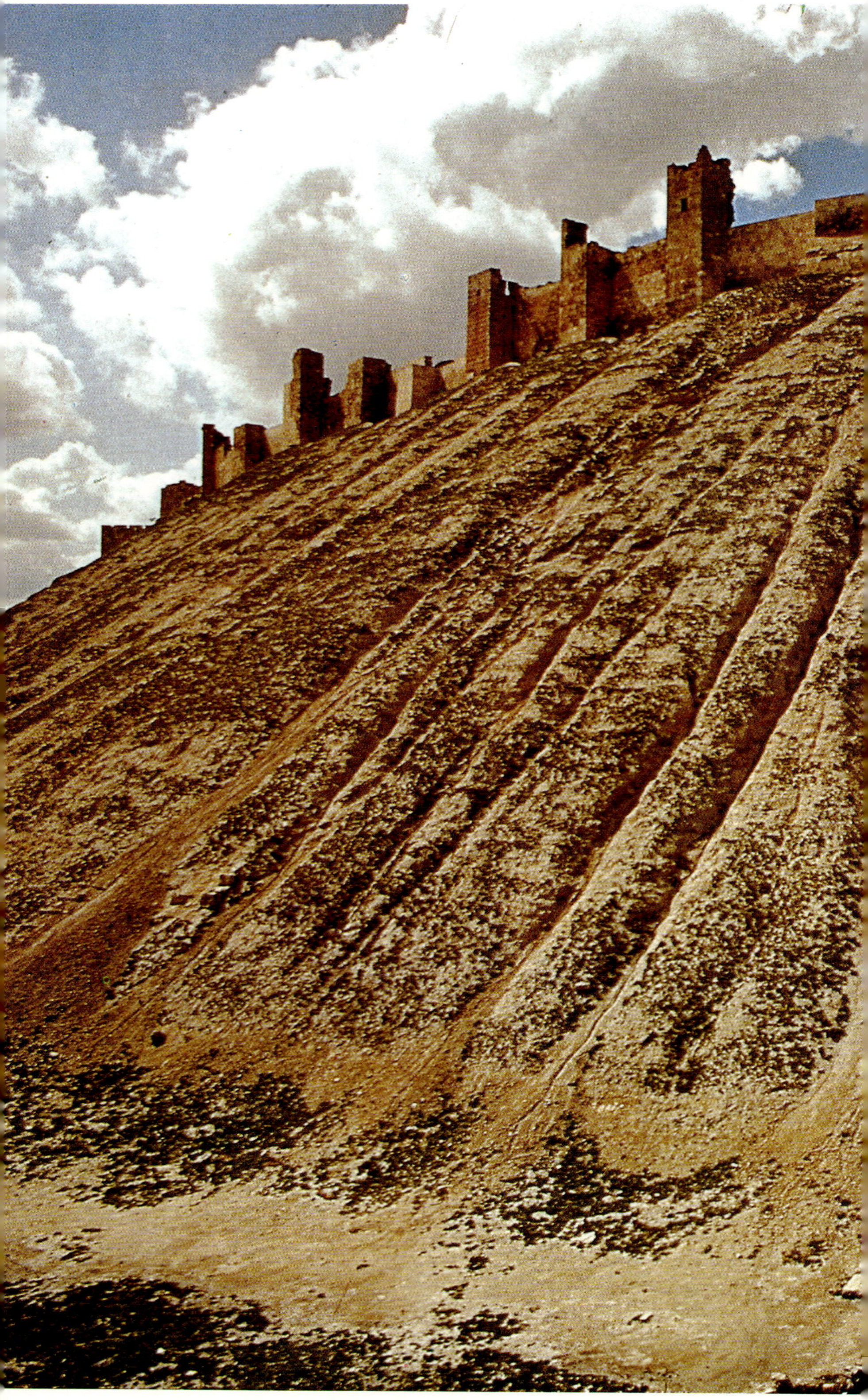

*Abraham is said to have camped here
on this acropolis which, long before his time,
served as the foundation for a fortress.
The lofty Citadel leaves a profound impression on every visitor
to Aleppo. Its ancient stone glacis is being restored.
(Photo Bruno Barbey, Magnum.)*

courtyards as warehouses with workshops around them: kilometres of narrow covered streets where traders and craftsmen congregate according to their various callings and specialities. This busy centre of the old city naturally had many public buildings: mosques, schools (madrassas), baths (hammams), hospitals and asylums (bimarstans), as well as the occasional foreign consulate—the Venetian one dates back to the beginning of the 13th century.

The labyrinthine Covered Souk

A visit to the souks thus enables the tourist to see something of the towns everyday life and at the same time see monuments which are often no longer used (the madrasas and bimarstans for example) but whose design and decoration is extremely interesting.

Along the main axis from Bab Antakia to the Citadel just about every possible kind of goods is offered for sale—food, clothing, perfumes, shoes... What does it matter if tinned goods and plastics are displayed beside freshly gathered vegetables and traditional spices piled up in great gaily coloured heaps, if Western detergents rub shoulders with red and green beeswax candles; if in the narrow passageway that is the al-Irakich souk reserved for the rope-makers, peasants and the last of the camel drivers hesistate between hemp and nylon... Of course it doesn't matter at all; change is a sign of vitality and the daily life of a people who are both faithful to their traditions and also fully up to date is just as interesting to watch as painfully preserved folklore. The visitor may be a little put off at first but he will soon get used to the setting and appreciate the company of these people—traders, artists and customers—who are so often prepared to be friendly.

As far as monuments are concerned, the visitor will wish to see the most characteristic ones.

The semicircular or pointed, slightly horseshoe-shaped vaulting, the domes where streets intersect, all built in fine limestone, are themselves an architectural masterpiece. The thickness of the structure ensures an even temperature all the year round; cool in summer, warm and dry in winter. Openings in the top of the vaulting let in sunbeams sometimes and a gentle light throughout the day.

Some 200 metres from Bab Antakia, on the right, there is a mosque of some importance: *djameh al-Bahramyah*, in the Turkish style with a great dome which is being restored; note the many beautiful small carpets in the prayer hall.

100 metres further on, a short passage (on the righthand side of the main souq which is called at this point al-Sakatiah) leads to the the largest khan in the old city: the *al-Joumrok* (or Gomrok) *khan*, literally the "customs caravanserai". It dates from the 17th century. French, English and Dutch merchants traded here and their consuls were obliged to live here.

Two windows have attractively carved stringcourses. Unfortunately, as in most of these warehouses, secondary buildings in quite unsuitable materials, as well as heaps of wrappings and rubbish, spoil the general impression of the original building.

Contiguous with the al-Joumrok khan, but opening onto a street at right angles to it, the *al-Mahmas souk*, is the *al-Nahasine khan*. Littered with bales and shaded by some scrawny trees in the centre this khan is occupied by shoemakers. In a corner a staircase leads up to a private house which was the Venetian consulate from the 15th to the 19th century when it became the *residence of the Belgian consul*. M. Poche, former consul and President of the Archaeological Society, rarely refuses to show visitors this typically Venetian house, in which many generations of men of taste have built up a priceless collection of works of art from every country between China and Egypt—yet another sign of Aleppo's transcontinental role.

Opposite the al-Nahhasine khan, a low door gives access to one of the oldest hammams of Aleppo; it is open for inspection—and use.

The *al-Doukh souk* (the first turning on the right as you walk up the al-Mahmas souk) houses leather workers, shoe merchants and carpet wholesalers and leads to the *Cotton souk and khan* (khan al-Ilabyah). Here there donkeys and carts all piled high with enormous bales crammed so full that the cotton spills out on the ground.

Opposite the souks and khans already mentioned, in relation to the central axis, (here called the al-Sakatiiah souk and the al-Attarin souk) stands the *jami al-Kabir*, the Umayyad or Great Mosque.

The entrance is on the western side, opposite an old Koran school, the *al-Halawyah madrasa*, installed in the former Byzantine Cathedral erected at the command of the Empress Helena. The tinsmiths of the rue *souk al-Hiddadin* share their street in the mornings with open air stalls full of fruit... and vine leaves.

The *Great Mosque* was founded in the early Islamic period but there is little to see that dates from that time. Its somewhat heavy style shows it to be mainly Mamluk, but its beautiful minaret, which rises straight from the street, dates from 1090 and is with its fine proportions and Kufic inscriptions a good example of the great period of Islamic architecture in Syria.

The north facade of the Great Mosque forms one side of a square crowded with hawkers and pedlars. On the square, to the right on leaving the mosque, a two-coloured gateway with a honeycomb vault and heavily studded doors beneath, leads into the ancient *al-Charafyah madrassa* which used to be a library. It would be comparatively simple to clear it of ugly accretions and Unfortunately its lovely decorated windows are half-hidden by ugly accretions—which it would be fairly easy to remove.

The same unfortunately applies to the neighbouring khan, the *al-Wazir*, with its monumental 17th-century gateway, which was cut into when the street was built.

A narrow street between the al-Charafyah madrasa and the east wall of the mosque leads into more covered streets where *jewellers and goldsmiths* abound. The goods they offer are little different from those sold everywhere from Cairo to Teheran—and beyond!

Popular art and traditions

Almost opposite the al-Wazir khan a little doorway leads into the *Museum of Popular Art and Traditions,* installed in a palace built in 1354—which has also suffered from recent town development.

The whole collection is not yet on display and only the central hall of the palace is open to view—a vast patio under a stalactite dome. There is an iwan opposite the entrance and three rooms in large alcoves on the other three sides.

The side rooms are furnished with decorated chests, sofas and chairs inlaid with pearl-shell, ebony and ivory. There are many mirrors, lamps, samovars and other objects in 19th-century Ottoman taste.

The displays in the glass cases are more interesting: blue and brownish glassware, ewers, plates and dishes of steel or damascened bronze, finely-chased silver. There is jewellery too.

An extraordinary painted wooden contraption

Finally there is an extraordinary wooden conraption, a sort of ancester of the modern cinema: covered with mirrors and spy-holes, with a sort of boiler at the back, it was taken from village to village and set up on the square. Three "viewers" crouched over the spy-holes, fascinated, as the "operator" produced a series of moving pictures with an appropriate commentary.

One always returns to the Citadel and its fortified entrance which is such a marvellous example of Arab military architecture. Here power by no means excludes beauty of decoration.

The Citadel

Abraham is said to have camped on this hill and milked his red cow there on his journey from Ur to Howran. But from even earlier the remains of more ancient civilisations have raised the level of this acropolis beneath which so many bloody and terrible events have taken place.

50 metres above the city a ring of crenellated walls and towers rises from a steep glacis, encircling a mass of ruins of every period.

On the north and south sides great towers rise above the moat. This moat, some 20 metres deep and 30 metres wide emphasizes the proud isolation of the whole fortress. This impression has been rather spoiled by the planting of a clump of trees right in front of the entrance gate. A steeply rising bridge, supported by slender arches, leads across the moat from an entrance tower on the lower side to the great and forbidding entrance fortifications above. These are both austerely beautiful and full of ingenious defensive devices which strike even a 20th-century visitor as sophisticated. Five great iron-plated doors—each set at a corner of the passageway—could be closed to trap invaders under a hail of arrows, fire and boiling oil (used in these parts since ancient times) from the lookout places, arrow-slits and machiolations above.

But such grim efficiency did not preclude decoration and reminders of the presence of God. The nailheads on the doors themselves beautifully worked, the lintels have comic or enigmatic carvings on them—intertwined serpents, a pair of lions confronting one another, one smiling the other weeping, and above all there are the fine kufic inscriptions calling upon the power and the mercy of Allah.

The interior of the Citadel shows all too clearly how it has been ravaged by enemies (the Mongols invaded it twice) and shattered by earthquakes (that of 1822 was particularly devastating).

As we follow the arrowed route the keepers will point out the various points of interest: the little domed Byzantine church converted into a mosque; a prison with dungeons dug out of the rock, a stretch of wall four metres thick which was the base of a Syro-Hittite temple; the remains of a great mosque built by Saladin's son, still flanked by its square minaret 20 metres high—from which there is a splendid view. A covered building contains fragments of sculpture and objects from various periods found on the site.

Wells 60 metres deep are said to have been linked up with mysterious underground passages. Gigantic cisterns and grain silos guaranteed the garrison's survival in times of siege.

The visit ends with the 13th-century royal palace, with its fine stalactite and honeycomb entrance porch, inlaid with white marble. The throne room, dating from the Mamluk period (15th-16th centuries) has been most tastefully restored. Syrian artists and cratsmen have here recreated the luxurious setting of the court: the ceiling with its decorated beams and caissons, the lighting, the windows, the polychrome columns—all are a tribute to their skill. It also illustrates the way the Department of Museums and Antiquities are going about their vast task of restoration and reconstruction.

Two hundred minarets

The commercial quarters are not limited to the souks whose grass-covered vaults can be seen from the rampart walk to the west of the Citadel. A netweork of narrow streets surrounds the castle mound itself. There are minarets in every direction—two hundred it is said —some squat like defensive towers, others slender as needles.

In the street leading to the entrance to the Citadel, opposite the al-Khousrawria mosque (a large building of no particular interest), is a more modest building with a dome. The Emir Zaher Ghazi (son of Saladin) is buried there in an annexe to a madrassa founded during the Crusader period (the *Sultaniya madrassa*).

Close—too close in fact—to these historic parts stand the Municipal Buildings, the *Seraglio,* an imposing modern structure with black marble columns.

Between it and the Citadel moat an old building has recently been cleared of accretions. Its facade, with a lofty entrace porch is decorated with stone of two colours; its roof is covered with cupolas which look like huge pimples. It was at one time a textile factory; at the moment it is being restored. This is the *al-Nasiri hammam,* one of the oldest "Turkish baths" in the city.

Other mosques and "the School of Paradise"

On the other side—i.e. facing away from the Citadel and the Seraglio—stands a fine octagonal minaret with a double wooden balcony and decorated with an attractive frieze around its base. It is part of the *al-Atroush (or Otrouch) mosque* which dates from the 15th century. Its porch forms an iwan, richly decorated and framed between twisted columns. Its courtyard is reminisent of a church cloister, with trees—figs, olives and pines—and a scattering of graves.

The rue *Bab al-Makkam,* lined with warehouses and enclosures containing sheep and even dromedaries, leads to an open-air morning market near the ancient town gate or bab. Continuiing in the same direction, crossing waste land and cemeteries, some 800 metres further on on the left (it is easy to miss it) lies the *al-Fardos (or Firdows) madrassa* (literally, and charmingly, "the school of Paradise")—one of the loveliest and most moving religious buildings in Aleppo. A dark twisting passageway brings us to a light and beautifully proportioned courtyard. It's a wonderfully peaceful spot; all harmony, sobriety and purity. The high pointed arches are supported on small columns with palm-leaf capitals. There is a great iwan on the north side. The sky is reflected in a pool in the centre. In a double domed chamber Mamluks lied buried under the floor in unmarked graves. The bustle of the city seems miles away...

More souks and the "old houses"

Due north of the Citadel, at right angles to the road which encircles the mound, the *rue al-Kawakbi* leads to a quarter where craftsmen abound and the coppersmiths' hammers can be heard all day. Great sheets of copper are transformed into jugs and pans by their well-aimed blows; a rough outline drawn on the wall is their only pattern. They sell their goods by weight. At the end of this street of copper a beautifully carved entrance leads into a vulgar warehouse.

A little covered souk brings us back to the centre, crossing the rue al-Kouatly near an old gateway, the *Bab al-Nasr* (victory), and joins the rue al-Moutanabi on which stands a small mosque, the *al-Mahmandar*. It has a curious minaret—a square base becomes first octagonal then cylindrical and each stage is decorated in a different style. It is surmounted by a hideous iron watchtower.

We now come the *Jedeide, or* "old houses" quarter, bounded by the rue al-Gassaniynn on the west and the al-Kouatly on the south. All the houses here are built of fine limestone, lining narrow streets with no shops and sometimes vaulted. They are all most beautifully kept by their owners who are mainly Christians of Armenian origin.

A guide is useful here to point out the courtyards which are completely invisible from the street. Little anonymous doorways lead into courts whose general style and decoration exemplifies the epicurean tastes of the bourgeois of Aleppo in the 16th and 17th centuries. There is always a fountain in the centre and sometimes a little garden planted with jasmine and roses. A high deep iwan, simply furnished for relaxation or for dining, generally occupies the cooler north side. The other facades, with living rcoms behind, have beautifully carved surrounds to their doors and windows. There is a whole variety of motifs—rosettes, ribbons, and garlands—which look like lace made of golden stone. The roofline is emphasized by a carved frieze and gargoyles. It is all essentially Syrian and unique to Aleppo.

The inhabitants are proud of their beautiful houses and very kindly disposed to visitors and photographers. Many of these houses are now owned collectively and run as institutions and schools. Unfortunately they are sometimes marred by later accretions—ugly chimneys and other incongrous eyesores.

The new Archaeological Museum

Five fantastic animals and two giants—two men and one woman, with bulging black and white eyes—all made of black basalt, greet the visitor—as they used to greet priests and pilgrims, in Syro-Hittite times, as they entered the temple-palace at Tell Halaf near the river Khabur in the 9th century B.C.

A mythical beast with the head of a man, an eagle's body and the tail of a scorpion joins with them to plunge the visitor straight away into that mysterious period, four or five thousand years ago, which be studied here—and in Damascus—better than anywhere else in the world.

Mari (Tell Hariri) has pride of place; with statues of Prince Istup-Illum and of the "Goddess with the Vase" and dozens of smaller figures, men and women, with long beards and robes of plaited wool, and their names in cuneiform script on their bare right shoulders.

There are tables illustrating the similarities between the ancient scripts and even the Greek and Roman alphabets.

The sculptures found at *Hama* occupy a series of rooms; there is a splendid pair of lions almost more comic than terrifying. The excavations at *Ras Shamra-Ugarit* have yeilded many bronze statuettes of which the most famous is of a prince or warrior with a craggy face and huge eyes, wearing a golden loincloth and bearing a gold sceptre in his right hand.

Sphinxes, lions and buffaloes

From *Tell Halaf*, near present-day Ras al-Ain on the Khabur, come not only the monsters near the entrance but also many enigmatic figures carved from massive blocks of black stone—sphinxes, lions, buffaloes, men and women with goats' bodies... Excavations at *Arlan Tash* (near Ayn al-Arab on the Turkish frontier) have yielded similar basalt figures, from the Hittite period and showing Assyrian and Egyptian influences.

Tell Ahmar, on the right bank of the Euphrates, halfway between Jarablus and Qalaat Najm, consists of the remains of the capital of a small Aramean kingdom of the 10th century B.C. From here come stelae of Assyrian manufacture and pottery than looks astonishingly modern.

Upstairs there is a display devoted to the rescue of sites threatened by the rising waters of Lake Al-Assad. (see under Al-Thaura). There are several cases showing work under way or completed by various foreign expeditions.

Finally a long gallery contains the beginnings of a collection of modern Syrian painting and sculpture. Since the artists' names and the titles of the works are not transliterated the visitor has to remain content to note and compare various expressive works by artists who are still feeling their way. This impression is confirmed by the sculptures in the *public gardens* by the Queiq; where he will no doubt wish to relax in the shade after his wanderings through this fascinating and lovely city.

ALEPPO

Name: Variant names: Halab, Haleb. The French form Alep is frequently used. Hittite period, Halap (2nd millenium B.C.), Capital of the Kingdom of Yamhad. Hellenistic Period: Beroia (2nd century B.C.).

Location and access: Principal town of governorate. Altitude 300 m. 350 km north of Damascus, by motorway and four-lane highway, via Hama (140 km), Homs (185 km), 180 km north-east of Latakia, by motorway as far as Sarâqeb (60 km) and then by excellent but hilly road. 320 km north-west of Deir-ez-Zor, by excellent road as far as Al-Thaura (140 km), afterwards good. Turkish frontier post at Bab al-Hawa, 50 km to the west. (Antakya, 95 km, Iskenderun, 130 km).

Railway: Aleppo-Al-Thaura-Raqqa line (two trains a day); Aleppo-Beirut line; Aleppo-Jisr ash-Shughur extended since 1975 to Latakia (very fine mountain route). Connection with Turkish railways at Azaz.

Airport: The city has an international airport on the Raqqa road. Offices of Syrian Air Lines and main international airlines, rue Baron.

Taxi services: Firms running taxis to Hama, Homs, Damascus, Beirut: Al-Syaha, tel. 44439; Al-Salam, tel. 22722; Al-Baba, tel. 11322; Al-Nahda, tel. 10836; Mass, tel. 14808; Al-Jinedi, tel. 15814; Chouha, tel. 15175 To Latakia: Al-Sahel, tel. 11703; Al-Dinany, tel. 11723. To Al Thaura, Raqqa, Deir ez Zor: Al-Raqqa, tel. 11153; Al-Chahba, tel. 15624; Omaya, tel. 11002; Aziza, tel. 11486; Port-Said, tel. 11428; Al-Sourie, tel. 26887. To Azaz, Afrine: Al-Jetimal, tel. 14306; Al-Sourie, tel. 26887. To Manbij, Jarablus: Al-Naser, tel. 14699; Aziza, tel. 11486. To Bab el-Hawa, Turkey: Al-Chabba, tel. 15624; Halap, tel. 14290.

Bus services: Macharka Bus Station, opposite the old city. Bus companies: Karnak, offices Baron street, tel. 10248, services to Damascus, Latakia, Beirut. Ayn Arag, offices rue Yarmouk, tel. 15086, minibus service to Ayn al-Arab. Various other companies, offices at Macharka: tel. 15292, Hama-Homs service; tel. 27308, Al-Thaura service; tel. 25284, Idlib service; tel. 26547, Latakia service; tel. 10915, Deir-ez-Zor service; tel. 26635, Damascus, Ayn al-Arab, Azaz-Afrine services.

Information: Tourist Bureau, Baron street, opposite Archeological Museum. Tel. 21200. Open Fridays and Holidays 9 a.m. to 2 p.m., all other days 8 a.m. to 8 p.m. Warm welcome, multilingual staff, leaflets and brochures in good supply. Official guides available. See plan, page 000.

Accommodation: Méridien (Air France hotel)****A, west district, near University; opening 1977. *Tourism'Hôtel* (Al-Syahi)***B, Saadalah al-Djabri street (opposite public gardens, tel. 10156/58, 95 rms.; *Baron****B, Baron street (next to Air France offices), tel. 10880/81, 46 rms. garage, excellent welcome, French-speaking staff; *Les Ambassadeurs***A, Baron street, tel. 10231, 18 rms.; *Granada***A, Baron street, tel. 24959, 36 rms.; *Heliopolis***A, Bab Faraj, tel. 17104, 45 rms.; *Ramsis***B, Baron street, tel. 16700, 41 rms.; *Semiramis***A, Kuwatly street, tel. 19990, 38 rms.; *Omaya Jadid***A, Al-Chahbandar, tel. 14104, 38 rms.; Phenicia (Venicia)**A, Al-Masaben, tel. 25909, 17 rms. Plus many other hotels (see list, Chapter "Syrian Journey").

Youth Hostel: on the square in front of the railway station.

Restaurants: Open-air with swimming-pool: *The Oasis (Al-Waha),* Al-Midan street, tel. 48609; *Gondoul,* Ayn Al-Tal, tel. 49555; *Rabiah,* Damascus road, tel. 16052; *Riviera,* Ayn Al-Tal, tel. 45660. There are a dozen or so especially well-known restaurants mostly situated in the area bounded by Baron street, Gul-Ab street, Saad Alah al-Djabri street (detailed list from Tourist Bureau). There are about a hundred plain, popular, inexpensive restaurants in different parts of the city.

Discotheques: Blow-Up, Saad Alah al-Djabri street, tel. 24755; *Chanel,* Pensilvania street, tel. 18966; *Mogambo,* Al-Omran street, tel. 22888; *Touring-Club,* Ayn Al-Tal, tel. 45847; *Venus,* Al-Nadi street, tel. 12809; *Gold Finger,* in Muslimieh, 18 km north of Aleppo.

Festivals and Fairs: Cotton Festival, every year in September, an international gathering with many artistic, folklore and popular events. Industrial and agricultural exhibition in July. Autumn Plastic Arts Exhibition in November.

Souvenirs: Locally produced craft work (see text).

A PASSIONATE LOVE OF STONE

■ *The Citadel of Aleppo, its deep moat, its splendid steep glacis, is the true symbol of a city which, throughout its long history has resisted ruin and death. Beneath it lies a dense network of beautiful and functional buildings. By contrast with Mesopotamia, built of poor brick and mud, Aleppo has used her splendid limestone with almost prodigal abandon and at the same time with great skill. The very nature of the stones imbues her buildings with life and vigour as does the use of water in Damascus, animating the architecture with fountains and pools...*
                    From a Unesco report on the preservation of historic buildings in Syria

apamea

■ In the month of June, on the stroke of two o'clock, when the wind stops blowing down the Orontes valley and sultry heat settles down on the plain, heavy tractor-drawn floats can be seen bringing back the workers from the fields—a lively medley of smiling faces and brightly-coloured scarves.

In the heart of the golden Ghab

Here half-way between Masyaf and Jisr ash Shughur, *the Ghab* can be seen in all its lush new fertility (see under Jisr ash Shughur). Wide irrigation canals now contain the waters of the Orontes which only yesterday flowed to waste in insalubrious marshland. (Although the maps haven't yet caught up and still indicate marshes here.)

Behind a clump of trees the water-tanks of a fish-farm give the impression of an oasis—a green spot amid the golden cornfields. As late as 1955 as one can see from photographs—the area abounded in pools of dirty, stagnant water, the remains of a vast lake much esteemed in ancient times for its stocks of catfish.

Heavily-laden lorries make their way slowly down the road, leaving hot furrows behind them in the tar which has melted in the heat. Most of them are making towards a great brown castle whose massive towers rise from high cliffs to survey the valley, at the point where another ravine joins it. This is *Qalaat al-Mudiq*, "the fortress on the defile."

Beneath the town stands a khân, dating from the Ottoman period, a vast square blank-walled building which used to receive caravans and pilgrims as they made their way up and down the Orontes corridor. One of the best-preserved khâns in all Syria, with high vaulted rooms around a vast courtyard, scheduled as an historic building and restored by the Department of Antiquities, it is intended that this caravanserai shall become a museum.

The fortified town above has lost its role as a refuge and mercantile staging post. Yet the lorry-drivers of today still stop at the bottom of the cliffs to refresh themselves with drinks and fruit from the little booths, and to exchange news.

There are steep paths leading up from the caravanserai to the ramparts and a little mosque, half-way up the slope. But it is more convenient to follow the surfaced road as it winds round the town to the north.

Like many another acropolis, Qalaat al-Mudiq is impressive from outside but less so within—a network of half-abandoned streets and houses in need of repair. But the view from the ramparts, of the Ghab in its valley and of the ravine which gave the town its Arabic name, is well worth climbing up for.

An Arab castle

A link in the chain of medieval fortresses which formed a continous line of defence along the Orontes valley, the "fortress on the defile" suffered the same reversals of fortune as its neighbours, from the 10th to the 13th century. Like Sheizar to the south and Jisr ash-Shughur to the north (see entries) it was the scene of battles between Arabs and Byzantine forces, and between Crusaders and Saracens (Nur ad-Din finally recaptured it from the princes of Antioch, in July 1149). But the earthquakes of 1157 and 1170 did even more damage. The fortress was nevertheless restored at the beginning of the following century. Its square towers, the use of sections of columns to bond the stones in its walls, its steep even-sloped glacis—all these are characteristic features of Arab castles of this period.

This similarity in appearance and situation to other Syrian fortifications would lead to the neglect of Qalaat al-Mudiq (it is some distance from the main highways) were it not for the fact that it is also a most important archaeological site and the living remnant, as it were, of ancient *Apamea*. A Belgian expedition has patiently excavated what remains of this city, in the neighbouring valley and on the plateau to the east of the medieval town.

Apamea: a fine Hellenistic and Roman city

The excavations here (begun in 1930 and continuing annually since 1965) have only partially revealed the secrets of the city, as yet. A casual passer-by would be quite unaware of the extent of work to date. From the road even the scanty patches of wheat that battles against the thistles on these chalky slopes is enough to hide what has been uncovered of a city which used to contain up to 120,000 inhabitants.

Apamea had seven kilometres of ramparts around it. The city's water tanks were filled by an acqueduct 120 metres long. The theatre—with a facade of 139 metres—is one of the largest known. The Seleucids kept a reserve of six hundred elephants here, as well as a breeding stud of thirty thousand mares and three hundred stallions...

A crossroads for the East, Apamea received many distinguished visitors. Cleopatra came here on her return from a visit to the Euphrates, accompanying Antony who was campaigning there against Armenia; Septimus Severus arrived in 179, when he was legate of the 4th Scythian Legion and later, in 215, the Emperor Caracalla called here on his way home from a journey to Egypt. In the 4th century Apamea was still conscious of a pagan past, of the glory that her school of philosophers had brought to the city, and that despite the vigour of her bishops who were well known even in distant Constantinople. Somewhat later the city became a centre of Monophostism, the doctrine denying the duality of the nature of Christ, which shook the eastern episcopate to its foundations and led to the establishment of the Syriac-speaking Jacobite Church.

Unfortunately—or perhaps fortunately—the ruins of Apamea, open to all the winds that blow, speak a poetic rather than an historic messahe to the non-specialist visitor. So perhaps it is better to simply wander around...

The most important features of the site are: the theatre, in the lower part of the valley, opposite the Arab castle, on the right-hand side; the churches, in the other direction entirely, on the eastern fringe of the city, to the right of the surfaced road from Qalaat al-Mudiq to Khân Sheikhûn and about a kilometre from where it crosses the *decumanus*; finally and above all the decumanus itself, the main artery of the city, running north-south.

The ruins of the *theatre*, so many times shaken by earthquakes, are a great mass of huge blocks of stone. However, a part of the stage wall, the lower ranges of seats with their stone mouldings, and the south wall with a fine barrel vault—an entrance to the theatre, do give some idea of the severe beauty of this great open shell facing the fortress. Excavations have ceased for the time being but are due to start again.

The *Christian quarter*, in the south-west part of the city, contains the foundations of many buildings, the most important being a church, known as "the Cathedral of the East" and a palace which was probably the Governor's residence at the end the 4th and beginning of the 5th century. The church, which is preceded by an *atrium* (an interior courtyard surrounded by a portico) was built at the same time, over the remains of a synagogue which had been pillaged and burned. The palace contained nearly eighty rooms, grouped around a vast peristyle and two interior courts. The floors were covered with fine *mosaics*. Alas, some of them have found their way to Brussels, where a room in one of the royal museums of art and history is devoted to Apamea. Others have been preserved in the museums at Hama and Damascus. (In the latter, worthy of special note, there is a section from a pavement, dated 469, which depicts a noria; thus proving the existence in this region, from Byzantine times, of these great wheels by which water was raised to irrigate the land.)

Quite a number of mosaics remain in situ, but to preserve them they are covered with a layer of sand—the visitor has to be content with a glimpse of a small patch here and there.

Order out of chaos

A Hellenistic and Roman city, Apamea is laid out in chessboard fashion, like so many other imperial cities. The siting of the various buildings and quarters of the city was all determined in relation to the decumanus, the central axis. Along this splendid thoroughfare flowed most of the public life of the city and it, almost as much as its temples, symbolised a city's pride and prestige. It was lined with shops and linked the principal gates of the city. The decumanus was crossed by the *cardo,* the main street at right angles to it, usually somewhere about mid-way along its length and close to the agora or forum.

The *decumanus* at Apamea was almost two kilometres long (1,850 m. to be precise) and 37.50 metres wide. Quite a respectable boulevard for even a modern city! It was lined throughout its length with porticos which rested on lofty columns. Monotony in the general perspective was avoided by subtle differences in the various sections of the colonnade; smooth columns with twisted mouldings at the base, columns with straight or twisted fluting. All the capitals were elegant Corinthian ones.

This great colonnade was erected in the 2nd century A.D. and was still standing in the 12th. It took the earthquakes of 1157 and 1170 to demolish it.

The ground is littered today with a chaotic jumble of pavingstone, great drums which were once parts of

*Dominating the tumbled ruins of the city
a series of columns with twisted fluting has been re-erected;
their capitals and entablatures have been put back in place.
Instantly all became orderly once more,
perspective returned and both reason
and instinct were satisfied.*

columns, huge capitals, lumps of broken frieze and metope. Here in the centre they are piled high, so that the visitor has to clamber over them —farther out, especially towards the north gate, they cover the ground as far as the eye can see. Vast areas, to the south of the decumanus particularly, are still covered by the earth that has hidden them for centuries

A choatic spectacle, indeed! But dominating the tumbled ruins of the city, transcending the disorder, a series of columns with twisted fluting has been re-erected; their capitals and entablatures have been put back in place. The steps separating the mosaic-covered floors of the colonnades from the traffic of the street have been freed from the soil which had buried them... All has become orderly once more, perspective has returned and reason and instinct are satisfied. Thanks are certainly due to the Belgian archaeologists and to the Syrian Department of Antiquities for this modest, appropriate and exemplary piece of restoration which alone would justify a visit to Apamea.

One or two interesting details

To left of the decumanus, facing north, towards the reconstructed colonnade, shortly after the point where it crosses the cardo, the ruins of a great building with a courtyard surrounded by a portico can be seen. This was the Temple of Fortune, or *Tycheon*, which dates from Roman times. It replaced an earlier, Hellenistic, building of which traces can be seen on the back wall; there is a niche with a finely-sculptured surround.

Behind the temple stretches the lengthy *agora*, accessible from the cardo through a monumental gateway and on the other side through propylea with curious bulbous columns whose highly-wrought bases seem to spring from stylised acanthus calyxes.

To the right of the decumanus and a little to the right there are first of all the remains of the baths, then the brick foundations of the last arcades of the acqueduct and, by the side of the road approaching the north gate, a square-based pillar decorated with bacchic motifs.

The earliest monasteries of Syria

Doubtless the next series of excavations will reveal new and fascinating things, and perhaps solve some old problems—in the same way as the discovery in recent years of a monastic complex which has been almost certainly identified as Nikertai (4 ½kms north-east of the ancient city).

Nikertai in Apamea, founded about 370, played an important role in the spread of Christianity in Northern Syria, and then again in the following century (paganism having been defeated) in the doctrinal battles which marked the detachment of Syria from the influence of Byzantium. The monks of Nikertai founded numerous daughter-houses throughout the region. Yet the actual site of their headquarters had been lost. Today the walls of churches, monasteries and their dependent buildings are appearing once again on the bare plateau. Sarcophagi, door lintels and a chancel stone have been unearthed, all bearing the engraved chrisma. The archaeologists have also discovered a great olive-press and even olive stones—signs of the past fertility of these parts where not even stunted bushes grow nowadays.

The discovery of a "hoard" of 534 gold coins dating from a much later period has shown that it is likely that the site was still inhabited 45 years after Apamea had been conquered by the Arabs, and that Byzantine and Christian institutions persisted here into the second half of the 7th century.

See Information p. 107.

baniyas

In all the 90 kilometres between Latakia and Tartous, the coast-road gives us only one glimpse of the sea. This view comes as we approach Baniyas.

The town appears suddenly, spread round the curve of a small bay formed by the alluvium deposited by a shallow coastal river. It is far from compact in appearance, like so many military centres and ports, and would seem at first glance to depend more on agriculture than on the sea. There are great clumps of trees between the white houses with their pink roofs, and the slopes around enclose the town like a shell. The white domes of tombs mark the tops of some of the surrounding hills whilst the dark mass of the castle of Marqab crowns the highest, set a little way back from the others.

Gardens and oil

All around the orchards, fields and crops are protected from winds blowing in off the sea, by tall rows of cypresses. From time immemorial Baniyas has been famous for its gardens and for many years the town drew its wealth from great forests which have completely disappeared today. The port, which lost all its military importance after the reconquest, depended entirely on its exports of wood. Today it is silted up and used by only a handful of fishing vessels. But, a sign of the times, gigantic oil tankers are taking their place.

Balanea under the Greeks, La Valénie to the Crusaders, Baniyas is enjoying a new boom as an oil-pipeline terminal.

Enormous storage tanks, drawn up on the plain like pieces in some gigantic game of draughts, mark the ends of a cluster of 33 inch pipes which stretch across mountain and desert all the way to the oil wells at Kirkouk in Iraq. A refinery, its towers dazzling silver in the sun, treats six million tonnes of crude oil every year. Harbour installations have been built out into the sea to permit continuous loading of tankers.

A little beyond this industrial complex, nature takes over once more. A vast stretch of water, half hidden behind dense trees, is the clue to the luxuriance of the plantations—particularly the nearby orange groves. It is fed by an an underground spring whose waters flowed to waste, until very recently, into the *Sinn*—the shortest river in Syria, only 6 kilometres long.

It seems quite likely that the economic revival of Baniyas could lead to some development of tourism.

Bathing and History

Like many other towns on the Syrian coast, Baniyas could attract tourists. If one or two decent hotels were built, and a modicum of resort facilities developed, visitors would certainly stay here.

The beach is narrow but extensive. The surrounding countryside, as we have seen, is attractive. If Baniyas itself has no picturesque reminders of its past, its hinterland contains many relics—some of them considerable—of the wars between Arabs and Franks. The *castle of Marqab* (see special entry) is one of the most impressive and the best preserved.

Another important fortress is that at *Masyaf* (see entry under this name too). This was the stronghold of the Ismailis; it can be reached in less than an hour by car, taking the attractive Baniyas-Hama road which skirts deep ravines to climb up to the desolate ridge of the Ansariya, before plunging down towards the fertile Ghab.

Almost every ridge and peak in that range was fortified by someone. The "Old Man of the Mountains" ruled over the heights for a long while (see under Masyaf). Unfortunately those eyries are often difficult of access—a jeep and a good guide are essential.

See Information p. 107.

bara (al)

■ Al Bara, a modest village living from the cultivation of cherries and olives, lies forgotten at the bottom of a valley in the province of Idlib.

The brightly-dressed women of the place can be seen fetching water from fountain, in copper or tin cans which they carry on their heads. Schoolchildren walk about the little country roads, learning their lessons as they go. Small boys lead the family's donkey back from the orchards. But it isn't for its bucolic charm that Al Bara deserves a place on the visitor's itinerary. Indeed very few visitors do come up here. —So few in fact that they are received as honoured guests by the notables of the village, who hasten to offer them tea and to guide them around the ruins of "the largest ghost town in Northern Syria."

The village nestles half-way up the slope overlooking a wide valley. The whole of the valley floor and the slope opposite are covered with the remains of a vast number of houses which can be see between the olive trees. The ruins, though indeed at first sight they seem too large to be ruinous, spread over at least three kilometres.

The largest "ghost town"

The landscape seems tinged with a faint sadness. The silence of the grave seems to hover over the depopulated valley. The village urchins usually so full of life when visitors appear, are few and timid. The dark-brown, almost black soil is scattered with dull grey rocky outcrops. Pieces of broken building stone everywhere mutely proclaim the life that has departed...

For Al Bara was once an important town, known from the 2nd century B.C. and still active after the Frankish invasions. The Crusaders took the place in 1098 and were driven out of it twenty-five years later. Muslim tombs, small mosques and inscriptions in Arabic, indicate that rural and even intellectual life continued here for several centuries more. The town was evidently abandoned gradually, as the arable soil was gradually eroded and washed away down the valley—a process that is still going on. (The same thing happened more dramatically elsewhere—(see entries for Kalb Lozé and Qalaat Samaân.)

A detailed visit takes several hours and is quite a tiring business, due to the terrain, the vegetation invading everything, and the number of low dividing walls that have to be clambered over. Yet since there are no really imposing and important buildings it is not easy to restrict oneself to just one sector. The young men of the village willingly act as guides; their help is most useful.

Villas, churches, monumental tombs

There are three types of building to be seen at Al Bara.

The dwellings in many cases still have their double-storied facade. Some have porticos in front of them. Over the doors there are great stones, set at an angle, which act as porches. The house that is furthest away the west is also the best preserved, not having been used as a quarry for other building. It is known as *Deir Sobat,* "the convent", despite being merely a farm and dependent buildings. In some of the houses there are still olive and winepresses in the cellars. One of these has a Latin inscription on it, just over the hole through which the wine used to flow down into the basement, in which Bacchus is mentioned (although the building dates from the Christian era) "This nectar that you see—gift of Bacchus—is the fruit of the vine, fed by the warm sunshine."

The three main *churches* are laid out on a basilican plan, with three aisles. Their fallen roofs and the luxuriant vegetation that clings to them make it difficult to study them in detail. Their decoration is extremely sober—merely a few acanthus leaves, sometimes stylized, and the occasional chrisma on some of the lintels. There are no delicate carved borders—as at St. Siméon for example (see under Qalaat Samaân)—to soften the transition from the rounded arches to the rough grey walls.

The *monumental tombs* are the most surprising buildings at Al Bara—both by their size (they are sometimes very large) and by their unusual designs. Square bases made of large blocks of stones are (or were) surmounted by pyramidal stone roofs.

The outside walls of the most important tomb are encircled by mouldings and cornices which certainly help to lighten its otherwise massive structure. These features, as well as the doorway, are decorated with vine-branches, ivy and scroll patterns. The central chamber is littered with blocs of stone from the collapsed roof; at least they make it possible to climb up to the higher cornice and enjoy a view of the whole of Al- Bara.

Not far away there is a more modest tomb whose pyramidal roof has remained intact. Here every stone projects like a little console: whether this was intended to be useful, symbolic or merely decorative, remains a mystery.

Crosses and chrisms make it possible to date these funerary monuments as 5th and 6th century.

From here it is easy to get back to the present-day village, via an Arab castle, *Qalaat Abu Sofian*. This fort predates the Crusades and is said to be one of the oldest in Syria—a proof that these forts existed before the Frankish castles. The ramparts afford a fine view of the ruined town.

Forgotten villages all around

Al-Bara is by no means unique. The entire mountain between the valley of Al-Bara and the Aleppo-Hama highway, to the east, is covered with Roman and Christian ruins. Unfortunately it is really only possible to explore this arid and desolate region on foot, on horseback, or by jeep, and with a local inhabitant as a guide.

It is fairly easy however, to reach the site of *Al-Maghara*, which lies about an hour's walk, by a good path, from *Meriane*—the last village we passed through on our way up to Al-Bahra. Apart from other ruins there are some astonishing hypogeum tombs to be seen there, with porticos in front of them.

Another interesting possibility is to make for *Maarat ann Numân* (see entry), a small town on the Aleppo-Hama road, across the mountain. There are two ways of getting there.

The route to the north follows the track to *Delloza*, a village surrounded by Byzantine ruins, and *Serjilla*, and ancient town strung out along a ledge above the central plateau, where the shepherds make temporary use of the ruins for shelter. Two kilometres to the south-west lies *Rebeia*, where there is a baptistery and a pyramidal mausoleum.

The second route is easier to follow and the track soon becomes a road again. It leads first to *Hass* (basilica and pyramidal tomb) and, an hour's walk further on, to *Khirbet Hass* (six churches, a hypogeum tomb with a portico) and then *Kfar Rûma* (ancient bridge). *Maarat an Numân* itself is worth a visit, mainly for its Islamic monuments.

BARA (Al)

Name: 2nd century B.C.: Kafra N'Barta. Roman period: Karropera. Crusader period: Bara. Arab period: Kafr al-Bara, Al-Kefr, Al-Bara.

Location and access: Idlib governorate. Altitude about 850 m. 350 km south of Idlib by Jisr ash-Shughur-Latakia road as far as Urum al-Jawz (20 km), then right turn to Meriane (12 km) and Al-Bara. The asphalt road continues for 2 km beyond the village (first turning right) to the edge of the valley and from there access is easy to the north part of the dead town.

Information and guides (almost exclusively Arabic-speaking): At the village hall in the centre of the village on the main street.

Accommodation: A at Idlib, Aleppo, Hama, Latakia.

bosra

■ A pile of roughly-hewn blocks of stone, black houses amid black rocks, Bosra seems to have fallens asleep. The vast plain of the Howran all around—golden with wheat and barley from May onwards—only serves to emphasiez 'Bosra's isolation. The place remains a prisoner of its glorious past.

The ruins of this past rise incongruously among the houses of the present town; columns vith splendid acanthus capitals and minarets that once were bell-towers; gigantic arches which now span unimportant streets; great pools, built to supply a metropolis with water, now seem out of all proportion; the main street is being dug up to find the paving of the former *decumanus*. Groups of patriarchal figures, white-turbanned and moustachioed, pursuing their endless conversations in shady corners, only serve to heighten the impression of timelessness given by this extraordinary town.

Mentioned in the lists of Tutmose III and in the letters of Al-Amarna (in the archives of the Pharaoh Ahkenhaton, 1334 B.C.), Bosra, also refered to in the Bible, became one of the leading Nabatean cities (1st cent.) before being made the capital of the Province of Arabia by its Roman conquerors (106 A.D.). As a crossroads on the caravan routes and residence of the Imperial Legate, the city flourished and many fine buildings were erected. It still continued to expand and flourish after the decline of the Roman Empire. As the seat of an archbishop, Bosra played an important role in the history of early Christianity—as well as having links with the beginnings of Islam. According to tradition, Muhammad greatly enjoyed his conversations here with a Nestorian monk named Bhira, who is said to have predicted his prophetic vocation.

Bosra was the first city in Syria to become Muslim. Her square minarets are no doubt the oldest, still standing, in the whole of Islam. The significance of the city as an important halt on the way to Mecca, and the prosperity that this brought, lasted until the 17th century. By then the region was becoming unsafe and the pilgrims began to take a less dangerous route further west. Bosra never recovered.

Today, the international highway to Amman and Arabia crosses the Syrian frontier at Deraâ; Bosra, forty kilometres away, is now merely the terminus of a narrow-guage railway with a little old-fashioned train which runs twice a week. But this ancient train comes to a halt at the foot of one of the most extraordinary monuments in all the Middle East—the fortress-theatre, recently and beautifully restored, where the best ballet, theatre and folklore companies give performances every summer. This remarkable building is gradually bringing new life to Bosra through tourism.

A Roman theatre in an Arab citadel

From outside it could be an Arab fortress similar to many others. On a semi-circular front, great square towers built of enormous blocks of stone (some of the corner ones are more than five metres high), project from the blind ramparts. A deep ditch, the first line of defence, is crossed on a six-arched bridge. An iron-bound gate, a series of vaulted rooms, twisting passages, rampart walks, and all kinds of defensive works give an impression of the military quality of the castle—it resisted invaders on more than one occasion—but nothing prepares us for the discovery that right at its heart lies an enormous and splendid ancient theatre!

The two structures, both equally fine, are closely engrafted into each other. The 13th enclosing wall completely encircles the cavea of the theatre. When the Arabs entered Bosra in the 7th century they immediately blocked all the doors and openings of the ancient theatre with thick walls, thus transforming it into an easily-defensible citadel. But the new threats posed by the Crusaders rendered these early defences inadequate; so, in the mid-11th centhury three towers were built, jutting out from the Roman building; nine other bigger ones followed, between 1202 and 1251. Later accretions overlaid the interior of the theatre and its ranges of seats, but at the same time preserved them. This interior has now been fully uncovered and restored in all its majestic entirety by the Department of Antiquities, which began its work here shortly after Syria became independent.

There is room fifteen thousand spectators to face a stage 45 metres long and 8,5 metres deep, and a stage wall whose base is emphasized by a series of Corinthian columns. Many details of its architecture proclaim the perfection of its construction—and the concern of its 2nd-century builders for the comfort of the audience.

The fortress, too, is worth a visit. In the central tower there is an interesting *Museum of Art and Popular Traditions*; there are many dioramas with life-size figures. The rural and nomadic life of former days is is vividly depicted, using original objects, furniture and costumes.

A *cafeteria* has been installed in the largest tower—the one to the west. On the terrace leading to it a selection of classical sculptures have been arranged to from an *open-air museum*. There are some fine female figures similar to those at Suweida (see entry), carved in hard lava stone, reddish in the brilliant sunshine.

Where Rome, Byzantium and Islam all meet

Present-day Bosra is a confusing place and the visitor is well-advised to find a local guide to show him round—the ancient remains lie scattered in all directions and over a wide area.

From the theatre-fortress a narrow road with ancient pavingstones leads into the decumanus, near a triple arch known as *Bab al-Quandil* (the Gate of the Lantern). It was built in the 3rd century, in honour of the Third Legion, garrisoned here at Bostra.

Following the decumanus to the left, towards the west and the Damascus road, we pass first of all a series of small basement windows set in a hundred-metre wall which turns out to be the outside of a vast *cryptoporticus* which has survived almost intact. It is a vast dark vaulted passageway and served as a warehouse for imported goods and as a store for products destined for export. This great cellar had three doors opening onto the *forum*. A *tetrapylon* (a building with four pilasters) whose foundations have been recently excavated, marked the junction of decumanus and the cardo—the two axes of the city—which were both lined with porticos that have disappeared. A double-storied archway marks the western entrance to the city: *Bab al-Haoua*, the Gate of the Wind.

If, on coming down from the theatre and the central arch, we turn right rather than left along the decumanus, our eye is caught by a group of tall slender columns. The first four, set at an angle to the street, are supposed to be the only surviving elements of a *nymphaeum*. On the other side of the street, two columns 25 metres apart one of which is joined to the neighbouring wall by a rich entablature, are said to have been part of a "*kalybea*", a religious building unique to this region. The eastern exit to the town was marked by an archway which, unlike the Gate of the Wind (to the west), is said to date from the first century, the Nabatean period, of which nearly all traces are now lost, the Romans having transformed the entire city. This *Nabatean gateway* is unique in all Syria. Petra (in present-day Jordan) is the only place where there are similar ones, indicating the existence of pre-Roman Arab civilisation.

Beyond the Nabatean gateway a network of streets leads, on the right, to a large double-storied house which may have been an *imperial palace* at the time of Trajan. Beyond the walls lies the great southern reservoir, *birket al-Hajj*, a pool 155 metres by 122, and 4 metres deep, although half silted up. From there it is easy to get back to the theatre-citadel. Leaving the Nabatean gate on the left we soon arrive at the ruins of a great building whose walls are pierced by many round-headed arches. This is the *Cathedral*, built in 512, the first domed building to be built on a square ground plan. The Emperor Justinian was inspired by this cathedral in the building of St Sophia at Constantinople.

Some delightful rustic mosques

About thirty metres to the north of the cathedral there is a building whose walls, intact up to roof level, plainly indicate that it is a church. This is the 3rd-4th-century *basilica*, site of the famous encounter between *Bahira* and Muhammad. The *al-Mabrak Mosque*, which recalls another visit by the Prophet to Bosra (for both episodes see box p. 000), is to be found outside the city, to the north-east. Thousands of graves, with great stelae of black basalt on them, keep watch at the foot of its walls which rise unadorned like those of some isolated bastion.

There are other Muslim buildings in Bosra which impress by their extreme simplicity, harmonionius proportions and the sharp outlines of their stepped roofs.

The *Abou I-Fida madrassa*, close to the birket al-Hajj (south-east of the city), consists of one great rectangular room with its ceiling supported by six simple arches resting on engaged columns. The minaret has neither roof nor staircase.

All that remains of the *Fatima Mosque* (which stands between the cathedral and the church of Bahira) is its minaret, pathetic in its isolation but elegant nonetheless, with little twin openings high up on its walls.

MUHAMMAD AT BOSRA

■ *A legend—but aren't all legends based on fact—attaches to the ruins of an ancient basilica (4th or perhaps 3rd century) near the Cathedral and known as the church of Bahira. Bahira was a Nestorian monk of Bosra (then known as Bostra) whose company Muhammad had greatly enjoyed when he had met him at a caravanserai. The monk is said to have predicted the Prophet's future vocation. This is not the only legend linking Muhammad with Bosra. A depression in a tile in the Mabrak an-naqa Mosque is said to be the print of the knee of a camel ridden by the Prophet or—according to another version—a camel that stopped here while bringing the first copy of the Koran to Syria. The mosque itself is said to be built on the spot where the Prophet pitched his camp during his visits to Bosra. These stories soon spread and Bosra became an important halt on the pilgrimage route from Damascus to Mecca. After the three day journey from Damascus caravans would often stop at Bosra for at least ten days.*

The *Mosque of Omar* in the centre of the town (called jami-al-Arous, "the bridal mosque," by the Bosriots), was a pagan temple to begin with. It is the only mosque surviving from the early Islamic period to preserve its original facades. All its columns remain in place, many bear inscriptions in Greek, Latin or Nabatean. Its fine square minaret dates only from the 12th century. Like most of the ancient buildings of Bosra the Mosque of Omar is being restored by the Department of Antiquities, with the seme scrupulous care as was devoted to the theatre-fortress. It will then only remain to provide the town with a modern hotel—a facility which is sadly lacking.

East of Bosra

An hotel at Bosra would make it possible not only to visit the town itself at leisure, but also to venture into the extreme south of Syria—where there are roads, narrow but drivable, linking many small centres rich in historical remains. Some sites are of interest mainly to specialists, but many could be more generally appreciated.

Salkhad (23 km east of Bosra on a surfaced road) has a citadel dating from the time of the Crusades. A circular structure rises above a steep glacis to crown a volcanic hill.

At *Al-Inat* (26 km south east of Salkhad by track) there is a great reservoir (birket) dug out of the rock in 1238-1240, as an Arabic inscription informs us. Further out, at *Oumn al-Qotein*, almost on the Syro-Jordanian frontier, there are extensive ruins.

Another track leads from Salkhad south to *Anz* (13 km) where there are also ancient ruins.

But more than all these villages Suwayda itself, Kanawât, Shahba, Shaka and Ezraa, are all very much worth a visit; they are all easy to reach by good roads. A special entry will be found for each of them.

BOSRA

Name: Variant names: Bosra ech Cham (esh Sham), Boçra: the "fortress". Nabatean period (2nd century B.C.): Bossora; Hellenistic period: Bostra; Roman period under Trajan (105 A.D.): Nea Trajana Bostra.

Location and access: Deraâ governorate. Altitude 850 m. 145 km south of Damascus, through Deraâ (40 km) or 130 km through Suwayda (35 km). By rail from Damascus, twice a week.

Information: At the museum is the citadel-theatre.

Accommodation: A at Damascus. Meals: cafeteria inside the fortress.

APAMEA

Name: Archeological site near the Arab city of Qalaat Al-Mudiq (var. Al-Moudik), the "citadel in the gorge". Variant names: Apamée, Apamé, Appamé. Persian period, 5th century, Pharnake (after Pharnakes, son of a Persian satrap). Macedonian occupation (393 B.C.), Pella (as a tribute to Alexander and his birthplace). Seleucid period (2nd century B.C.), Apama, Apamea, the name of the wife of Seleucus Nicator, a decendent of Pharnakes). Roman period, Antoninopolis (in memory of Antony, who stayed there in the company of Cleopatra during a campaign against Armenia). Crusader period: Afamiya, Famya, Fémie. From the 17th century: Qalaat Al-Mudiq.

Location and access: Hama governorate. Overlooking the Ghab Depression on the right bank of the River Orontes. Altitude 300 m. 55 km north-west of Hama; 45 km south of Jisr ash-Shughur, by good road. 25 km west of Khân Sheikhûn on the main Aleppo-Damascus road.

Accommodation: *A at Hama.

BANIYAS

Name: Variant names: Banias, Baniâs, Banyâs. Greek period: Balanea; Graeco-Byzantine period: Leucas; Crusader period: Valenia.

Location and access: Tartus governorate. Oil port. 50 km south of Latakia, 40 km north of Tartus by good road, 50 km west of Masyaf, 90 km from Hama, by good but hilly road as far as Masyaf.

Accommodation: A at Latakia. On the spot, Hotel *Homs**B, Kuwatli street, tel. 408.

crac des chevaliers

■ Every European child struggling to build a sandcastle on the beach tries instinctively to copy this marvellous castle, which he knows from pictures in his history books. Perhaps he doesn't know that Crac des Chevaliers is called *Qalaat al-Hosn* today—but it's still the paragon of castles.

If he had the chance to see it as it really is, he would find it bigger, more beautiful, more complete, than he had ever dreamed. Other castles may be more dramatically situated or their ruins may be more romantic—in Syria itself there are Margat and Saone, to name only the most famous—but none evokes as well as Crac those two centuries of implacable warfare. Elsewhere battles may have been bloodier, sieges more dramatic; but Crac by its size, its technical perfection, the bitter struggles it witnessed, remains the symbol of an entire epoch. In its very stones it demonstrates the will of the invaders to hold on to their distant possession and also the stubbornness of the forces of Islam as they fought for their land and heritage.

Tribute must be paid to the skilled work which has gone on since 1934 to restore the castle to its former beauty and power. The visitor would get a very different impression with heaps of rubbish which used to litter stairways, courtyards and chambers. But fortunately the restoration has not been overdone. Accessible right to the most secret places within its three enclosures, Crac remains a vast empty tomb without even "Son et Lumière" to bring it back to life.

The wind whistles through its galleries, the sun beats down on the high walls, grass grows between the stones and the damp is slowly causing the sides of the twenty-one great water tanks to flake away. But yet there are vast areas of passages, rooms and access ramps covered by vaulting that is still perfectly intact and extremely beautiful. The steep stone glacis from which the great ramparts rise will obbiously see out many more centuries. The windows of the great chamber, with their simple delicate pointed arches and slender columns are almost like a smile at the very heart of this austere fortress. And if the towers have lost most of their crenellations yet it is still possible to climb to the top and take in a vast and splendid view of the green countryside around, over which so much blood was shed.

The Homs Gap: the gateway to Syria

To the north lie the Ansariya ranges—steep inaccessible cliffs on the Orontes side, and a mass of valleys and ravines running straight down to the sea (see under Latakia).

To the south the Lebanon range is even more impressive, with the 3,088 metres Kornet as-Saouda—its snow-covered peak glittering in the summer sunshine.

Thus between Antakya (Antioch) and Beirut, a distance of 250 kilometres, there is only one place at which the mountain barrier can be easily crossed all the year round. This is the Homs Gap, cut by a coastal river, the nahr al-Kabir, in whose fertile valley lies the frontier between Syria and the Lebanon.

It is through this passage that inland Syria communicates with the Mediterranean. world. Of course such geographical accidents are not so important in an age of air transport, tunnels, viaducts and mountain motorways. However it seemed quite natural to use the Homs Gap to take the oil pipeline linking the wells of Mesopotamia with the Mediterrean ports.

In ancient times the importance of this strategic corridor was immense. To control the Homs Gap was to control Syria by isolating its hinterland from its maritime outlets. It was of crucial importance to the Christian in their conquest of the coast, and rather more. Crac des Chevaliers was its most important stronghold.

Built on the site of a former Kurdish castle (hence its name—see box), Crac stands on a hilltop some distance from the main road from Homs to Tartous and Tripoli—27 kilometres away, down a narrow winding road. It is not dramatically sited and disappoints perhaps at first view, especially if the visitor has just been to Margat. Halfway up the hill lies the village of *Al-Hosn* which used to serve and furnish Crac with provisions.

The fertile *plain of la Boquée* which connects with the upper part of the Kebir valley served to maintain a garrison of two thousand, their servants and horses and an enormous reserve of provisions. Somewhat away from the "Gap", but at an altitude of 650 metres, Crac served as an entrenched camp, commanding outlying posts and visible from the castle at *Akkar* in the Lebanon foothills opposite and whose ruins can be clearly seen from the top of the keep at Crac. There were also almost permanent links with Margat and Chastel Blanc (see Marqab and Safita).

The model castle

Before entering the labyrinth of courtyards and passageways it is a good idea to get an overall view by climbing to the top of the hill, taking the metalled road which winds round it on the south side. Seen from this height, on a level with the highest parts of the building. Crac does indeed look like one of those childhood sandcastles. There it stands on its levelled hilltop, sloping down steeply on three sides, with its high walls, its round towers, bigger at the corners, its machiolated galleries, its groups of bratizans and the fine lines of its arrow-slits.

The south side of the castle faces onto what one is tempted to call "terra firma" so much does the whole resemble a little peninsula. Here are the most massive defences. A square tower juts out from the outer rampart to cover, it would seem, a narrow and delicately-arcaded bridge, which is in fact an aqueduct.

An inner enclosure with great blank walls rises impressively above the outer one. Its gigantic towers (the southern one again the most massive) spring from a glacis steeper than the pyramids of Egypt and made of perfectly-fitting blocks of stone. These high towers rising higher than the rampart walk of the inner castle, but communicating with the building inside it (which are not visible from the observation point on the hill) virtually form a third system of defences.

A two-hour visit

Two hours is the minimum time that should be allowed for a visit accompanied by one of the official guides (they are friendly, competent and speak French or English).

The tour is so fascinating that it more than makes up for all the dark corridors, steep steps and uneven passageways.

The following are some of the highlights.

An ordinary gangway, replacing the former drawbridge, leads to a *postern* gate high on the eastern side of the outer rampart. There is a long inscription in Kufic lettering on the wall above the entrance, extolling the Sultan Beybars who captured Crac after a comparatively short and skilful siege (3 March—8 April 1271).

A *ramp of wide shallow steps*, up which cavalry could ride, leads into the heart of the fort. This long dark passage bristles with defences; elbows and portcullises, a hairpin-bend covered by a gangway and a corner bartizan, as well as many loopholes from which raking shots could come. Finally portcullises and gateways with machiolations above them and guardrooms on either side give access to an irregularly-shaped *inner courtyard* with much building overhanging.

Opposite the entrance five pointed windows and a gothic doorway lead into a fine *gallery* which in turn opens into the *Great Hall*, a magnifi-

110 CRAC DES CHEVALIERS

*Every European child struggling to build
a sandcastle on the beach tries instinctively
to copy this marvellous fortress,
this paragon of castles: Crac des Chevaliers.
(Photo Jacques Guillard.)*

cent room 27 metres long and 7.5 metres wide, composed of three vaulted aisles with pointed arches. The capitals and corbels are decorated with simple stiffleaf carving. Two inscriptions can be made out: one, in French, on the south pillar, tells us that "this work (labor) was done in the time of Brother Jorgi..." (warden of Crac); the other, in Latin, on the north pillar, is a maxim: "Have riches, have wisdom, have beauty, but beware of pride which defiles everything it touches."

The Great Hall was used for military gatherings and also for meetings of the Chapter of the Hospitallers, the governors of Crac. The loggia served as a cloister as well as a passage from which the mere knights could follow, at a distance, the proceedings of the councils of the leaders of the Order.

The *chapel*, built into the rampart itself, lies on the right-hand side of the courtyard. Its plain and simple nave leads into a half-domed apse and is roofed with transverse-ribbed, slightly pointed, vaulting. The side walls are hollowed out into great pointed arches with rib vaults and arch mouldings which lighten the building whose only decoration is a moulded string-course at the base of the arches. A stones mirhab placed against one of the lateral pillars serves to recall that the Chapel was immediately converted into a mosque after the capture of Crac by the Sultan Beybars.

On the same level as the chapel and the great hall, and communicating with the latter, a vast corridor a hundred and twenty metres long, down the western side of the fort links up with other rooms to the north and south. It is a marvellous construction with its vaulting coming right down to the ground. Light comes in throught apertures at regular intervals along the top of the vault. This *"Hundred and Twenty Metre*

CRAC AND KRAK...

■ *The form "Crac des Chevaliers"—generally used today, is a comparatively recent one. Many historians write "Krak des Chevaliers"—a spelling never used in medieval texts and which should therefore be rejected. It would seem that the Franks derived their form "Le Crat" (the oldest to be found in French and Latin documents) from Akrad (Hosn al-Akrad: the Kurdish castle). This was later written "Le Crac"—by analogy doubtless with the great castle built by the Franks to the east of the Dead Sea and which they called "le Crac." This latter castle lies at one end of the ancient city of Kérak or Karak. Now the name Karak derives from a Syriac word Kark(â) meaning "fortress". Influenced by this word the chroniclers changed Crat into Crac. In medieval chronicles the castle is sometimes called "le Crac de l'Ospital" and the one near the Dead Sea "le Crac de Montréal (being close to Montréal) to differentiate between them.*

PAUL DESCHAMPS
(adapted)
"Terre Sainte romane"
Coll. Zodiaque, 1964

Hall" (for such is its name) contained a well, four bread ovens, and served as a warehouse. Latrines were cut into its north wall. On the same level, but on the other side of the central tower a similar but smaller room housed the castle's stores of provisions which were considerable as they were calculated to sustain the garrison for five years. Enormous wine jars were found there, and the remains of an olive-press.

Another structure which is astonishing both in its proportions and its architecture is the socalled "*Hall of the Massive Pillars*". It lies on the southern side of the courtyard and has a pointed vault which rests on massive square pillars. It housed kitchens, refectories and storerooms. Light filters in through openings in the flat roof which forms an upper courtyard or *esplanade* linked to the lower one by a handsome flight of steps.

Overlooking and shading the esplanade, the three highest towers protect the south flank of the castle. They form a kind of complex keep which could defend itself independently. It is a colossal structure. The loophole in the first floor of the central tower is cut through a wall 8.5 metres thick. It is the most consummate achievement of 13th century fortress building.

The round tower on the southwest corner contained *the lodgings of the Grand Master* of the Order. From his vast rectangular bays he could survey the interior as well as the outside surroundings of the fortress. The roof of is chamber forms a perfect hemispherical dome.

Between the Inner and Outer Castles

In order to see the external defences the visitor must make his way back down the entry ramp to the point where it turns. *The fivefold system* which controls this passageway includes, on the lower level, a gate and portcullis together, set in a wall five metres thick and opening onto the moat, full of water, which separates the inner and outer walls.

This *stone-faced moat* is dominated by the stone glacis on which the inner castle stands, and by the wall of a gallery, 60 metres long, which links the outside towers and ramparts of the southern flank. The moat was fed from the aqueduct which ran under the ways and by rainwater through drainage pipes; it served as part of the castle's defences if it was attacked and also to water the garrison horses.

The *square tower*, in the middle of this south face, as well as most of the surrounding structures were built by the Arabs, the brunt of the attack in April 1271 having been directed here. Inscriptions in Arabic recall the qualities of the attackers.

There is another inscription on the polygonal central pillar supporting the upper floors of the *south-west tower*. In beautiful calligraphy it records the name of the man who defeated the Hospitallers of Krak, the Sultan Al-Zaher, or, more exactly and completely: "Al-Malek al-Zaher Rukh al Dunya wal din Abou alfath Beybars". "Beybars" (the Panther) being only a splendid—and familiar—abbreviation. From the top of this tower there is a view over the whole castle.

From the rampart walk of the outer fortifications there are splendid views of the towering walls and slopes and general massing of the whole construction. It is essential to walk all the way round.

On the northern corner there is a structure quite different from the rest —an *oblong tower*, i.e. one whose facade is longer than its depth. It has indeed a magnificent facade with a triple range of three point arches supported by pilasters and concealing the machiolation. A wide abutment protects a small postern gate opening into the "hundred and twenty metre hall". Its base may well be a remnant of the eleventh-century Kurdish caste.

11th, 12th, 13th centuries...confronted by this perfect construction and the scientific intelligence and skill of the men who built it, it is all too easy to forget the great age of Crac des Chevaliers.

The inner castle was completed in 1170, more than eight centuries ago, despite two terrible earthquakes. By the year 1200 Crac looked very much as it does today except that then it was brand new, white and clear in all its lines and humming with life as a monastery, workshop and front-line fort.

St. George Al-Houmayra

Twenty kilometres east of Crac, on the road to Safita (turn left at the bottom of the hill instead of turing right toward Homs) there are some big modern buildings in the hollow of the walley. These unattractive walls house a monastery which goes back to the sixth century.

It was dedicated to "Gorgeos", the St. George who killed the dragon, patron saint of England and of the Knights of the Garter. It is often forgotten that he was martyred at Lydda in Palestine and was venerated first by the Christians of Egypt and Syria. The Muslims know him as Lord Al Khodr Abou Al-Abass and call the monastery by the name of a neighbouring archaological site, Al-Houmayra. The monks, who are Orthodox, hold regular services and receive pilgrims, who come in great numbers on May 6th, the Feast of St. George, and on September 14th, the Feast of the Holy Cross.

The church, surmounted by a dome, was rebuilt in the nineteenth century. The ikonostasis, one of the largest in Syria and Lebanon, was carved and decorated at the same time. Of greater interest are the ancient ikons, silver crosses, chased chalices and dishes, in the "Treasury" which can be visited on request.

The ancient underground chapel can also be visited. Here one can see, by candlelight, beautiful 13th century woodcarving, in a remarkable state of preservation, and, behind bars, a series of ikons depicting the life of St.George.

In a green hollow on the next hillside there are mineral waters noted for their curative properties. They are known to the local inhabitants as *Al-Faouar Al Ajib,* "the miraculous gushing spring".

CRAC DES CHEVALIERS

Name: The French name is generally used, though the official name for administrative purposes is Qalaat al-Hosn after the nearby village of Hosn (Hussein). First Arab name: Hosn es Sath (Castle on the Slope), and later Kurd: Hosn al-Akrad, hence Crat, Crak and sometimes Krak (see box in text).

Location and access: Homs governorate. Altitude 650 m. 65 km west of Homs; 75 km south-east of Tartus by good, very busy road. Coming from Homs, the road to the village of Annâz and the Crac turns right off the Homs-Tartus road, immediately after crossing a small hump-back bridge on leaving the Lebanese enclave (see text).

Information and guides: At the entrance to the castle.

Accommodation: At Homs or at Tartus. Meals: cafeteria inside the castle.

damascus

■ Damascus in an exceptional example of the timelessness and universality of a great city.

A modern capital whose voice —discreet but assured, moderate but yet not lacking in feeling—is having a decisive effect in the Arab world and in the Mediterranean area today, Damascus is said by its citizens to be "the oldest continuously inhabited city in the world." One other Syrian city, Aleppo, disputes this title however, recent excavations have shown that it is Hama which really deserves it.

The mamluk minaret framed between two Corinthian columns dating from fourteen centuries earlier (an ensemble chosen for the cover of this guide), symbolizes the extraordinary mixture of influences that have gone to make up this city of nearly two million people.

The Umayyad dynasty made Damascus the political, religious and cultural centre of early Islam; but the Great Mosque built by Caliph Al-Walid (708) included within its walls a church which had itself been built on the site of a pagan temple. Salah-ad Din, the hero of Islam, lies buried in this city which the Crusaders were never able to invest; and it was not far from here that Paul of Tarsus was converted.

Damascus is mentioned in the earliest historic texts—Egyptian records of the 19th century B.C., and the archives of Mari, dating from the 25th century B.C.

Further back, history gives way to legend and speaks of "Dimachq ach-Sham", the "town of Shem", son of Noah. Legend too, gives way to poetry, in which it is said that when Christ returns to Earth to do battle with the Anti-Christ, He will make His way down by the highest minaret of the Umayyad Mosque.

The oldest city in the world?... To be sure, but is it not so because the secret of longevity is change, and because timelessness can only be achieved through evolution?

In our day Damascus is once more undergoing many changes, and successfully at that.

A new Damascus

No matter what his route, the visitor is struck by much that is new in Damascus. Arriving from the International Airport he sees many recent technical installations, ultra-modern hotels, and the improvement of the arid zones on the edge of the desert. If he comes by motorway —from Homs, Hama or Aleppo, he sees a vast new industrial area, wide avenues and clearways right to the heart of the city. Coming from Beirut he passes the University Residences, the extensive duty-free zone, the International Fair with its great concrete arrow bearing the colours of many countries. If he comes in from Qnaytra he sees a satellite-city under construction—Dimachq ad-Jadineh, New Damascus.

There is also the new mountain road, leading into the city from the north after having climbed almost to the summit of the jabal Kassioun; it offers a splendid panoramic view of Damascus and the green slopes around it. Other new features include the three sports complexes, finished in 1976 to receive the Arab Olympic Games.

There will be major building works in the city centre for some years yet—to reshape it to cope with heavy traffic and to provide the business premises, offices, hotels and administrative buildings that are urgently needed.

Despite the country's recent troubled history and the dangers it still faces, the city of Damascus, capital of a mature nation, faces the future unflinchingly.

A sea of cars and people

Left to himself in this city whose layout is not easy to grasp at first, the visitor may find himself lost, even panic-stricken to begin with, submerged at all events amid a welter of crowds and traffic.

Early in the mornings, and above all in the evening, the old city and the central quarters overflow with a human tide that surges from the pavements into the roadways, causing furious hooting from the motorists and vain shouting from the traffic police. Chains and protective barriers would seem to have been devised merely to serve as a training ground for obstacle racing... Very often the tide loses momentum and people drop out to stand in bus queues, to stop at the news vendors' stalls, and to stand around in little groups and discuss the news in front of "super palatial" cinemas with advertisements all over them...

If the pedlars' trays—laden with geegaws, edible seeds and cigarettes sold individually—rarely attract the attention of the passers by, the same cannot be said of the shop-windows, crammed transistor radios, tape-recorders and, the latest craze, cassettes.

Garlands of oranges and lemons, great glass jars misted over from the ice-cold juices they contain, proclaim the narrow shop where you need little encouragement to buy freshly-squeezed fruit juices. In the neighbouring roast-meat shop they tend to prefer a modern automatic spit that can take fifty or a hundred chickens at a time, to the traditional kebab skewers and the vertical "chawerma" introduced by the Ottomans. And there behind the window stands a man with a big knife who, quick as a flash, will cut you one, two or ten slices from an apricot and semolina gâteau as big as a millstone...

Vanishing turbans and Fezzes

The crowds are dense, but peaceable; even the children rarely get excited. The people are pleasant, courteous and helpful when necessary, but rarely demonstrative or spontaneously familiar. A stranger in their midst does not arouse excessive curiosity; they show a reserve that it would be wrong to interpret as indifference—being more often the result of the difficulty of communication.

Dress is also a cause of astonishment to the foreigner encountering an anonymous crowd here for the first time.

The galabiehs and jelabahs, the turbans and the fezzes, that used to be worn, are being rapidly replaced by somewhat dreary European clothes. Even the "qûfieh", the head-dress consisting of a piece of red or black check towelling held in place by a plait—so practical for desert travel—is seldom seen. In the general monotony the occasional sheikh's turban, or the soutane of an Orthodox priest, stands out.

Fortunately the younger generation of Damascene women have the secret of blending simplicity with elegance—consigning the black veil, worn closed like a monk's hood, to folklore.

The city in its setting

See plan and key p. 242

Damascus owes everything to the river Barada. Descending like a torrent from the Anti-Lebanon range, this narrow but abundant river, joined by a hundred smaller streams, cascades down the gorges of Aïn al-Fijeh. Then it meanders for a while beside the Beirut road, giving pleasure to the patrons of restaurants and cafés along its lush green banks, before losing itself in myriad branches, canals and ditches. These fertilizing waters have produced the *Ghouta,* a vast expanse of gardens, fields and orchards, the oasis from which Damascus gets much of its food.

The Ghouta is a place for recreation too (there are many swimming pools, "casinos" and sports arenas there), and is very much appreciated by the inhabitants of a city that suffers all too often from the drying dusty winds that blow over it from the desert and the nearby mountain.

To the north-west, the mountain

By channelling the Barada it has been possible to create gardens right to the very heart of the lower town. To the north-west however the city has flung itself far up the rocky slopes of the *jabal Qassioun*, whose summit (1,155 m) is topped by a television mast. These higher parts of the city are populous and poor, with the exception of the district known as *Al Mouhajarine* (bounded to the south by the rue Beirouny, and the rue Nazem Bacha), where great modern blocks face out over the vast urban panorama extending away to meet the green Ghouta. *Saahat Khorchid,* a small square where many trolleybus lines have their terminus, offers a similar view; there is a café there with several terraces from which to enjoy it. A new road has now been built up the mountain from the other side, emerging near the summit to command another fine view over the city.

From the west, towards the city centre

The place des Omayyades marks the entrance to the city from the west; the road from Beirut and the motorway from Qnaytra, which also serves Dimachq al-Jadineh ("New Damascus") both converge there. The hotel "Sheraton" is there also, standing slightly back from the square itself. To the left there is a residential and administrative quarter (new ministries, army headquarters, embassies), whilst the continuation of the Beirut road, the avenue Choukry Kouwatly leads to the busy centre of the city, an area which is being completely reorganised. The *avenue Choukry Kouwatly* is bordered on the left by the gardens surrounding the Officers' Club and the hotel "Méridien"; on its right the waters of the Barada flow sluggishly along an excavated channel across which can be seen, on the other bank, the buildings of the International Fair, the theatre, various sports facilities, the gardens and the buildings of the Museum, and finally, the domes and tapering minarets of the Takieh Sulaimanieh (the "pilgrims' haven"), dating from the time of Suleiman.

The centre and the ramparts

There are many landmarks to help the visitor in the *centre of the city,* despite all the works that are going on. The avenue Choukry Kouwatly ends at a sort of esplanade, crowded with taxis and buses. From here, on the right (near the hotel "Semiramis" and the Air France office), the *boulevard al Jabry* begins (General Post Office, Syrian Air, Railway Station); on the left is the *boulevard Port Saïd,* which becomes the *boulevard du 29 Mai,* ending at the *place du 17 Avril,* facing the imposing marble colonnade of the Central Bank. These wide boulevards are lined with restaurants, cinemas, the monument to the glory of the Syrian peasant (Mydaan Youssef al-Azmeh), the city Tourist Information Bureau, and commercial buildings of many kinds. If, leaving the boulevards, we take one of the streets continuing the avenue Choukry Kouwatly to the east, we arrive at *Saahat al-Chouhadaâ* ("the Square of the Martyrs"), still commonly known as *place Merjé.* This square is easily recognised by a curious bronze colonnade wreathed in electric cables. This monument was erected to commemorate the opening of first telegraphic link in the Middle East—the line between Damascus and Medina.

On the Saahat al-Chouhadaâ and in the streets nearby there are travel agencies, middle-range hotels, some government offices (including the Ministry of Tourism) and... some very good cake-shops. We are now very close to the western tip of the "old city." The old city of Damascus is still three-quarters surrounded by its *rampart walls* which are ringed by streets crowded with traffic and people. To the north runs the boulevard Al-Malek Fayçal. To the south there is the rue Zaghloul (lined with fine mosques and madrassas: *Darwich-Pacha, Sinan Pacha* and others, with green-tiled minarets; then the rue Badawy, rue Chaghour and the boulevard Ibn Assaker.

The best-preserved section of the walls is along the *boulevard Ibn Assaker,* with Bab Toumaa (at the north), Bab Charqy (a restored Roman gateway) and Kanissat Bab Kassane (the Chapel of St. Paul: see below). Opposite the latter is the beginning of the motorway to the International Airport.

Approaching from Aleppo or Palmyra

The motorway from Aleppo enters the city from the north, at the *place des Abbassides* (new 45,000 seat stadium) which corresponds to the place des Omayyades to the west. From this square the *boulevard al-Nassirah* leads to the boulevard Ibn Assaker, the city walls and the old city, whilst the boulevard d'Alep leads to the place Tahrir ("Liberation Square") which has a modern monument, a sort of triple totem, in the centre. To the right the *boulevard de Baghdad* and the *boulevard Dr Mourched Kater* (parallel one-way streets) give acess to (or from) the place 17 Avril and the western and central quarters of Damascus. The city is extended on its southern side by some three kilometres of suburbs.

To the south, Al-Midân

The straight line of the *boulevard Khaled Ibn al-Walid* leads from the city centre, near the railway station, to join the Jordan highway at a roundabout, the *Saahat al-Achmar,* marked by a handsome fountain. Formerly the axis through this quarter, known as *al-Midân,* ran to the west of the present-day boulevard; this is a rather dull street now; a few domed madrassas were built along this pilgrimage route during the Mamluk period.

To the south-east, the Airport and Saiyida Zenab

It is twenty-three kilometres, along a modern motorway, from the new International Airport and its modern "hotel-casino" to the old city-walls and the Chapel of St. Paul. The visitor, fresh off the plane, will the surprised to see so many orchards and gardens, still wonderfully green even in July.

The road to Suwayda and the jabal al-Arab branches off from the airport motorway to the right, about 1,500 metres after leaving the city. Just on the other side of the first village, *Yalda,* there is an astonishing mosque, built in the centre of a vast courtyard. Seen from the outside this building with a metal dome, gives no hint of the rich decoration within. It is a Shi'ite mausoleum, the tomb of *Saiyida Zenab,* a man particularly venerated by the Iranians. With its wealth of crystal, blue ceramic tiling, rich carpets and decoration in pure gold, it makes quite a contrast to the more sober Sunni shrines—recalling rather those of Mashad, Teheran or Shiraz.

The Old City within the walls

The oldest part of Damascus is virtually a city within a city, with walls enclosing it on three sides and a branch of the Barada acting as a moat to the north-west. Unfortunately the river looks more like a drain at this point, while the walls are breached by incongruous openings and the fortified gateways are often half-hidden under later accretions...

First levelled by the Mamluks, then demolished by the Mongols, the

*Recognisable as a Shi'ite shrine by its showy
and luxuriant decoration,
the tomb of Saiyida Zenab,
in the southern suburbs of Damascus,
attracts many pilgrims—from even distant countries.
(Photo Robert Azzi, Magnum.)*

ramparts were rebuilt in their present form in the 13th century on the boundaries of the old Aramean city.

With its long straight streets, intersecting at right angles, the present internal layout follows the ancient plan. The *Madhat Bacha souk,* continued by the rue Bab Charqy, is the ancient via Recta, the *Street Called Straight* (this term is still used). This is a sort of decumanus, fifteen hundred metres long, joined at intervals and at right angles by streets leading from the various gates of the city. Thus the town is divided according to the Hellenistic notions imported by Alexander, into regular blocks, roughly forty-five metres by one hundred; this methodical urban plan is impressive even today.

The Great Mosque, hub of the city and of the Umayyad Empire, was fitted into this plan without disrupting it. It incorporates many elements of more ancient buildings—parts of porticos, a temple colonnade, the foundations of a church. These astonishing juxtapositions are in themselves one of the major sights of Damascus.

Through the centuries corporations of craftsmen and merchants established themselves around the Great Mosque, while the important Christian minority consolidated itself in the north-east quarters of the city, around the churches and sites associated with the Conversion of St. Paul.

Around the Umayyad Mosque

Coming in from the Saahat al-Chouhadaâ our first impression of the old city is one of noise and crowds. The roads are full of taxis and lorries, porters and deliverymen of all kinds, with all kinds of vehicles. Merchandise spills out of the shops

THE FLORALIES AND THE DAMASK ROSE

■ *Since 1973, the Floralies, an international flower festival, has been held in Damascus on the banks of the Barada, during the month of May.*
This event, so characteristic of the Syrian way of life, takes as its symbol "the Damask Rose".
Rosa Damascena, its essences, its perfumes and its oils, have for centuries carried the fame of Damascus all over the world. This is the rose we see in mosaic in the aisles of the Alhambra at Granada. The people who live in the Valley of the Roses in Bulgaria claim that theirs are "roses of Damascus that have migrated across to live amongst us." It was this same Rosa Damascena that a knight of the Sixth Crusade so carefully took back home with him, in 1238, and which became the French "Rose de Provins". On 6th August 1968 two young Frenchmen arrived in Damascus after retracing his steps, bearing a cutting of it as a tribute to the city: a bush grown from this cutting now graces the gardens of the National Museum.

onto the pavements—every possible sort of thing, from ropes and leatherwork to wicker and tinware. In the *rue al-Malek* the blacksmiths and coppersmiths work right out onto the pavements, whilst the roadway is lined with the fruitsellers' carts piled high with apricots, almonds, cherries and limes—all gaily decorated with green leaves, poppies and carnations...

The first gate through the walls, on the right-hand side of the rue Malek, *Bab al-Faraj* (Gate of Deliverance), leads us (if we turn sharp left under the gate) through some little winding streets to the north side of the Great Mosque itself.

If, on coming from the place Merjé, we do not turn down the rue al-Malek, but take an iron-roofed passage through the walls instead, we soon come to the entrance to the *Citadel*. It is the Headquarters of the National Guard, and is therefore closed to the public. There are plans in hand to restore this building—its foundations date from Roman times—and to transfer to it the Army Museum and the Museum of Syrian History (see below).

The main entrance to the old city, its market hall so to speak, is the *Al-Hamidieh Souk,* slightly to the right of the passage mentioned above. This is a pedestrian zone, a wide covered way into which light filters down from bays in the lofty iron vaulting, a roof so ancient, rusty and roughly repaired that the light shows through like so many tiny stars. A far cry from the fine stone souks of Aleppo! The artificial light, the succession of shops overflowing with colourful merchandise, the big signs all written in Arabic lettering, the tenacious shopkeepers who spot the visitor's nationality in an instant... it all takes one's breath away at first; however, one soon recovers from the shock and begins to enjoy it.

No sooner are we becoming accustomed to the setting than it begins to change. The vaulted roof gives way to two gigantic Corinthian columns, complete with sculptured entablature, which rise high into the sunlit sky. They are what remains of the *propylaeum of the temple of Jupiter* built on the site of the temple of Hadad the Aramean (9th century B.C.). Between the columns, to the rear, rises one of the minarets of the Umayyad Mosque. (The entrance to the mosque is 30 metres further on, on the left.)

As we approach the sanctuary the drapers, shoe-shops and ironmongers give way to little shops selling perfumes, wax, red and green candles, holy pictures of scenes at Mecca and calligraphy proclaiming the One True God.

The souk to the right of the Great Mosque is the home of carpenters and cabinet-makers, who are sometimes to be found working in little trellis-shaded courtyards. Band-saws and electric lathes are fast supplanting the old manual techniques. However there are still a few craftsmen who know how to use an old-fashioned turn bench and guide the chisel with their big toe. Amongst all the pots, bowls, spoons, and cake-moulds decorated with stars and rosettes, it is easy to find plenty of cheap and attractive souvenirs.

On the east side of the Great Mosque some steps lead down to a street open to goods vehicles. There is a little cafe there, where old men sit, apparently letting the world go by; but in fact observing it very closely as they draw meditatively on their hookahs.

Still keeping to the left along little streets bounded by a wall built of great blocks of stone, we arrive at the north gate of the Great Mosque, marked by the *al-Arous (bridal) minaret.* This is a high tower with a lantern with a projecting roof and three ranges of balconies rising up to a sphere at the very top. The porch of the minaret iself is preceded by an impressively-proportioned Byzantine colonnade.

Somewhat to the right is the mausoleum of Salah ad-Din and, a little further on, the Museum of Epigraphy (see below).

Continuing round the Great Mosque to the left opposite a former madrassa, we finally arrive at the visitors' entrance to the sanctuary.

*In the new quarters of the expanding capital,
as here around the Place Tahrir,
the new mosques are still built in the traditional style—
modern art shows itself
in purely decorative structures.*

The Umayyad Great Mosque

The non-Muslim visitor first enters a room where he pays his admission charge and takes off his shoes. There is a showcase here containing some beautifully lettered and illuminated copies of the Koran.

The preliminaries over, we are now ready to plunge from the everyday world into that world beyond time, the courtyard of a mosque. It is a deeply impressive experience. We are entering a world of peace and silence. Human figures, crouching under the arcades or out in the great marbled spaces, seem tiny and almost insignificant. Yet the building does not really crush or overwhelm them; it is conceived on a human scale, as a place to which men may come, freely and alone, to commune with God.

As visitors to this sanctuary, whether we be Christian or agnostic, we can only truly experience its atmosphere by sitting down under a shady portico and letting a little time go by... In so doing we shall grasp, imperfecty no doubt, but surely, something of the true quality of Islam. This essential atmosphere is wonderfully conveyed by the Umayyad Mosque of Damascus, despite its apparent newness. (It was largely reconstructed, according to the ancient plan, after a disastrous fire in 1893.)

After these few moments of re-adjustment, perhaps of meditation, we are ready to look around. The mosque has three minarets, the one at the north-east is known as the Jesus minaret. The mosaic panels, one of the treasures of the building, were executed in the ancient Byzantine manner and are made of coloured and gilded glass rather than stone. The main motifs are scenes of nature and the countryside; only those compositions on the left as we enter the west arcade of the courtyard date from the earliest period, the 8th century. The small isolated building, standing on small slender columns and with its walls covered with mosaics, was the "treasury" where public funds were kept, safe from robbers and from fire.

The prayer hall, 130 metres long (non-Muslims are not admitted on Fridays), was conceived as a basilica with a double range of arcades resting on Corinthian columns. One third of the way along it there is a domed shrine, set between two pillars, which contains a relic venerated by both Christians and Muslims, the head of St. John the Baptist (the Prophet Yahia to the Muslims). It is said to have been found in 705 (the 83rd year of the Hegira), in the crypt of the previously-existing church, at the time of the building of the mosque, under Caliph Al-Walid.

Saladin's Tomb and the Museum of Epigraphy

On leaving the Great Mosque by the north gate we turn to the left. The little mausoleum, half-hidden in a small garden and covered by a red-ribbed dome, contains the *tomb of Salah ad-Din,* who rallied Islam at one of the most critical periods and defeated the Crusader invaders (see Panorama: history). The building, which had been neglected at one time, was restored at the end of the last century, thanks to the interested generosity of the German Kaiser, Wilhelm II, who had his monogram placed on a lamp hanging over the tomb. Next to the Sultan's green marble memorial-stone, in accordance with his wishes, lies that of his faithful secretary. The latter's tomb is of white marble, attractively decorated with pampres.

The *Museum of Epigraphy,* recently installed in a former madrassa built in 1421 at the expense of the Governor of Damascus, is worth visiting—as much for its setting as for its collections.

The whole interior is decorated with polychrome marble mosaics. The square central room has a dome, directly under which there is a pretty octagonal pool, reached down three steps. There are display cases all round. They contain manuscripts and printed works, marvellous examples of calligraphy and lay-out; there are also stones which show how the graver's chisel can ally the rigour of Arabic script with artistic fancy to produce most beautiful lettering. There are objects here too—blue faïence inkwells, a reed pen cut as finely as a scalpel, and engraved metal stamps. Tiles from the pre-Islamic period show the development of Arabic script. A large table illustrates the development of the alphabet from earliest antiquity to the Arabic script of today. Richly illuminated arithmetical and astronomical tables conclude the display of this original and interesting museum.

There are other ancient monuments in this area, between the north facade of the Great Mosque and Bab al-Faraj. They are not regularly open to the public. It is worth mentioning two, to which the visitor can gain admission on request; two madrassas of the Ayyubid period (dynasty of Salah ad-Din, 13th century). The *Zahiriya madrassa* was founded by Saladin's father and is now the National Library. Opposite stands the *Adiliya madrassa,* conceived and executed according to the style and methods of Northern Syria; it has been termed a masterpiece of masonry and construction and has a fine gateway with a hanging keystone. The building now houses the *Arab Academy,* the most important cultural body in the country.

The Azem Palace and the Popular Arts

Close to the Umayyad Mosque, on the southern side, this palace was designed in 1749 for *Assad Pacha al-Azem,* Governor of Damascus. It exactly fulfils the expectations the foreigner may have gained from romantic literature, about the Damascene "douceur de vivre." Pretty rather than grandiose, even slightly finicky it has a wealth of polychrome stone, cascading fountains in basins of immaculate marble, and a riot of flowers and greenery—bougainvillea and roses and the mingled scents of jasmin and the cypress trees.

It was in this ravishing setting that the Minister of Culture decided, in 1952, to establish the *National Museum of the Arts and Popular Traditions of Syria*. Two years later the Department of Antiquities opened the doors of the *Azem Palace*, whose collections today contain almost ten thousand items. There is even more in store. Specialists often come to study and gain inspiration—dress designers have made extensive use of the splendid costumes here in order to create new fashions.

The display is both educational and extremely attractive; life-size dioramas are a frequent feature. Furniture, tools, utensils—everyday items as well as more unusual ones—are used in settings in which highly realistic wax figures re-create natural scenes with almost uncanny accuracy. This series of glimpses of Syria as it was, often until very recently, brings to life scenes as divergent as massaging or making a cup of coffee, a wedding ceremony or a Pasha's reception.

A comprehensive catalogue, compiled by M. Chafic Imam, the Director, expertly guides the visitor through the fifteen rooms of the Azem Palace.

In this same part of the old city (i.e. between the Great Mosque and the rue Droite—the Street Called Straight) hammams and khâns were built during the Ottoman period. The most noteworthy of the latter, *khân al-Goumrok*, has in the centre—instead of the usual courtyard—a hall enclosed by six great cupolas on pendentives. It is proposed to use this magnificent building to house the largest craft centre in Syria.

Two thirds of the way along the rue Droite are the bays of a reconstructed Roman monumental arch. They indicate more or less the beginning of a quarter in which many Christians—of various denominations—still live.

The churches of the old city

Of the half-dozen churches which survive in this quarter (mainly around the *rue Bab Touma*, Thomas Gate), the *Chapel of Ananias (Kanissat Hananya)* maintained by the Franciscans, is virtually the only of historic interest and associations. This was in fact the cellar of the house of Ananias, one of the early Christian disciples, one of the "Seventy-two" of whom Saint Luke wrote, who was charged to go and lay his hands upon St. Paul, sheltering in a house on the via Recta, in order that he might regain his sight. The incident is recounted in the Acts of the Apostles, and elsewhere; Ananias's incomprehension at first, his scepticism, and his final submission to the Divine will... There followed the first preaching by the new apostle in the Synagogues of Damascus, his condemnation by the Jewish community here, his taking refuge in the house of a Christian right against the city wall, and his flight. One night, with the aid of disciples, he climbed through a window, was let down the wall in a basket, and escaped. He had spent three years in Damascus.

The house on the walls has been converted into a chapel, dedicated naturally, to St. Paul. Its entrance is from the south-east corner of the ramparts, some three hundred metres to the right of *Bab Charqy*, from the outside of the walls.

In the church to the left of the entrance, there is a bas-relief depicting the descent the basket; the building is modern and unattractive. It is called in Arabic *Kanissat* (church) *Bab Kassane*.

Bab Sharqy (the East Gate) at the far end of the rue Droite is an imposing structure with Roman arcading. It has been recently and impressively restored.

An ordinary doorway in an unimpressive building, on our immediate left on leaving Bab Charqy, leads into a treasure cave: the workshops, salesroom and the home of M.

Georges Naassan. The present head of a family who have been artists (and businessmen!) for generations, Georges Naassan is a major supplier to the bazaars of Damascus and beyond. He stocks the cheaper lines because he has to, but his real love is for high quality things—exquisite uncrushable silks, chessboards inlaid with mother of pearl and rare woods, fine gruns and other weapons—damascened of course!

High quality craft work

Even in this machine age, Syrian craftsmen, often as skilful as they are talented, still understand and prize fine workmanskip. This can be seen not only in Georges Naassan's establishment. A few years ago the Syrian Government opened its own official *"Bazar de l'Artisanat"* (Craft Bazaar)—a highly successful adaptation of an historic building to modern use. (It is adjacent to the Takiyeh Mosque, between the last stretch of the Barada embankment and the *rue Al-Baroudi;* entrance opposite a large taxi park.)

This "Bazaar" in fact occupies a former caravanserai or hostelry, built by the Ottoman Sultan Selim, hence its name, *Salimiyeh.* Running the length of a whole street and all around an arcaded courtyard with a marble pool in the middle, the former pilgrims' quarters, kitchens and offices, have been turned into workshops. There are weavers' rooms where fine brocades are made, furnaces where glassblowers make all sorts of beautiful vases and jugs, and workshops where goldsmiths inlay silver wire into copper, steel and gold. The lofty room on the far side of the courtyard, an iwan (or liwan, as it is more often known in Syria), houses the carpenters and makers of decorated woodwork. Here they make chairs, chests and other furniture, all gaily decorated with flowers. Plaster-relief work, paintings on glass, illuminated manuscripts, damascened weapons, wood mosaics, woollen caftans and silk dresses—a host of lovely things, beautifully designed and executed, are all temptingly laid out in this attractive setting... temptations both for the eye and for the pocket! (See chapter "Syrian Journey: a thousand souvenirs.")

Two slender minarets with conical tops rise above the greenery. A cluster of little cupolas interspered with tiny towers (they are in fact chimneys) surrounds a vast dome. A few scattered tombs at the foot of the building and the flowerbeds of a deserted garden—this completes our picture of the back view of one of the finest buildings in Damascus. It is the view we have from the top of the *rue Moussallam Baroudy* (the continuation of the rue El-Nasr, on the other side of the railway station).

The main facade is of course on the other side. We get a good view of it as we approach either from the National Museum (to the left) or the Bazar de l'Artisanat (to the right). The arrangement of the building now falls into place. The great central dome covers the prayer hall of the mosque, while the smaller ones to the sides cover the porticos and rooms of what was once a Dervish hospice. With its fountains, trees and flowers this whole architectural ensemble is a vivid evocation of the taste and styles which originated in Constantinople and readily acclimatized themselves in Damascus towards the end of the 16th century.

Al-Takieh al-Suleimaniye an Ottoman transplant

The *Suleimaniye* dates from 1554; it was built by the famous Turkish architect, Sinan, who had already built an imperial madrassa in Constantinople. The neighbouring Salimiyeh (see above) was built twelve years later. It exemplifies a whole range of decorative motifs of the period: marble veneers and vast areas of tilework on the walls and over the doorways and windows, black and white stone arcading; an abundance of complicated shell and

*More examples of happy coexistence between tradition
and modernity: from left to right,
the monumental entrance to the International Trade Fair,
a policewoman, a craftsman woodworker.
(Photos Hureau, Azad Ministry of Tourism, Azzi Magnum.)*

DAMASCUS 127

stalactite niches and polychrome stone arches of ever-increasing complexity. The capitals are often heightened with red and blue. The astragals of the columns and their bases are made of gilded bronze. Every surface is decorated in alternating colours... And yet, paradoxically, the total impression is one of calm and repose. Plants and flowers too add to the delightful, almost feminine, atmosphere. The few old wise men who come here to meditate, the students who find it a setting conducive to study, and the occasional pairs of lovers—they might all be obeying the commands of some inspired and unşeen theatrical producer, so perfectly do they complete the scene.

The Historical and Army Museum

If one looks away from the domes and minarets of the Slamanieh the spell is quickly broken. By a curious and incongruous irony the lower part of the gardens is occupied by war planes, howitzers, guns and rockets, which have nothing at all to do with the Ottoman minarets.

Friendly and courteous military personnel invited us to step inside and inspect the neighbouring buildings.

A military museum may seem a strange and unlikely tourist sight, but we ought not to miss it. *The Historical and Army Museum* provides an occasion to recall the military highlights of five thousand years of Syria's history.

There is a series of dioramas which look inevitably somewhat stilted and artificial, but they are most carefully composed. The weapons and objects on display, together with a wealth of maps, make it possible to follow developments from Qadasch right up to the recent battles in Golan and in the skies over Damascus. For once, we are in a museum which does not stop short at the 19th century; the events most vividly depicted are the most recent ones.

The National Museum of Syria

The entrance is in the *rue du Dr Rida Saïd* on the western side of the Takieh al-Slamanieh. The museum is closed on Tuesdays. See the guide-plan on p. 245.

To provide even a summary catalogue of this museum would require more pages than there are in this whole guide-book. To make a selection from the thousands of items worth studying would be arbitrary and unjust. In fact the only question worth asking about this monument of Syrian culture is: "how many times should it be visited?" The answer is, of course, "As many times as possible!" It is ideal to visit the various sites around the country and then come here to see the relevant collections—there is so much here to deepen and illuminate what one has already seen on the ground. At the end of one's stay in Syria a final visit to the National Museum will help to put everything into perspective... and everyone will by then have his or her favourites among its masterpieces.

One's visit, or rather visits, to the National Museum, are greatly enhanced by its thematic and chronological classification, and by the excellence of its display in general (see guide-plan p. 245). The labels are clear and detailed, and frequently translated into French and sometimes English as well.

A few sections which could perhaps be better signposted should not nevertheless be missed: the garden where there are mosaics, statues and a lapidary collection; the facade of Qasr al-Hir ash-Sharqi (rather cramped between the two wings of the museum) which was brought here stone by stone and re-erected (see under Palmyra); the frescoes from the synagogue at Doura Europos (on the extreme left as you enter the museum, right at the back of a courtyard), dating from 235 A.D. (marvellously preserved despite the destruction of the city by the Persians in 256, they are figurative frescoes, contrary to Hebraic tradition);

the hypogeum of Yarhaï (in the basement, straight ahead of the entrance) which was brought from Palmyra, an astonishing collection of funerary sculpture which gives a remarkably vivid impression of the Palmyrene bourgeoisie; finally, following the stairs from the hypogeum to the first floor of the building, we come to the "Homs Treasure", a fantastic hoard of jewellery found in a royal necropolis dating from the reign of Augustus (the first half of the 1st century A.D.).

But all these wonderful things must not prevent us from lingering to look at the alphabet of Ugarit (the original this time, not one of the numerous copies), the "great dancer" from Mari, the "Chinese horseman" from Raqqa, and the Arab astrolabes, the copper terrestrial globe and the tenth-century ceramic dish on which the whole world is depicted as centring on Maqqa (Mecca). The whole collection is a marvellous stimulus to the imagination of any traveller worthy of the name—as indeed is the whole of Syria... and Damascus in particular.

DAMASCUS (DIMACHQ)

Name: The French version of the name Damas is frequently used. Variant names: Dimachk, Dimachq ech Cham (or esh Sham). On the Mari tablets: Apum. Hittite period: Upi. Aramean period: Aram, then Damascus.

Location and access: Capital of the Syrian Arab Republic. Principal city of governorate. Altitide: 690 m to 1,155 m. Population of Greater Damascus, approaching 2 million inhabitants.
International crossroads, 110 km south-east of Beirut, by excellent, but hilly road (motorway planned); 210 km north of Ammân, by good road. 600 km north-west of Baghdad, by road and track under reconstruction.

Modern international airport: 25 km southeast of the city by motorway: Syrian Air Lines and many foreign airlines. Syrian Air Lines Terminal: S. Al-Jabry street (opposite General Post Office). Warning, the old airport, to the south-west of the city is no longer used for civil airline traffic.

Taxi and bus services: For all destinations inside the country, consult the Tourist Bureau and travel agencies (list in the Chapter "Syrian Journey").

Railways: Damascus-Zabadani and Damascus-Deraâ (Bosra)-Ammân lines.

Information: Tourist Bureau, boulevard du 29-Mai, tel. Ministry of Tourism, Abi-Faras Al-Hamadani street (small square in the city centre near the Martyrs square: see city plan p. 242). Tourist plan of Damascus on sale in hotels.

Accommodation: Méridien (Air France hotel)****A, Choukry Kouwatly Ave. (opposite the grounds of the International Fair), tel. 229200, telex 11379, 300 rms. *Sheraton*****A, Choukry Kouwatly Ave., near the Omayyades square, 336 rms. *Damascus International (Al-Dawli)*****A, Bahsa street, renovated district of the city centre, tel. 112400, telex Interho 11062, 133 rms. *Damascus Airport and Casino (Al-Matar)*****A, opposite new international airport, tel. 225402, cables: Airportotel Damas, 44 rms. Plus 4 ***A and B hotels, 13 **A and B hotels and many * hotels: see list at the back of the guide.

Holiday centre with bungalows, swimming pool, sports facilities, on the Beirut road at Ayn el-Fijeh road crossing planned for 1977.

Youth hostel: Salah Al-Ali street, Al-Mazraah district, tel. 118200.

Camp sites: Harasta Camping 7 km along the Aleppo road. Sahara Tourist Camping 10 km along the Beirut road. Al-Dajani Camping 10 km along the Deraâ road.

Summer resorts: Bloudane, Al-Jirjanieh, Zabadani (see article under the latter heading).

Entertainment: Many cinemas, cabarets, night-clubs in the city centre (boulevards de Port-Saïd, du 29-Mai, Youssef Al-Azmeh square). Dancing and shows at Hotel Semiramis and various others.

Festivals and fairs: April, drama festival; May, Plastic Arts Exhibition; May, International Flower Show; July-August, International Fair.

Souvenirs: High-quality, varied and original craftwork (see text). Main shops: New Bazar de l'Artisanat forming an entrance to the Takiyé Mosque; in the souks, mainly around the Umayyad Mosque; Ateliers Georges Nassan, near Bab Charquy, rue Droite.

deir-ez-zor

■ A town, a river, a bridge.

The town is the only important urban centre in the East of Syria. Its position, far from the capital and from the nerve-centres of the country, at the entrance to a vast and developing region, gives it a very considerable local importance and is enhancing its sense of its own identity.

The river is the Euphrates, lifeline of the region and a corridor of civilisation throughout the ages. With the filling of Lake Al-Assad it has become possible to regulate its hitherto capricious flow and to make plans for new harvests.

A town set amidst gardens

The bridge, or rather bridges —there are five of them, as the locals proudly point out—are the historic reason for the very existence of Deir-ez-Zor. Countless armies, conquerors and merchants have come this way. There are wide concrete structures to carry the cars and lorries of today, but a light suspension footbridge, dating from 1924, with as many stays as an ancient sailing ship, is floodlit in colour at night-as if to underline the significance of this thousand-year old crossing.

This historic, economic and social context gives Deir-ez-Zor an initial interest for the visitor. It is well placed for easy access to highly-important archaeological sites (see below and also entries for Doura Europos and Mari). The improvement of arid lands (45,000 hectares have already been irrigated since the filling of the dam), the technical problems raised by the the regulation of the flow of the Euphrates (fertilizers, salinity, etc.), the introduction of new crops (fruit, ground-nuts, rice) which are being studied in an Institute of Agronomy, the development industry in the wake of increased cotton production, ...these are some of the topics which any technician, Syrian of foreign, whom the visitor may meet, as he takes his tea in a riverside café, would be happy to discuss. The visitor will also be agreeably surprised by the pleasant appearance of the town. There are decent stone houses (a front garden is de rigueur in the newer areas), fine trees on the river banks, flowers in the public gardens, and well-designed administrative buildings. A "corniche" is being built along the river and a "hotel-casino" is at the planning stage.

The *Cultural Centre* provides a meeting-place for many young people—and an opportunity for friendly rivalry between the sexes in the many activities it offers—painting, modelling, drama and folk-dancing. Its library already has a stock of fifteen thousand books. A theatre is now under construction.

Paradoxically it is the Euphrates itself which is somewhat disappointing at Deir-ez-Zor. The waters of this majestic river which used to surge past, undermining the pink cliffs on the right bank, now flow sluggishly along, with not a boat or a sail to bring them to life. There aren't even any fishermen—which seems strange as there are fish in abundance, growing peacefully bigger and bigger!

Halabiyé and Qalaat Rabâh

60 kilometres upstream, on the right bank, from Deir-ez-Zor (signposted from the ME 4 highway) stands a most impressive castle. This is *Halabiyé*, called *Zenobia* in Palmyrene times, which for hundreds of years was bitterly contended for. Outer walls, on a triangular plan extending down to the river bank itself (there used to be a ford at this point), rise in a series of closely-set square towers to the top of a basalt spur, which is crowned by a massive keep. Inside the ramparts there is nothing but ruins, but the lovely grey stone, flecked with glittering gypsum crystals, lends a fairytale beauty to the silent scene. Slightly downstream from Halabiyé, on the cliffs on the left bank, stands its counterpart, the

*The Euphrates, river of life and corridor
of civilisation, is romantically beautiful in the evening
at Deir el-Zor; making us forget the castles
along its banks and the dams that are in
the process of taming it.*

doura europos

castle of *Zalabiyé*, whose simpler rectangular curtain wall is rather better preserved. The outline of its towers is clearly visible from Halabiyé. Since there is no ferry across the river, access to the latter fortress is long and difficult; it can be reached by a track along the left bank, from Dor-ez-Zor.

On the right bank 45 kilometres downstream from Deir-ez-Zor, a legendary castle seems to rise from the pink and ochre cliffs, level with the village of *Mayadin*. This is *Qalaat Rahbâ*, an Arab fortress perched on a rocky spur, which looks formidable from a distance but on closer inspection turns out to be sadly dilapidated.

The countryside around Mayadin and *Ashârâ* (the next village) is extremely colourful in July. Melons, particularly watermelons, are almost exclusively cultivated in these parts. Great mountains of them lie piled up in special storage yards; in the nearby cafés deals are concluded for tons at a time—the whole crop runs into millions of tons. If you wish to buy some you have only to ask. The boot of your car will soon be filled to overflowing with green and yellow melons, as big as Rugby footballs and as hard and dense as stones.

DEIR-EZ-ZOR

Name: "The Convent of the Groves" (the tamarisk groves on the banks of the Euphrates). In ancient times: Auzara, Azaura.

Location and access: Principal town of governorate. Altitude 600 m. Bridge across the Euphrates. 320 km south-east of Aleppo, by excellent road as far as Al-Thaura, afterwards good. 135 km north-west of Abû Kamal (Iraq frontier); 410 km from Baghdad, by asphalt road; 210 km north-east of Palmyra, by unsurfaced track unsuitable for motor vehicles (no filling-station along the way, asphalt surfacing planned for 1978). 175 km south-west of Al-Hasseke by surfaced road.
Airport: Syrian Air Lines flights to Damascus and Aleppo.
Railway: planned.

Information: Tourist Bureau and Syrian Air Lines office. Guide for groups: Official in charge of Tourism, Archeology and Cultural Affairs, Mr. Ibrahim, at the cultural centre.

Accommodation: Al-Raghdan**B, Al-Nahir street, tel. 2053. Plus a score of *A, B and C hotels. Modern hotel planned for 1980-81.

■ From Deir-ez-Zor to Abû Kamal a continuous line of steep cliffs marks the boundary between the great Syrian desert plateau and the alluvial plain of the Euphrates. The ancient river valley sometimes found these cliffs an obstacle, and the river now describes big meanders from time to time—occasionally swinging out several kilometres across the plain. The international highway, from Baghdad to Aleppo, runs almost straight across the country —sometimes at the foot of the cliffs, sometimes along the water's edge.

At one point however, the mountain and the river meet and the road is obliged to climb steeply. For a short distance it runs across a stony plateau before plunging down into the green valley once more, the cliff reverting to its general north-west, south-east orientation. In the centre of this spur and right on the edge, overlooking the Euphrates 90 metres below, stands the fortified town of Doura Europos. It was established by Alexander's lieutenant Seleucos (the founder of the dynasty) and its name is taken from the village in distant Macedonia in which Alexander (conqueror of Syria in 305 B.C.) was born.

Occupied by the Parthians, then by the Romans, the town was closely linked with Palmyra (see entry) which it served as an important forward line of defence against the Persians. It was captured and destroyed by the Sassanids in 256 A.D., shortly before the fall of the great Syrian metropolis itself.

The sands covered it and it was forgotten.

The site did not attract significant attention again until 1921 when some mural paintings were accidentally discovered there, in a temple dedicated to the gods of Palmyra (at present in the National Museum at Damascus). Many other discoveries followed, notably frescoes on the walls of a synagogue built in 235 A.D.; discovered in a remarkable state of preservation they too were transported to the Damascus Museum in 1936. Despite these transfers, for which there was a lot to be

ezrâa

said, Doura Europos still has much to interest visitors.

The site, which has now been completely excavated, is very impressive. As at Halabiyé further north (see under Deir-ez-Zor), it is very clear here how important a frontier the Euphrates was, in the ancient world.

Vast enclosing walls, with three fortified gateways, enfold within their towers a town extending over 73 hectares. These defences, as well as the citadel right above the river and having its own system of rampart walls, are still impressively intact. By contrast there is very little of the town itself left standing. A church, a dozen temples, a market and several baths have been located and excavated. Inscriptions, sometimes in three languages, Parthian, Palmyrene and Latin, have been found. At the bottom of the ravine between the town and the citadel the customs area, spread out along the bank of the citadel serves to remind us that Doura Europos was not merely of strategic importance, but that as guardian of the river crossing, it was also a halt for caravans and a river port as well.

An attractive feature of the place is that, like Rasafa, Doura Europos was partly built of gypsum stone—no doubt because it was considered to be a good insulator; the framents that litter the ground glitter like a carpet of diamonds.

DOURA-EUROPOS

Name: Doura: wall; Europos, birthplace of Seleucus I, in Macedonia (Seleucus founded the city in 312 B.C.). Archeological site near the Arab village of Salhiye.

Location and access: Deir-ez-Zor governorate. Right bank of Euphrates. 40 km upriver from Abû Kamal (Iraq frontier). 95 km downriver from Deir-ez-Zor.

Accommodation: At Deir-ez-Zor.

■ A sprawling agricultural village on the fertile Hawran plain, slightly off the Damascus-Deraâ road, Ezrâa's only claims to the visitor's attention are its two churches, dating from the 4th and 5th centuries.

They are friendly laughing people in Ezrâa (Catholics for the most part), and willingly guide the visitor to the northern part of the village where a large, isolated building stands; it is built on a square plan, its facades are austere and it is surmounted by an incongruous metallic dome. This church, built in 410 on the site of a pagan temple, is one of the earliest examples of a basilica with a central dome supported by an internal octagon. The proportions are good and it would be an impressive ensemble were it not so neglected, and if an early attempt to strengthen it with a great concrete support had not been done so clumsily. This Orthodox church is, moreover, said to contain the tomb of St. George, a saint venerated throughout the East by Christians as well as Muslims.

The second church is in the heart of the village; it is dedicated to Mary and is served by Catholic priests. Architecturally it is similar to the church of St. George and is almost as dilapidated. Both buildings are decorated with Greek inscriptions and friezes of grapes around the doors and windows.

Half-way between the two churches there is some partly excavated arcading with sculptured decoration and kufic inscriptions.

The black lava stone of which the centre of the village is built is relieved by colourful little gardens, while further out extensive vineyards make a pleasant transition between the village and the flat cornlands of the Hawran.

EZRAA

Name: formerly Zorava.

Location and access: Hawrân region. Altitude about 600 m. 80 km south of Damascus, by road No. 5 as far as Shaykh Miskin and road No. 109, to the left. 40 km west of Suwayda by road No. 109.

Accommodation: None. At Damascus.

Hama is an industrial city of tomorrow, the centre of Syria's steel industry. Yet a romantic beauty and an Eastern charm still linger on the banks of the Orontes, where the norias continue to turn for ghostly occupants of forgotten palaces.

hama

■ An unceasing sound, like the creaking of a bullock cart, rises from the river banks to permeate the narrow streets and pervade the whole town—it is audible even as far away as the citadel. This is the noise made by the norias of Hama—a "cry" almost, like the muezzin's call to prayer, harsh, plangent and timeless.

A noria is an undershot Vitruvian waterwheel which raises water from a pool or a well to a channel or a cistern above. It is a very ancient technique.

Its yield is, of course, pitifully small, compared with modern hydraulic installations, but being powered by the flow of the river itself the noria is cost-free and lasts for ever.

These ancient waterwheels are depicted on stone, payrus and mosaics (one of the latter, found at Apamea, is on display in the National Museum in Damascus). Even today these wheels are still used—sometimes fitted with great earthenware pots to collect the water—in Spain, Portugal, Greece and in Egypt. None can compare with the norias of Hama. Here the smallest is ten metres in diameter, and there are some as big as twenty metres. But their size is not the only thing that makes them impressive—nor the robust complexity of their construction. They have a rustic beauty indeed, but it is their blind power and apparent timelessness that really capture the imagination. They seem to churn up the waters of the Orontes, but it is of course the Orontes that is causing them to turn, day and night, unceasingly.

Although these actual wheels are no more than two or three, perhaps four, hundred years old, their groaning and splashing—like that of the river itself—seems to go back to the very beginning of time.

They have a charm that it takes some time to appreciate. It simply can't be captured by the tourist who makes a hurried stop to photograph "his" first noria. Especially since, in all probability, this will be the noria near the aqueduct by the Sérail bridge, in the gardens in the middle of the town—near the Tourist Office, opposite the scenic café on a jetty in the river.

It needs more time and patience than this to get a true impression of Hama.

Not one noria, but ten

Of the citadel—the qalaat—of Hama, there is not a stone left standing. It stood on a tell which excavations have shown to consist of at least ten distinct archaeological layers, from the neolithic period to the Middle Ages.

Every single stone of the medieval fortress was carried off and used in other buildings; but the hill on which, like all other Syrian strongholds, it stood, is still there and has been developed as public gardens from which, at sunset especially, there is very good view of the whole town. The winding course of the Orontes, between its banks of greenery, is laid out beneath us as if on a map. We can easily make out all the well-known norias. There are at least ten of them, two or three are no longer working. Those farther out from the centre of the town, often half-hidden among gardens, are difficult to locate from the river level itself.

A new circular road around the foot of the citadel hill makes it easy to find the group of norias that are furthest downstream; they are almost concealed by the luxuriant gardens that lend to Hama something of the atmosphere of an oasis. A rustic bridge on which there is a mill crosses the river at this point. The highest waterwheel, which dates from the 14th century, is known as the *Al-Mouhammadiya;* it supplies water to the *Great Mosque* a hundred and fifty metres away, marked by an elegant octagonal minaret with a double lantern and wooden balcony. This mosque was built on the site of a Roman temple, later occupied by a Byzantine church; many re-used ancient capitals indicate its earlier history. It contains the mausoleum of two princes of Hama who reigned at the end of the 13th century; their cenotaphs of ebony inlaid with ivory are marvellous examples of fine woodwork.

Following the Orontes upstream, from the bridge with the mill and the Mouhammadiya, keeping to the streets near the river we come to the other norias and the main buildings of the town.

On the bend of the river, as it winds round the north of the citadel hill, a bridge leads across to a small mosque; beside it stands a short squat minaret, built of large blocks of white stone underlined by narrow bands of black. A little dome, bare of all ornament, marks a tomb adjacent to the mosque. Here lies *Abou al-Fidâa* (or Abi Fidaa), King of Hama from 1310 to 1332, who was famous above all as an historian and geographer. The mosque is sometimes called *djemaa al-Hayaât*, "the snake mosque", from the interlaced designs around one of its windows, which look like snakes intertwined.

White domes and charming minarets

At the very foot of the citadel, but in the south-east corner of the town, there is another mosque that is worth visiting: *Al-Nouri*, with little ribbed domes, over which rises a fine square minaret, the bands of darker stone half-way up give it its typically Syrian character. The minbar (pulpit) inside in the prayer hall is another fine example of the taste and skill of the craftsmen of Hama; it is made from rare woods finely carved in geometric patterns. The delicacy of this decoration contrasts particularly well with the reflective sobriety of the courtyard with its simple arcading which harmonizes perfectly with the white domes close by. There are three inscriptions worth noting, on the outside wall: the first, in Greek, praises the bravery of the inhabitants in the face of the Roman invaders; the second, framed within a finely sculpted border, records, in Arabic, the name of the builder of the mosque, Sultan Nur ad-Dîn Zanki, and the date of its construction, the 558th year of the Hegira (1129); the third, also in Arabic, notes that students used to gather here to work and that their expenses were paid by the municipality.

A glimpse of the Orient as it used to be

Less than a hundred metres from the Al-Nouri mosque there is a scene that might have been taken straight from an old print.

Here the Orontes flows over a weir and then under a grey, arched bridge near which a noria creaks away, hard up against a house by the riverside. A cluster of domed houses with projecting verandahs supported on great beams, overlook the blue-green waters. Their sharply-angled walls rise in succession straight out of the river and give a fortress-like air to the whole scene. The only access to this quarter is across the bridge and through a pointed archway whose heavy door looks as if it could once again be closed against the world, were the need to arise. From there, dark gateways, winding passages, irregular courtyards tiny culs de sac and mysterious stairways finally lead one out onto the single street, lined with dwellings which could be princely or could be hovels.

The tallest of these houses, its terrace splashed with water from the noria, did in fact belong to a noble family, one of whose sons became one the most venerated saints of Islam...

Syrians indeed often make the point that Hama, even today, is famous for the piety of its citizens. The visitor will no doubt already have noticed how much more common it is to see men wearing the

A GARDEN ON THE ORONTES

■ *We went and sat down in a little cafe under the poplar trees by the Orontes. A few Arabs began to arrive, for the sun was low on the horizon and the doves and swallows were starting to wheel about in the evening air... Under the trees—like our trees at home, but twice-blessed here for the coolness that they bring—beside the life-giving water and the mill-wheels, like poems come to life, I tasted all the sweetness of the old oases of Asia as it filtered in through the pores of my soul. An unexplicable nostalgia! What is it that evokes these disquiets in a setting so poor and yet so strangely powerful? What is it about Syria that I love? What am I seeking here? I think I am breathing in, here above the four rivers, a lost memory of that garden which long ago was closed to us by the flaming sword of the Keroubs...*

MAURICE BARRES
"Un jardin sur l'Oronte" (1921)

traditional gandourah, and completely black-veiled women, in Hama, than in the rest of Syria.

The charming old-world Azem Palace

On the other bank of the Orontes a tall lanterned dome above the trees marks the *Azem Palace*. This splendid building was the residence of the Governor, Asaad Pacha el-Azem, who ruled the town from 1700 till 1742.

The Azem Palace is reached from the bridge by a narrow street along the right bank of the river, between the wall of the Al-Nouri mosque and the imposing stone piers of a former noria. The palace, which has been converted into a Museum of Islamic Art, is open every day.

The first shaded flowery courtyards has all the charm of a little secret garden, with its tiny fountains and open summer salon under the north-facing iwan.

There are ancient sculptures scattered about; there are more in the rooms to the sides, and displays of coins, glassware, and weapons. There are Roman Hellenistic and Byzantine remains, from the time when Hama was called Epiphania. But there are older and more precious things too, reminders of those distant times when the Kingdom of Hamât (or Hamah) dealt on equal terms with King David and King Solomon, and of the time when, allied with its neighbours, it made war on its Assyrian occupiers and halted the troops of Samalnasar at Qarqar-sur-l'Oronte, north of the town, in 853 B.C. Unfortunately another revolt, in the following century, failed, and in 720 Sargon II (see chapter: History) deported the whole population.

In another room enormous photographs illustrate a more recent revolt—the one against the Turks.

A staircase leads from the gardens to a courtyard terrace and the first floor of the palace. The facade is preceded by a portico and the enor-

*On the airy slopes half-way between the blue skies
and the green valley floors, men have
built houses as red as the earth itself...
but sometimes they delight in painting
them mauve...or white.*

mous central room is roofed by the red dome that we saw from a distance.

The displays on this floor exemplify an art of living of great refinement and delicacy. Windows of stained glass and alabaster, marble paving, carved woodwork, deep-piled carpets and mosaic and marquetry all combine to create an atmosphere that is both stifling and yet subtle, the Orient beloved of so many nineteenth-century romantics. The richness of it all is almost vulgar, but soon, as one manages to concentrate one's eye upon one object at a time —a vase, a chandelier, a painting, or a miniature then satiety is overcome and it becomes ever more tempting to linger.

Restaurants in a park

Continuing along the left bank of the Orontes we arrive at the centre of the town, the place de la Liberté and the Sérail bridge, crossed by the Damascus-Aleppo highway. It is easy, and pleasant, to spend an hour or so wandering through the public gardens, noisy with the sound of water cascading down from an aqueduct, or to linger by the norias—perhaps at the same table in the café where Maurice Barres heard the charming medieval fable that he told again in his "Jardin sur l'Oronte."

But times have changed since Barres was here. The din of traffic often drowns the sound of the norias and modern white buildings loom over the pines and cypresses. So it would perhaps be a good idea to continue our walk quite a bit further upstream, to the place called "*The Four Norias of Bichriatt*" (or al-Maksaf), some twelve hundred metres from the bridge. Here is another riverside garden, much more peaceful than the one we have just just left. In the evenings craftsmen woodworkers come here and use the stream as it flows down a small channel, to turn their lathes, dimly lit with just a single lamp. At the end of the gardens two pairs of norias turn unceasingly. Until nightfall urchins play there, clinging to the blades of the wheels and then when they reach their highest point falling into the churned-up waters. A large café-restaurant, the "Casino des Quatre Norias", stands a little way back from the river. It is a pleasant place in which to spend the evening twilight: the enormous waterwheels seem to grow to giant proportions in the shadowy dusk and their insistent sound becomes ever more unreal.

There are other norias too, outside the town, among the orchards and the market-gardens.

Two "khans," the Asaad Pacha el-Azem and the (more recent) Rustom Pacha, figure among the more minor attractions of Hama, with gateways and courtyards built of stone in alternating colours. They are near the souks, in the rue Al-Mourabet, the second street on the left as you leave the place de la Liberté in the direction of Damascus.

Hama as an excursion centre

Hama used to have one single hotel which was welcoming and spotlessly clean though somewhat spartan and rather small; a modern hotel is being planned. Apart from the interest of the town of Hama itself it makes a good base from which to explore a large number of interesting sites: places of outstanding interest like Apamea, Crac des Chevaliers, Masyaf, Sheizar, Maarat ann-Numan, Homs and even Palmyra (see entries under these names), but also less well-known sites, or ones more difficult of access, for which guides (obtainable through the Tourist Bureau or in the hotels) are useful. Here is a selection of the latter, with an outline of points of interest.

Rastân, on the Homs-Damascus highway (26 km south of Hama) stands on a promontary overlooking the Orontes, on which there is a dam at this point (photography forbidden). Its houses are built of basalt but frequently plastered in various bright colours; they form a picturesque ensemble with a good view over the lake and the fertile plain below.

On the road to Masyaf, at *Deir Sheib*, the *monastery of La Croix* (25 km west of Hama), there are some semi-ruined Byzantine buildings.

To the south-east there are Salamiyé and Qalaat ash-Shamamis. *Salamiyé*, which is benefitting from the irrigation works under way in the Orontes basin, is scattered around its National Agricultural College and its horse-breeding centre. The mosque and most of the houses are built of black basalt. The whole region bristles with small volcanic cones. One of these, 4 km north-west of the town, is corwned by the *fortress of Shamamîs* (or Chemamis), the "Castle of the Sun," an Arab building restored in the 12th century. Its ditch is cut out of solid lava and its curtain wall encloses the crater at the top of the hill. To the north-east lie Qsar ibn Wardân, Stalb Antar and Aanjarîn, castles and a stronghold which today stand isolated out in the desert.

A track suitable for motor vehicles passes through the villages of *Taybet att-Turki* and *Al-Hamra*, with their characteristic sugar-loaf style houses; it then deteriorates though remaining clearly visible. 55 kilometres from Hama the ruins of *Qasr Ibn Wardan* come into sight, on a terraced hillside. The ruins of several buildings, a palace and a church show their original construction of brick and lava stone, with limestone and marble decoration. Dates on two of the facades, 561 and 564, place the buildings during the reign of Justinian, Christian Emperor of the East.

10 kilometres beyond Qaâr ibn Wardân lie the remains of an ancient fortress of the same period, *Stalb Antar;* its towers are gradually being evoded away by the desert winds.

Finally, 15 kilometres further along this same track brings us to the ruins of ancient *Androna*, present-day *Al-Andarîn*. The remains cover a wide area. The enclosing wall, two churches, a great square building with walls 80 metres long which was used as a barracks, and a vast cistern are all easily recognizable. The town was supplied with water through underground channels or "qanats" (cf. "Iran Today" in this series), whose ventilation shafts are still visible across the desert. Like her neighbours, Androna did not long survive the loss of Northern Syria by the Byzantine Empire. The poet Anor ben Kalthoum wrote of the decline of this city around the year 600.

The ancient palace of *Esriyé* is even more isolated; among these splendid reddish ruins of a former Roman mansion there are walls still standing, supported by engaged columns with Corinthian capitals. Esriyé marked the crossing point of the tracks Emesa (Homs)—Ressafe—Raqqa and Tadmor (Palmyra)—Aleppo. Lying as it does 80 kilometres north-east of Salamiyé (100 kms from Hama) it is essential to have both a vehicle equipped for desert conditions and a local guide in order to visit it.

Syria's iron town

Hama has an assured future as a tourist centre, this has been known for a long while. The economic development of the town is more recent and will accelerate in the next few years. The development of the valley of the Orontes and the Ghab plain will certainly continue to have an impact on Hama (see entries for Apamean Masyaf, Homes), but the immediate future can be summed up in a single word: iron.

The iron-ore deposits of the Masyaf region, estimated at about 100 million tons will be treated in a great steel complex, under construction near Hama, that will employ four thousand workers, technicians and engineers. The first steelworks, opened in 1971, is producing 110,000 tons of reinforcing steel each year, as well as other constructional components; it is the largest plant of its kind in the Arab world.

homs

■ Coming from Damascus you turn right here for Palmyra, left for Crac des Chevaliers, and you cross the whole town from south to north to get to Hama. The visitor very often remembers Homs merely for its traffic jams. A crossroads, an industrial town, a town repeatedly struck by earthquakes throughout its history. Homs seems to lack tourist "attractions" insofar as the word implies the picturesque or the unique. The fact is generally recognized, but it is not necessarily a serious shortcoming.

Industry, the key to the future

The citizens of Homs accept the situation philosophically; for their concerns and their hopes lie elsewhere—in the economic development of their town which is the natural consequence of its geographical situation. Half-way between Damascus and Aleppo and at the beginning of the rich Orontes valley, Homs moreover commands the famous "gap" that takes its name—the sole easy line of communication between Syria's coast and her hinterland. History is now paralleled by economics. The modern oil-pipelines follow the route taken by the armies and caravans of old. The most important oil refinery in Syria, on the western outskirts of Homs on the road to Tartous, has already been enlarged on two occasions. Petrol trucks leave Homs in all directions.

A sugar refinery, spinning mills, silk and rayon weaving, the hydroelectric works at Rastân all show the way in which the region is developing. Soon metallurgical industries (complementary to the steel complex under construction at Hama; see entry), fertilizer plants for the treatment of phosphates from Palmyra, new textile factories to process the cotton from around Lake Qattiné, the new lake upstream from Homs itself, all these activities assure the economic future of the city.

It is already a busy place with more than 130,000 inhabitants.

The projected complex will produce an initial 300,000 tons of sheet steel, bars, pipes, etc., annually. Its capacity will gradually reach 600,000 tons. Syria is expected to consume 730,000 tons of steel products in 1980. To quote one of its leading managers: "the Hama steel complex is to Syrian industry what the Euphrates Dam is to Syrian agriculture."

HAMA

Name: The French version of the name Hamaâ is generally used. Variant names: Hama on the Orontes. Aramean period: Hamât; Seleucid period: Epiphania (in the reign of Antiochus IV Epiphanes, circa 175 B.C.).

Location and access: Principal town of governorate. Altitude 308 m. 140 km south of Aleppo; 45 km north of Homs; 200 km from Damascus, by motorway and expressway. 90 km east of Baniyas; 140 km south-east of Latakia.

Information: Tourist Bureau, Al-Djabri Bd (Aleppo road), left after the bridge, near the garden, tel. 000. Syrian Air Lines offices, Choukri al-Kouatly street (near the main square, Liberté Square, tel. 1213).

Taxis: Al-Naouahir, Choukri al-Kouatly street, tel. 2485. Al-Sharmini, Choukri al-Kouatly street, tel. 2980. Garage de Salamieh, Liberté Square, tel. 1133. Safariat al-Sahel, Mouraibet street, tel. 2566. Garage Al-Sari, Choukri al-Kouatly street, tel. 1393. Garage New Omayat, Choukri al-Kouatly street, tel. 1968.

Accommodation: Basman**B, Choukri al-Kouatly street (right of the Liberté Square coming from Damascus, 100 m on the left-hand side of the street, near a fruit-juice bottling-plant), a plain, clean, fresh, quiet establishment; good welcome; English and French spoken; 28 rms., without restaurant; tel. 12838. Cairo*A, Choukri al-Kouatly street, 9 rms., tel. 12096. *Al-Raid*A, Choukri al-Kouatly street, 12 rms., tel. 12843.

Open-air restaurants: Casino des Quatre Norias, known as "Al-Maksaf", left bank of the Orontes, 1 km upstream from the place de la Liberté, adjacent to the public gardens (avoid taking the right bank: neither the gardens along the river nor the gang-ways shown on the very rough plan provided by the Tourist Bureau are open to the public). Al-Marah and Al-Oumara, quite simple restaurants in the gardens around the artesian well, right at the east end of the town (take transport). Worth noting: the broad, shaded terraces of the cafés along the Orontes near the place de la Liberté.

Traffic is heavy even on the outskirts and grows even denser around the rather curious concrete clock-tower which marks the centre of the city. It also marks the end of the boulevard *Choukri al-Kouwatli,* tree-lined and bright with flowerbeds. Along this road, as broad as an esplanade but not particularly long, there are cinemas, restaurants and attractive cafés.

There are not many buildings of interest, and even they are somewhat dubious esthetically... An army barracks now occupies the site of the former citadel, on a rocky eminence in the south of the city. The fortified walls have disappeared apart from two half-ruined gateways incorporated into neighbouring buildings—the Damascus and the Tadmor Gates. The Great Mosque, on the continuation of the Hama road, near the eastern entrance to the souks, has a minaret of some elegance. The souks themselves are nothing very special, though there are many brocade merchants to be found there.

A gigantic mausoleum

The only truly spectacular monument is the mausoleum containing the *tom of Khaled Ibn Al-Walid,* the great commander of the Muslim armies who brought Islam to Syria in 636. The building, a recent construction, has enormous metal domes which are dazzling in the sunshine. It is situated in the northern part of the city, to the right of the Hama road, behind an esplanade planted with flowers. Two very tall white stone minarets lend a certain lightness to the imposing structure: rising from a square base the octogonal shafts splay out towards ruff-like balconies, then rise again, slender and fluted, to terminate in bulbous lanterns. The courtyard of the mosque, adjacent to the mausoleum, is bordered by delicate arcading whose supporting walls, decorated with alternating bands of black and white stone, echo traditional Syrian motifs.

Unknown frescoes and enormous catacombs

Homs has a numerous Christian minority which has long been established in the eastern part of the city. There are many churches there, small modest buildings for the most part. One of them claims to possess "the girdle of the Blessed Virgin." The *Church of St. Eliân* commemorates the only son of a high Roman official, governor of Homs (Emesa) at the end of the 3rd century, who died a martyr for his faith at the hands of his own father. His ancient, purely local cult was revived after centuries of neglect, when a series of fine frescoes was discovered in the church in 1970. They bear inscriptions in Greek and Arabic and date from the end of the 12th century; a layer of plaster had fortunately preserved them for posterity (see leaflet by George Saadé, available in the church). There are traces of 6th century mosaics under the painting. In 1973 the whole church was completely restored and its walls were covered with more frescoes—depicting more than a hundred figures—of rather a different order artistically from the earlier medieval ones.

There was another discovery in this same quarter, in 1957, when roadworks revealed the entrance to a network of *catacombs.* The locals of Homs had long been accustomed to talk of the "magarats" (cellars) under their houses, but no excavations had been conducted to test these rumours.

Only the beginnings of a few underground passages have been explored so far, but experts agree that beneath ancient *Emesa* there was a whole network of galleries where the Christians buried their dead, from the 3rd to the 7th centuries. Some of these tombs had mosaic decorations. Coins, glass, liturgical vessels, and gold jewelry from this site are on display in the National Museum in Damascus. The actual excavations are closed to the public for fear of the danger that the vaults may collapse.

These recent discoveries shed a new light on the history of Homs which was not particularly brilliant, apart from the dubious glory of having been the birthplace of the man who was proclaimed Emperor by the Roman Legions stationed in Syria, in 218. He was fourteen years old and was a priest in the Temple of the Sun God Baal at Emesa. When he was made Emperor, in Rome, he took the name of his god: El Gebal, hence Elagabalus in Latin, Heliogabalus in Greek. A somewhat mixed-up adolescent, passionately absorbed by mysticism, *Elagabalus* remains famous for his bloody executions—these became so outrageous that he himself was finally murdered by the Praetorian guard. In a rare moment of lucidity he adopted his cousin, Alexander Severus, as his successor.

A lake dating back to Egyptian times

Out along the road to Tartous, just after passing the oil refinery, an enormous expanse of blue comes into view on the left and seems to extend right to the outlying hills of the Anti-Lebanon range. This is the Lake of Homs, or *Lake Qattiné*, which extends over 60 square kilometres—a tenth of the area of the new Lake Al-Assad on the Euphrates. It is fed by the *nahr al-Assi* (the river Orontes), swollen by the snows and torrents of the nearby mountains. Its waters are famous for their abundance of fish. One main canal, 60 kilometres long, supplies the whole city of Homs with drinking water, and a whole network of secondary channels provide for the irrigation of some 20,00 hectares.

The banks of the lake are steep in places and rather inaccessible; there is no road right the way round. Yet this is not an entirely modern reservoir. The retaining dam and many of the ancillary works have been consolidated and extended in recent years, but the first dam to regulate the flow of the Orontes is said to have been built in the middle of the second millenium B.C., after the defeat by the Egyptians of the powerful neighbouring city of *Qadesh* (the victory of Tutmose III at Megiddo, about 1468, and the campaigns of Amenophis II, 1438-1412, against the Hittites). At Karnak, in Upper Egypt (see "Egypt Today" in this series), there is a battle scene entitled: "the ravaging of Qadesh."

The site of Qadesh has been identified as *tell Nabi Mand,* some 6 kilometres upstream from the lake, on the left bank of the Orontes, overlooking the river about thirty metres away. (It can be reached by track from the village of *Qûsayr,* 25 km south of Homs.) Diggings have recently been started there again and have revealed mudbrick walls; archaeologists have shown that the site was occupied at least from the Hyksos period up until Roman times.

Another ancient site demonstrates the importance of this region over thousands of years. This is *Qatna,* near the present-day village of *Mushrifa,* 15 kilometres north-west of Homs on the road to Salamiyé. The town, perched on a rocky hillock, was surrounded by four kilometres of rampart walls, with gateways and defensive works, built of enormous blocks of stone—all characteristic features of Hyksos fortification (mid-2nd millenium).

Another place of interest, a modern one this time, is the village of *Fûrqlos,* 40 kilometres from Homs on the road to Palmyra. Almost all the houses are built in the sugar-loaf style, characteristic of Northern Syria. The oldest are used to house pigeons and poultry but the more recent are lived in and are indeed marvellously well-adapted to the local climate. Their interiors are kept spotlessly clean. They are dark and the temperature inside never varies. The main—often the only—item of furniture is a huge chest, often beautifully painted, with applied decoration. The local inhabitants are most hospitable to passing visitors who will often be invited to visit their homes.

Information p. 147.

idlib

■ Idlib is one of those towns that motorists usually drive through without stopping. There are no famous monuments, the setting is not particularly beautiful and there is little in the way of accommodation—so perhaps such an attitude is justified. Nevertheless, with its wide streets, landscaped roundabouts and tall modern blocks, it is evidently a rapidly developing place.

Idlib is the capital of a mouhafazat, and this province or, more accurately, governorate, possesses many tourist sites of considerable interest.

Seven million fruit trees

The surrounding countryside is most attractive: gently rolling uplands where the red soil contrasts with the green of the plants and trees. There are fruit trees everywhere: olives, carefully pruned and tended; apricots, bearing succulent fruit we may meet again in gâteaux in Damascus; plum trees, with small hard green fruit; pomegranates, whose orange-red flowers used to be a symbol of power and whose heavy fruit is made into a delicious and refreshing drink in the little juice-bars of Aleppo and Damascus. But above all it's for cherries that the Idlib region is famous. Towards the end of spring small boys on every roadside offer great handfuls of bright gleaming fruit to the passer-by... for a few pence.

From its seven million trees the region provides for nearly all Syria's requirements of fruit and olives.

In the hillier areas of this delightful region there are many sites that could be developed as "summer holiday centres." At an altitude of 800-900 metres the air is stimulating and the general climate most agree-

AN UNKNOWN SEMITIC LANGUAGE

■ *The tablets found at Tell Mardikh have enabled us to identfy the most ancient written language which was also the spoken language of the Syrian population, by contrast with Sumerian and Akkadian which in Syria were languages written only by educated people. Secondly, everything leads us to suppse that this "Ancient Canaanite" was the language of the first great urban culture of Syria, that is of the first Syrian civilisation that was both autonomous and original in its thought—which developed during the 3rd millenium B.C. Finally, this discovery of Ancient Canaanite necessitates a general revision of our historical notions of the role of other ancient semitic peoples in Syria, the Amorites in particular. The identification of the most ancient urban culture culture at Ebbla as a Canaanite one indicates that the role of Syria in the very foundation of Middle Eastern civilisation was far more important than had hitherto been imagined.*

PROF. PAOLO MATTHIAE
Leader of the Italian Expedition
to Tell Mardikh

able. There are some holiday centres here already, but they are not many and their facilities are modest—they certainly indicate that much more could be done.

Among existing holiday centres there are: *Ar-Riha* (15 km south of Idlib on the road from Jisr ash-Shughur and Latakia) with its "Casino Jebel al-Arbain" embowered among trees; the village itself is pleasant with a square minaret and blue limewashed houses; *Ain al-Zarqa* (30 km east of Idlib) is attractively sited overlooking the Orontes, among pine and oak woods, with streams and waterfalls; *Salqîn* with its "Casino" on a scenic terrace (41 km north-west of Idlib); *Sheykh Obed* (14 km north of Salqîn), overlooking the Turkish frontier, near the charming village of *Harim*.

Highly favoured by Nature, this corner of Syria has always been heavily populated. Many of the "ghost towns" of Northern Syria, those evocative bare ruins on ridges that have become so arid now, are in fact within the province of Idlib.

Tell Mardikh, ancient Ebla

The most important groups of them: *Al-Bâra* (40 km south of Idlib) and *Qalb Lozâ-Kirk Bizâ* (70 km north of Idlib) have entries of their own—as does *Qalaat Sâmâan* in the very north of the province.

But settlements far older than these have been discovered. Excavations at a tell 25 kilometres south of Idlib (south of the village of Sarâuib, near the Aleppo-Hama road) have made it possible to establish the site of the important ancient city of *Ebla*, destroyed in about 1600 B.C. The site is known as *Tall Mardikh*. There are some astonishing finds from here in the National Museum in Damascus: finely-engraved cylinder-seals, charming female figurines holding their naked breasts in their hands, great double stone cisterns carved in bas-relief with banquetting scenes, military parades, and the heads of extraordinary open-mouthed animals.

The site itself, as so often, is disappointing to the layman. Indeed visitors are not at all welcome while digging is actually under way. In August 1974 forty-four cuneiform tablets were discovered here at Tall Mardikh. They revealed a language, hitherto unknown, current around 2300 B.C., the ancestor of Canaanite. In the opinion of Professor Paolo Mathiae, leader of the Italian mission to Tall Mardikh, this language is the oldest semitic language of Western Syria, corresponding to Akkadian in Mesopotamia, the oldest semitic language of the East. Further excavations here in 1975 and 1976 increased the tally from forty-four to some fifteen thousand!...

Authentic craftwork

As in many essentially agricultural regions, crafts have been practised here for centuries. The products have a simplicity and beauty born of generations of experience.

At *Armanaz*, near Idlib, there are families of craftsman glassworkers in which sons have succeeded their fathers for more than two hundred years; their furnaces have not gone out within living memory. In the town itself there are also potters who make elegant jugs. In the villages along the Orontes other craftsmen make dishes, trays and bowls from rushes and straw.

IDLIB

Name: Variant names: Hidleb, Idelb.

Location and access: Principal town of governorate. Altitude 000 m. 55 km south-west of Aleppo, by motorway as far as Sarâqeb (62 km by old road). 130 km north-east of Latakia, by good, winding road.

Information: Governorate Tourist Department.

Accommodation: Al-Kabir Al-Syahi (Tourist'Hôtel)**A, Malki street, tel. 20970. At *Salqîn* (summer resort, 40 km north-west of Idlib); *Casino,* with swimming pool, **A, al-Dawar street.

jablé

■ Jablé is a large seaside town, virtually in the middle of the Syrian coast. Although it was an ancient port there are no more ships to be seen at Jablé, apart from a few fishing vessels, and, although it is on the Mediterranean, it is far from being a tourist centre—there are no decent beaches and no hotel worthy of the name.

Perhaps, if the local inhabitants took stock of the situation and certain improvements were made, Jablé could yet have some future as a holiday centre. It does in fact possess an important ancient building which already causes the town to be mentioned on lists of sites worth visiting.

Of all the peoples who visited or occupied this coast, between the time of the Phoenicians and the departure of the Crusaders, the Romans were the only ones to leave a significant memento of their presence here: a *theatre*, built to accommodate between 7,000 and 8,000 spectators.

Despite unfortunate railings which mask the entrance, and the weeds which are already beginning to cover the stones that excavations revealed, only a few years ago, the building remains impressive. The site is completely flat, so that the cavea is entirely supported on a system of vaulting, each arch supporting a row of seats.

Not far from the theatre a minaret and a series of white domes indicate the presence of *a mosque*. This shrine contains the tomb of a major saint of Islam, Sultan Ibrahim, King of Afghanistan, who renounced his throne for a life of virtue and charity. He died at Jablé.

Tell Soukas, in the National Museum in Damascus

Two sandy coves on the coast, some 6 kilometres south of Jablé, mark the site of two basins of an ancient port.

Excavation of a nearby hill, known as *Tell Soukas*, has produced a rich harvest of finds: a fragment of the scarab of the Pharaoh Amenophis III (1405-1370 B.C.), Mycenaean figurines, Cypriot and Mycenaean pottery, a Ugaritic tablet (see under Ugarit), silver diadems found near skeletons in a tomb, etc.

All these objects are on display in showcases in the room devoted to "Antiquities from the Coastal Areas", in the National Museum in Damascus. Others are preserved in the Cathedral-Museum at Tartous. There is little to interest the layman at the site itself.

JABLE

Name: Variant names: Djeble, Jeble. Phoenician period: Gabala. Crusader period: Zibel.

Location and access: Latakia governorate. Seaside. 28 km south of Latakia.

Accommodation: At Latakia.

HOMS

Name: Roman period: Emesa.

Location and access: Principal town of governorate. Altitude 495 m. 160 km north of Damascus, 45 km south of Hama, 185 km from Aleppo, by motorway and expressway. 95 km east of Tartus, 190 km north-east of Beirut. Railway lines to Tartus, Beirut, Hama, Aleppo.

Information: Tourist Bureau.

Accommodation: Qasr Raghdan**B, Kuwatly street, 30 rms., tel. 25211. *Basman Al-Jadid***B, Al-Sham street, 16 rms. tel. 26977. *Basman Al-Kabir**A, Al-Maari street, 20 rms., tel. 25700. *Semiramis**A, Kuwatly street, 12 rms., tel. 21837.

Open-air restaurants and cafés: Town centre, Choukri al-Kuwatly street.

jisr ash-shûghûr

■ There are not many bridges across the Nahr al-Assi—literally "Rebel River", known to non-Arabic speakers as the "River Orontes"—along the corridor down which it flows between the coastal range to the west and the Zaouiyé to the east. There is one at Shaizar, one on the road to Masyaf, one opposite Qalaat al-Mudiq and another some fifty kilometres further north, at Jisr ash-Shughur. This lack of bridges was because of the river's liability to sudden flooding, which produced the marshes that until so recently marked its course. Consequently places where there was a river crossing tended to become places of some consequence. Hence the importance of Jisr ash-Shughur, which was also ideally situated on the route from Aleppo to the coast.

The town has a wonderful position and appeals to the visitor by being in itself quite picturesque.

After passing through the orchards of Idlib (see entry) and making a steep descent around an arid spur of the Zaouiyé, the road from Aleppo suddenly confronts us with a considerable township—a mass of small houses with green, blue and even violet plaster on their walls, ranged on terraces down a hillside still crowned by the remains of a defensive fort. At its foot the Orontes flows between banks of greenery; its dancing waters are delight of the small boys of the place all the summer long.

There is a bridge—the bridge—with a bend in the middle, to strengthen it against the strong current. From Roman times there has been a road across the river at this point. Since then the piers of the bridge have been repaired and reinforced in many different materials. It remains a handsome structure and fits perfectly into the landscape.

Unlocking the fertile Ghab

The economic importance of Jisr ash-Shughur can only increase during the coming years. Not so much now as keeper of an important bridge but as a natural link between the Ghab and the natural outlets for its new riches.

It is said that the Pharaoah Tutmose III used to come to hunt elephant in this humid valley, and that, a thousand years later, Hannibal taught the Syrians how to use the great beasts in war. Over the centuries this unhealthy plain was famous as an open door to invaders and also for the abundance of fish to be found in its fluctuating waters.

It is really only quite recently, around 1970, that things have changed. The task of making the middle reaches of the Nahr al-Assi valley healthy and fertile was one of the first that the new state of Syria set itself.

Embankments were built along 60 kilometres of the river's course. Two dams were built to complete the effect of the lake at Homs—at Rastan, between Homs and Hama, and at Mohardé, upstream from Sheizar. Hundreds of subsidiary canals drained the land and redistributed the waters; kilometres of concrete drains are still being laid, the roads are being improved. The result of all this is the attractive chequered landscape of yellow, green and red that can now be seen from the promontaries at Sheizar and Apamea (see entries). Wheat, barley, sugar-beet and thousands of fruit trees now cover more than 4,000 hectares.

So Jisr ash-Shughur now has a new role to play—that of transport centre to get all this produce away to market. Roads are important but the terrain is difficult and road-transport is slow. A railway has therefore been built, at enormous effort and expense, across the coastal chain. The line is an amazing series of tunnels, viaducts and corniches. But since 1976 the harvests have been able to reach Latakia without difficulty and the Ghab in return has enjoyed easy access to imported heavy goods.

Downstream from Jisr ash-Shughur the Orontes valley is less intensively cultivated than it is in the Ghab. Pastureland and orchards (cherries above all) become more common, contrasting with the arid hilltops all around. The road to Qnayé, on the frontier, and to *Harim* (see under Qalb Lozé) no longer runs along the river, which it crosses at *Darkhûsh*, but winds up among the hills.

Holiday centres and health cures

There are two places here that are of particular interest to the visitor. *Salqîn* (48km north of Jisr ash-Shughur, 11km south of Harim), at an altitude of 1,000 metres, is a typical "summer resort" which appeals to the people of the uplands for its bracing atmosphere, greenery, running streams and a pleasant "casino".

Hammam Sheykh Issa (25km north-east of Jisr ash-Shughur, via Qnayé) does not have the same attractions. At an altitude of only 240 metres and in a rather bare part of the Orontes valley, it is not a particularly inviting place in which to stay. But there are springs here, gushing out at a temperature of 39°C. (102°F.), which contain sodium, magnesium, sulphates, phosphates and potassium, whose beneficial effects have been known since antiquity for the treatment of rhumatism and skin diseases.

JISR ASH-SHUGHUR

Name: Variant names: Djisr (the bridge) ech Choghour (Chaghour), Djisr esh Shogr. Hellenistic period (2nd century B.C.): Seleucia ab Bellum. Roman period (2nd century): Niaccuba.

Location and access: Idlib governorate. On the Orontes, downstream of the Ghab Depression. Altitude 000 m. 75 km north-east of Latakia by fine but hilly road. 105 km south-west of Aleppo, by motorway and good road. 90 km north-west of Hama, via Apamea.

Accommodation: A few * hotels, or, better, at Latakia or Hama.

ST. SIMON STYLITES (386-459)

■ *He joined a monastery at the age of sixteen, but was eventually expelled because his exaggerated ascetic practices were too much for the brethren. Nothing daunted, he became a solitary hermit, and then, in 423 A.D., took up his post, on top of a ten foot pillar.*
The height of his pillars grew with his ascetic ambitions, and he spent the last thirty years of his life on the summit of a fifty foot column. ...A ladder permitted the monks to bring him his exceedingly meagre daily rations, and twice weekly to administer the Eucharist. At least once a day he preached to the crowds below and prostrated himself in prayer more than a thousand times. He didn't hesitate to make pronouncements on numerous points of religious policy, and to volunteer advice to the Emperor and to the ecclesiastical authorities. In the atmosphere of early Christianity, this fantastically ascetic way of life soon gained him a prodigious reputation for sanctity...

JULIAN HUXLEY
(adapted)
"From an Antique Land"
(Cedric Chivers, London 1954)

ladhiqiya (latakia, lattaquie)

■ Some thirty large cargo-boats ride at anchor off-shore. In a vast half-circle they come in to tie up at the quays under the giant cranes, with pilot boats and fishing vessels weaving their way in between. Along the corniche boulevard there are restaurants with covered balconies built out over the sea, with wonderful views of all this activity. The fish and shellfish—personally selected in the kitchens—taste all the better eaten here in the sea air, with all the colour and excitement of a big port laid out before us. Latakia is one of the lungs of Syria. Most of her imports and exports pass through Latakia, which is also the end of the overland route from Europe through Turkey.

It is only natural therefore that the Syrian government should have taken particular care to develop the city. Much has already been achieved: the construction of the rail link with the Ghab, opened in 1976 (see entry for Jisr ash-Shughur); the creation of a "duty-free zone"-covering 75 hectares it is the most extensive in Syria—a third of it is already open; the construction of giant refrigerated stores; as well as the development of the port itself and the improvement of its loading and unloading facilities. The city itself reflects this urge to expand. Wide two-lane boulevards have been built to take the increased traffic. A modern functional administrative centre now faces the sea from the centre of the city. A "Méridien" hotel is being planned.

The port facilities are already impressive—although still inadequate to take the increased trade. There are 45 hectares of basins, 1,700 metres of docks, 90,000 square metres of warehouse space and an immense silo that can store 35,000 tons of grain. The port has about a hundred service vessels of various kinds.

The Northern Quay is for passenger lines, connecting with Cyprus, Beirut, Alexandria and the western Mediterranean. There is a vast building housing Customs and Sûreté office as well as a Tourist Information Bureau and a railway station. No doubt one day car-ferries will be putting in here too.

A base for exploring the Syrian coast

Besides being important economically, Latakia has considerable tourist potential. Not so much for its own attractions but because it is well provided with accommodation and is well-placed as a base from which to explore the coastal regions of the country. There are beaches, mountains, lush countryside, archaeological sites and many relics of the Crusaders, all within, at most, a few hours' drive.

In the city itself there is pleasant walk along the corniche and the adjacent colourfully planted avenues; it is tempting to linger longer in the magnificent *public gardens*, right by the sea (near the "Casino" hôtel), with their fine palm trees and clumps of oleanders. There are not many ancient remains: four columns and a Roman arch from the time of Septimus Severus (circa 200 A.D.), a triumphal arch on four massive supports, at the bottom of an avenue in the south of the city.

There are *beaches* to the north of Latakia, beyond the unsightly installations around the oil-wharves. The road cuts across a small promontory and then follows the curve of a bay where there are several motels-cum-bathing-stations. There is a wide, gently sloping beach, with clean fine sand. The sea is calm and bathing is quite safe. (See list at the end of this entry.)

Lush countryside

The motel-bathing-station furthest from the city is the "*Club Ras Shamra*", 8 kilometres out, not far from the famous archaeological site at *Ugarit* (see entry). The countryside is particularly rich and fertile in these parts.

The orchards and market gardens are protected from the winds by great cypress hedges. The citrus groves are especially carefully tended. Irrigation channels and watering systems ensure bumper crops of vegetables. Cornfields alternate with fields of sunflowers over much of the landscape. Where it gets drier olives take over once more.

The first thirty kilometres of the road from Latakia to Antalya lie thus through very pleasant agricultural areas; as soon as we reach the first foothills of the northern mountain ranges the forests begin. They are evergreen forests of good-sized trees—an extremely unusual landscape in Syria and hence very strictly protected by the authorities. The forests have become a favourite weekend recreation place for the people of Latakia; every Friday there is an exodus towards the resorts of *Sastal Moâf, Nabhein* and *Kassab* as well as to the beach at *Râs al-Bassit* (see entry)—where there are few facilities as yet, but where the Syrian tourist authorities propose to develop a "holiday complex".

South of Latakia the countryside is quite different.

The so-called coast road in fact runs some distance inland and offers few glimpses of the sea. The narrow coastal plain is rather dull and the landscape is of no particular interest. The only place really worth visiting is Tartous and the nearby Isle of Arwad. On the way there it is worth while stopping briefly at Jablé (see entries under these names).

Shepherds, waterfalls and forests

The most interesting excursions from Latakia are into the mountains and valleys to the east and south-east of the city.

The *valley of the Nahr al-Kabir*—followed for a while by the road to Jisr ash-Shughur and Aleppo—is almost Alpine in feeling only a few kilometres inland from the sea. The river flows along a great pace between the wooded slopes, throwing up pebbly beaches beside its deep meanders. Small boys—some of them with astonishing fair hair—lead their herds of goats and cattle, and sometimes flocks of sheep, there to drink. The shepherds enjoy splashing about in the water too, of course, and they also collect any driftwood that happens to be about—wood is a precious commodity all over Syria.

The banks of a tributary of the Khébir, which joins it close to its mouth, just south of Latakia, are a very similar kind of terrain. Crops tend to give way to stock in these parts. The road along this river valley joins the one along the Nahr Al-Kabir after making long detours to *Haffé* (where there is a turning for the castle at Saône—see entry under Qalaat Salah ad-Dîn), and then to the charming "holiday centre" in the woods, at *Slenfé*, and finally to *Salma*.

Towards the Ansariya

The coastal range rises like an impregnable barrier parallel to the shoreline. Its ridge runs from north to south at a height of between 1,200 and 1,500 metres, the highest peak rises to 1,562 metres. There are very few roads across it, suitable for motor vehicles. Right to the last turning before the pass one wonders just how the road will ever make its way across. There are many roads which simply become dead ends or dwindle into goat tracks as they reach the top of the ridge.

These are the roads used by hardworking peasants, who often have to rebuild their stone walls flattened by storms and whose lives are a constant struggle to wrest a living from an exceedingly unwilling soil. As his road winds higher and higher it becomes obvious, even to the passing stranger that the land is becoming poorer and poorer and the crops less and less. Leaving behind the fertile orchards at the bottom of the slopes one gradually reaches a landscape where scanty patches of wheat stand out against the white limestone and the bare garrigue. Far below there is the sparkling sea, where an oil-tanker is making its way towards Baniyas and a cargo-boat is heading into Latakia.

These were often strategic routes —better suited to the horsemen of days gone by, the Crusaders or the warriors of Allah, than to the motor vehicles of today.

For those fighting men these mountains were witnesses of moments of glory and moments of defeat—not to speak of long hours of waiting and watching for friendly troops or a friendly sail, nor of the days spent dragging supplies up the moutainside to provision the strongholds perched like eagles' eyries on spurs of the Ansariya.

They are still there those citadels, that saw two centuries of bitter fighting. Some are now no more than shapeless ruins among the thistles: *Mhelbé, Bani Qatân, Qsaybé, Aalayqa, Kahf, Yahmûr...* Others—and they are among the greatest—still stand out against the Syrian sky, arrogant even though sometimes mutilated; among them are *Qalaat Salah ad-Dîn* (known as Saône to the Crusaders), *Marqab* (Margat), *Safitâ* (Chastel Blanc) and, proudly isolated, *Crac des Chevaliers.*

These by-roads, used by preasants and knights of old, are becoming major tourist routes today. This will certainly assure Latakia, important already in the economic development of Syria, of a significant role in Mediterranean tourism as a whole.

LATAKIA (AL-LADHIQIYA)

Name: The French version of the name, Lattaquié, is frequently used. Variant names: Lattakia, El Ladkiyé, Lâdhaqiyé. Phoenician period: Ramitha, Mazabda, Leuke Akte; Seleucid period (2nd century): Laodicea; Crusader period: La Liche«

Location and access: Principal town of governorate. Commercial port on the Mediterranean. 175 km south of Iskenderun, via Antakya (116 km) and across the Turkish frontier at Ordu-Yaladagi (60 km), by good road. 240 km north of Beirut, crossing the Lebanese frontier at Arida (120 km). 185 km northwest of Homs, via Tartus (90 km). Railway line to Jisr ash-Shughur (open in 1976) and to Aleppo. Boat services to Cyprus and Beirut. Syrian Air Lines: flights to Damascus, office, rue Al-Qouds, tel. 2050, 1244.

Information: Tourist Bureau, Martyrs Square, tel. 1861. Brochures in various languages. Official guides. Excellent welcome.

Travel agencies: Almanara, Adnan Al-Malki street, P.O. Box 207, tel. 12053, 12129, telegraphic adress Almanara 1320. *Karnak,* Al-Hourria street, tel. 11541. Rayess Tours, 8-mars square. Tel. 13565.

Public services: Post Office, Al-Hourria street (north area of harbour); tel. 11252. Passports, at the Seraglio, near the Post Office, rue Al-Hourria, tel. 11400. Customs, Baghdad street (by the harbour), tel. 1440.

Accommodation: Méridien****A, north coast, under construction (opening scheduled for 1977). *Tourist'Hôtel and Casino* (Al-Syaha)**A, Andalous street, by the sea, near the park, 32 rms., restaurant with terrace, tel. 13400. *Gondole* (Al-Gandûl)**B, Andalous street, 34 rms., tel. 13889. Venice (Venitia, Phénicie)**B, Al-Azmé street, 28 rms., tel. 11672. Plus some ten *A and B hotels (see list at the back of the guide).

Out of town, on the beaches to the north, clubs and chalet hotels. 4 km out, *Casino Aphamia,* tel. 3330. 6 km out, *Casino Jules Jammal,* tel. 4176. 6 km out, *Florida,* tel. 1380. 7 km out, *Casino Rivage Bleu,* (Blue Beach), tel. 1144. 8 km out, *Club Ras Shamra.* 50 km out, holiday centre under construction at Ras al-Bassit.

Summer resorts (altitude 600 to 1,100 m): At *Qastal Moâf,* 40 km north along the Antakya road: *Verte Montagne***B, 25 rms., tel. 4. At *Kassab,* 65 km north, four **B and C hotels. At *Nabhein,* 5 km from Kassab, one ** hotel. At *Slenfe,* 50 km east of Latakia, *Tourist* (Al-Syaha wal Istiaf)**B, 50 rms., tel. 6 and 14; *Valley View* (Al-Wadi)*B, 13 rms., tel. 15.

Open-air restaurants: Andalous street, along the sea-shore, and on the beaches.

maalûlâ

Maalûlâ is some 50 kilometres from Damascus. The first part of the route, a steep climb all the way, is by motorway, then, on top of the limestone plateau, it follows a narrow dusty road cut through the chalk, at the foot of a line of cliffs at an altitude of more than 1,600 metres. The light is blinding, the landscape is bare, there is not a single tree. There are only a few crawling vines here and there to relieve the stony ochre landscape, brilliant in the relentless sunshine. Suddenly a narrow fissure appears and widens soon into a deep valley. There are large patches of green again; fig trees sprout from the slopes, there are gardens surrounded by apricots, slender poplar trees appear, alive with birdsong—an oasis after the rigours of a desert crossing. Around the last bend in the road Maalûla appears.

To call it a honeycomb is really too hackneyed. Perhaps as many as a couple of hundred little cubes of masonry, all close together, seem to cling to the cliff-face—piled against it up to the point where it becomes a sheer wall. They are plastered in yellow, blue and sometimes mauve, making a bright contrast with the ochre of the rock, fissured in great dark stripes. Tiny windows and openings and little balconies on rickety wooden beams give some contrasting shadow to what seems like a vast cubist painting.

Saint Sergius and Saint Thecla

At the very foot of this township the road divides. The left-hand branch leads up a steep ravine and emerges on a plateau planted with vines and fruit-trees which ends in a sheer cliff overlooking the village. A low, blue-domed building houses a small community of monks who work as peasants and in their vine yards, and have a particular devotion to Saint Sergius: *Mar Sarkis*. A low doorway—defensive as well as being a sign of humility—leads to the monastery and the little Byzantine church, which are of little interest apart from the impressive view they afford of the country below.

The right-hand branch of the road at the foot of the township leads up to a terrace half-way up the slope; a stream gushes down a cleft at our feet and ahead there is good close view of the jumbled pile of houses. The imposing building. To the right, at the foot of the cliffs, is another convent, dedicated this time to Saint Thecla, venerated by all Orthodox Christians. A series of steps and terraces leads to the various levels of the building and to a modern domed church, of no artistic interest; from there we can reach a grotto where the water dripping from the roof is said to possess miraculous powers.

To the side of *Mar Takla* a path leads to a very narrow cleft—you can touch both sides of it—dug by the waters draining down from the plateau. This steep passage was for ages the only access to the upper monastery, Mar Sarkis. It is dangerous to use it during stormy weather.

The language of Christ

A mosque with a square minaret, evidently quite modern, stands at the foot of the township, but the majority of the people of Maalûlâ are Catholic Christians of the Greek rite.

The community has another feature that will interest the visitor. Both men and women in Maalûlâ understand Arabic, the national language taught in all the schools, but continue to speak among themselves in the old Syrian dialect known to philoologists as "Western Aramaic", an extremely ancient language current in the Mddle East during the first millenium before Christ. Two books of the Bible, Daniel and Esdras, were written in Western Aramaic. It was also the language of Christ. The Lord's Prayer, the prayer of Christians all over the world, was first spoken in Aramaic; the monks of Mar Sarkis have made a recording of it in this language for visitors.

As one hears it spoken by the baker and the grocer in Maalûlâ, Aramaic strikes the ear as being more fluid, less guttural, than present-day Arabic. This linguistic tradition is also preserved in the two neighbouring villages of *Jabaadîn Bakhaâ*. An excursion to Maalûlâ can be easily combined with a visit to another Christian site, the convent at Saydnâayâ, 30 kilometres to the south-west, towards Damascus, by a good, if narrow, road.

Saydnâya, the Convent of Notre Dame

To begin with there is the same plateau landscape like that around Maalûlâ. The road follows, at some distance, the rocky mountains of the Kalamoun range. Gradually the sparse cornlands give way to vineyards and olive groves. *Halbûn*, near Saydnâayâ, has been famous since ancient times for the quality of its wines (they are even given a favourable mention in the Bible).

The township of Sayadnâayâ is spread out over a hillside. While lacking the exceptional appeal of Maalûlâ it is however a fine prospect—though somewhat spoiled by a rash of concrete sheds and other erections... The squareish houses, with high airy arcaded fronts, rise like giant steps up the rocky hill, which is crowned by an imposing building rather like a fortress, despite its colonnaded galeries and the little blue domes indicating the presence of a Byzantine church.

Saydnâyâ has indeed grown up around an important convent which has been famous throughout the Christian East, ever since its foundation in 547. Dedicated to the Blessed Virgin (Saydnâyâ, Saydâ Nâyâ, means "Our Lady, Notre Dame" in Syriac), it contains one of the four paintings of the Virgin attributed to Saint Luke the Evangelist. This is called in Syriac, Chahoura or Chagoura (Chahira in Arabic): the Illustrious, the Celebrated, the Most Famous, the Best Known.

There are still some fifty sisters living in the convent; they belong to the Orthodox rite and come under the Patriarch of Antioch who has his headquarters in Damascus.

Visitors are generally received by the Mother Superior, a charming and highly-intelligent woman, who explains, in whispered French, that the convent is supported by its property in Syria and Lebanon and that its seventy-six sisters and novices look after two hundred orphan children of different faiths and nationalities. "The hungry child must be fed. The world does not consist just of Christians..." Syria has traditionally been a tolerant country, respectful of minorities; its modern laws in no way hamper the Community and their activities.

Tourists are admitted to the chapel containing the painting of the Virgin attributed to Saint Luke. A forgotten verse from the Book of Exodus (Chap. 3, v.5), over the entrance, recalls a commandment lost to the Catholic Church but still current in Islam: "Put off thy shoes from off thy feet, for the place whereon thou standest is holy ground." The walls of a tiny, low-ceilinged room, lit only by candles, are covered with very old icons. Unfortunately only the silver frames surrounding the paintings can be seen—the paint itself is so dirty that it is impossible to make out the pictures. The painting by Saint Luke is half-hidden in a kind of tabernacle. The main pilgrimage to Saydnâyâ takes places on the 8th of September. Visitors can buy lace and embroidery made here by the Community.

MAALULA

Name: Variant names: Maaloûla, Maaloûla. Aramean: "The entrance".

Location and access: Damascus governorate. Altitude 1,500 m. 56 km north of Damascus, by Aleppo motorway as far as Khân al-Arûs (49 km), then asphalt road left, or by Barzeh road on north side of Damascus, through Al-Tall, and Said Naya (the road between Said Naya and Maalûla is shown as a broken line on some maps, but in fact has a perfectly good surface).

Accommodation: At Damascus.

*The honeycomb village of Maalula.
Some of its 'cells' have been daubed
with blue plaster for hundreds of years.
(Photo Jacques Guillard.)*

maarat ann-nûman

■ Proudly standing on stop of a hill made higher by a steep glacis, the castle is rather reminiscent of the Citadel of Aleppo. Its fortified entrance works are similarly conceived as well. A typically Arab fortress, it occupies the site of a former Graeco-Roman castle.

Down below, the town forms a splash of grey on the tawny expanse of the high Syrian uplands. The houses are built of dark-coloured limestone, quarried from the mountainside nearby.

Here and there in the streets you can see ancient stones with Corinthian carving. Ancient columns have been re-used in the courtyard of the mosque itself, and there is a carved cross on one of the windows of the minaret. This minaret, square-based, soberly-decorated and very slender, is extremely elegant. It rises above a large arcaded square from which there are entrances into covered souks. On the edge of the town two 16th-century khans are still used for their original purpose.

A mausoleum, recently built in traditional style, contains the tomb of Abi Ala'a al-Ma'ari, a distinguished poet and philosopher born at Maarat, who died in 1058. It is much venerated.

Towards Al-Bara and the "Ghost Towns"

It is possible to visit several "Ghost Towns" from Maarat (see History, and entries for Al-Bara, Qalb Loza, Qalaat Samaân).

To the west Al-Bahra can be reached, by tracks which are difficult in places, passing through the abandoned towns of Kfar Ruma, Hass, Al-Bara, Delloza, Serjilla (see entry for Al-Bara). Al-Bara can also be reached easily by surfaced roads, via Ar-Riha, taking the road to Jisr ash-Shughur and turning left to Urum al-Jawz and left again to Meriane and Al-Bara (about 45 kilometres).

There is another group of ghost towns on the range that rises between the roads to Ar-Riha and Aleppo, north of Maarat. A guide is essential since the tracks are numerous and badly-signposted.

These towns, deserted today and far from all the busy centres, are in a remarkable state of preservation. They have stood here for a thousand years, these houses, monasteries and churches; it seems that they only need a bit of tidying up, the replacement of the odd wall or roof here and there, to make them perfectly habitable once again.

Taking them in order, there is *Dana* (not to be confused with another Dana, near Qalaat Samaân), notable for its tomb-shrine with a pyramidal roof and colonnaded peristyle, severely decorated and perfectly preserved; *Jéradé*, where the streets are littered with blocks of masonry, but still having its rampart walls and a six-storied watch-tower; *Rûeyha,* an extensive town laid out round a central colonnaded square; there is a monumental tomb there too, rather like a Greek temple, whose walls, columns and roof—all intact—rise above the surrounding chaos. The facade of a neighbouring church is also still standing; a three-aisled basilica, dating from the 3rd century; it is said to be the oldest in Syria.

From Maarat too it is possible to visit the excavations at *Tall Mardikh* (20km to the north-east, to the right of the main road to Aleppo, just before you come to the village of Sarâqib); they are described in the entry for Idlib.

MAARAT ANN-NUMAN

Name: Named after Noman Ibn Bechir, companion of the Prophet. Variant names: Maarat en Nomân, Ma'arret el-Noman, Maarat an Nouamn, Maarat an-Noman, Maaret en Naamân, etc. Graeco-Roman period: Arra. Crusader period: Marre.

Location and access: Idlib governorate. Altitude 400 m. 60 km north of Hama, 80 km south-west of Aleppo, 40 km south of Idlib.

Accommodation: At Hama, Aleppo or Idlib. On the spot, one *A hotel, Abi Al-Alal.

mari

■ "It will take another two hundred years to excavate Mari completely." Those are the words of the French archaeologist, André Parrot, who has pushed back the frontiers of history here at Mari.

Excavations have been conducted regularly every year since that day in August 1933 when a group of Bedouin, looking for stone to cover a tomb, dug up a statue weighing three hundred kilogrammes and reported their find to the nearby French military post. Thanks to that chance discovery a great ancient capital was to be recovered and a whole forgotten civilisation brought back to the light of day.

After only a few months the site was identified. In a temple dating from the third millenium before Christ, dedicated to Ishtar (the principal goddess of the Assyro-Babylonian pantheon), some thirty statuettes were recovered, amongst them one of a king: Longi Mari.

Each succeeding year has brought its haul of extraordinary discoveries. The most important has been that of the Palace of Zimri-Lim, King of Mari from 1782 to 1759 B.C., a dwelling consisting of some three hundred rooms, courtyards, stores and containing above all a library stacked with twenty thousand cuneiform tablets—a whole Foreign Ministry come to life again.

Beneath the Palace of Zimri-Lim another palace was discovered, dating this time from the first half of the third millenium (from the so-called pre-Sargonid period, before 2350 B.C.). Even deeper still two, if not three, royal residences have been found one on top of the other—they all go back to the third millenium—five thousand years, two hundred generations ago! Mari was destroyed in about 1760 B.C., by Hammurabi, the neighbouring Babylonian king.

On the site...

There are fine objects from Mari in the museums of Damascus and Aleppo (there are some in the Louvre too). In books by André Parrot himself, and in more popular journals, the layman can learn all about the diggings. Is the long journey down to this part of the Euphrates really worth while? Prior to 1976 the traveller could easily pass *Tall Hariri*—a few humps of stones and sand scarcely higher than those which surround them—without realizing that here was a world-famous site. Today there are 700 square metres of plastic roofing gleaming in the sun to draw our attention; they cover priceless things. Following a worldwide appeal for funds, it has been possible to build some sort of shelter to protect the most important parts of Mari from the weather. The transparent roof, less ugly than one might fear, covers the central hall of the palace, with its chapels one on top of the other, and the great courtyard.

All the buildings are of unbaked brick, covered with a fragile of clay that is no longer protected as it used to be by ceramic tiling.

This protected area is the only part that is open to the public. It is not grandiose, far from picturesque even. One should not even try to imagine the statues and frescoes that one has seen in museums back in their places here—nor to follow too closely the careful explanations of the guides. These grey walls, these corridors of clay and bitumen paths are five thousand years old and have served in their time as part of the backdrop to the human comedy. That is all, and that is enough.

MARI

Name: Variant name: Marat. Name of the archeological site: Tell Hariri.

Location and access: Deir-ez-Zor governorate. 125 km south-east of Deir-ez-Zor (11 km north-west of Abu Kamal), then follow track to the left to Sayyât, right bank of the Euphrates.

Accommodation: At Deir-ez-Zor.

marqab

■ Whether he approaches from Latakia or from Tartus, the traveller, even if he is pressed for time, cannot not stop as he nears Baniyas (see entry) and sees before him a tall hill with terraced gardens on its slopes and at the top a huge and glowering fortress.

It is enormous: there are no less than fourteen square and round towers jutting from the curtain wall that encircles the hilltop to form a triangular bastion. Its southern corner, sharper than the others and bristling with defences, has a keep rising above it like the prow of some great ship.

Glowering: from the massing of these great blank walls which looks as if they are good for a few centuries yet, but glowering above all because of the funereal black basalt stone of which it is built. These roughly dressed stones were dug from the hillside, itself an extinct volcano. The outline of each stone is heightened by the use of white mortar; weeds now grow lustily from cracks in the walls themselves and in the glacis—emphasizing still more the contrast between this grim fortress and the infinite gradations of blue and green in the setting all around—the scrub, the gardens and orchards, the distant mountains, the huge sky and the sea not far away.

Such is the impression made by *Qalaat Marqab*, the *Margat* (Lookout) of the Crusaders.

A fortress of funereal stone

A narrow tarred road now leads up to the base of the fortress, on the western side of the ramparts. Gently sloping steps lead up to a bridge which leads in turn to an entrance postern half-way up the wall, protected by a barbican. The outline of the fortress follows the convex line of the hillside just here and one has an excellent view of the best-preserved and strongest section of the castle's defences. Yellow gorse and red-flowered pomegranates in the ditches below seem to be launching a peaceful attack on the great black walls.

The affable keeper who, like some watcher of old, has seen us coming from a long way off, will greet us, offer us tea, post-cards and souvenirs and press us to sign an impressive Visitors' Book. Only then shall we be let in to explore the ruins.

Given that there is far less left standing inside the castle at Margat than at Crac des Chevaliers (see entry) the tour does not take long. After having accompanied us to the chapel and the keep, pointed out the gothic arches and the crenellations, the passageways and the tall arrow-slits, and after having given us a summary of the history and explained the lay-out of the fortress, our aimiable guide leaves us free to wander through the great vaulted halls and over the grass-grown and windswept rampart walks. Time passes swiftly as we dream in these evocative surroundings. The sun is now setting low over the sea, lighting upt the stones of Marqab with its last fiery rays.

The Lookout and the "*Assassins*"

The site of Marqab had caught the attention of strategists well before the Crusades. Byzantines and Arabs had fought over it throughout the 11th century.

This fortified lookout post was ideal for keeping watch over the coastal plain, it commanded one of the routes across the coastal range and had an excellent view of the complicated terrain from which the henchmen of the "Old Man of the Mountains" used to launch devastating and bloody raids on Christians and Muslims alike (see under Masyaf).

The original castle changed hands several times before 1140. That year saw the beginning of its major fortification by the Crusaders. The years that followed were the hey-day of Margat—especially when it was in the hands of the Hospitallers, that rich, enterprising, intelligent and courageous order of knights. Even Salah ad-Din himself avoided encounters with the defenders of Margat, during his campaign to re-conquer the Syrian coast after his victory at Hattin in 1188.

A contemporary chronicler estimated the permanent population of the fortress at "a thousand persons, apart from the garrison." "They have provisions," he said, "to withstand five years' siege." Around 1240 the Bishop of Valenia (present-day Baniyas) took up residence within the walls of the fortress.

But the days of the Christian strongholds were numbered. Sultan Beybars redoubled his attacks. In the spring of 1271, Crac itself fell, as well as satellite forts such as Safita (see entries under these names). However it was not until 1285 that the troops of the Reconquest under Sultan Qalaûn defeated the last of the knights at Margat. The surviving Hospitallers were granted "the honours of war" and allowed to withdraw under safe conduct to Tortosa (Tartus) and Tripoli.

There is an inscription commemorating the final victory of Islam, carved on a band of white limestone at the top of the "Tour de l'Eperon" under the keep.

The name of Qalaûn is to be found there, as well as that of Balbân al-Tabbakhi, Governor of Crac, to whom Margat—now Marqab once more—was entrusted also.

MARQAB

Name: Variant names: Merkab, Qalaat Marqab. "The fortress of the watch-tower. Crusader period: Margat.

Location and access: Tartus governorate. Altitude 500 m. 6 km south-east of Baniyas taking first turn left off the Tartus road (winding and steep, but with asphalt surface).

Accommodation: At Latakia.

THE SUCCESSFUL SIEGE

■ *In utmost secrecy in Damascus Sultan Beybars made ready a great supply of weapons, arrows, oil, siege machines and a great host of archers. He appeared before the gates of Margat on 17 April 1285. The fortress held out for five weeks, as had Crac. It was surrounded by siege weapons whose projectiles destroyed the mangonels of the besieged castle; but the defenders managed to repair them and in their turn destroyed some of the siege machines which fell on their crews and killed them. The besiegers then started to undermine the castle... the Tour de l'Eperon collapsed, causing chaos among the assailants. The Franks, exhausted and having discovered that other towers were undermined, realised that further resistance was futile... Signs of this terrible siege are still to be seen on the walls of the keep. Indeed we even found arrowheads still embedded in the mortar between the stones around the loopholes. This proves that in such sieges the archers aimed masses of arrows at these narrow slits. Those that did not go through, hit the stone and fell to the ground, but others buried themselves in the mortared joints.*

PAUL DESCHAMPS
(adapted)

masyaf

■ Our road descends desolate hillsides that even the goats seem to have deserted, follows a stream bordered by oleanders, and then brings us out at a small market town dominated by a great medieval castle that has been basking here in the sun for centuries. We are at Masyaf.

The castle rises half-ruined amidst its encircling walls and their towers open to the sky. The houses and their terraces form a sort of glacis stretching up to the first of the castle's defences. High walls of ochre stone continue the natural slope of the rock upwards to where, on a small platform on the very top, the keep of the castle stands.

Seen from the other side, with no houses to break the transition, the castle looks even more formidable —here peaceful orchards of figs, mulberries, pomegranates and almonds, heralds of those of the Ghab, make a striking contrast to the castle above them.

A visit to the qalaat, made more difficult by the piles of ruins that encumber it, has little to teach anyone who has already seen Crac des Chevaliers, Marqab or Salah ad-Din.

The entrance fortifications, between high square towers and with a rampart walk with arrow slits above them, are the best preserved part of the castle. Ancient columns which have been re-used here and there indicate that the Arab fort may well have replaced some earlier structure.

The H.Q. of the Assassins

Masyaf is interesting above all, not so much for its architectural detail or the beauty of its setting, but because it was one of the main command posts of "Sheikh al-Jebel", the famous "Old Man of the Mountains", whose deadly exploits were recounted by the medieval chroniclers. For this genial nick-name concealed the identity of none other than Rachid ad-Din Sinân, the redoubtable chief of the Assassins.

This sect (see box in text) grew up at Alamut, a fortress hidden in a fold of the Elburz Mountains in Northern Iran (see "Iran Today" in this series), where the religious dissident Hasan Sabbâh took refuge around 1190 in order to train a secret army to serve his ambitions and beliefs. He kept his men loyal and increased their fanaticism through the use of the drug, hashish, which gave them, so they said, a glimpse of the Paradise of Allah.

The old man of the mountains

From their base at Alamut the Assassins hived off in groups, almost like a monastic order, founding bases in the most inaccessible mountains. A dozen of these, between Khorrasân and Mount Lebanon, contained as many as seventy thousand of their followers, in the mid-12th century. Their chief stronghold lay in the southern part of the Syrian coastal massif, with its deep ravines and bare peaks covered with extraordinary rock-formations. *Ollaiqa, Qadmûs, Al-Kahf* and their secondary posts became points of departure for murderous raids; *Masyaf,* on the edge of the plain, served as a general headquarters. All that remains of most of these Isma'ili castles are a few inaccessible ruins, but during the wars between the Franks and Arabs these gangster hideouts were a significant embarrassment to both sides.

The Assassin-Isma'ilis knew how to play upon the rivalries within each of the opposing camps and how to take advantage of their relative weakness or strength; this gave them a certain power. Emissaries from both sides would come to ask for the "services" of the Old Man of the Mountains. Caliphs and Sultans came and went, as did Kings of Jerusalem and Crusader princes, but the Old Man survived them all, up here at Masyaf. He "reigned" for fifty years! The Templars chose to come to an agreement with such a dangerous rival. The Count of Tripoli was one of the Assassins' victims. The Crusader Frederick Barbarossa and the Saracen Saladin himself both had narrow escapes from them.

It would be interesting to know what the present-day citizens of Masyaf—who are said still to follow Isma'ili teachings—think about all this!

MASYAF

Name: Variant names: Massiâf, Qalaat Massiaf, Mesaif.

Location and access: Hama governorate. Altitude 400 m. 40 km west of Hama. 50 km east of Baniyas. At the southern end of the Ghab Depression. 90 km south of Jisr ash-Shughur.

Accommodation: At Hama. On the spot, two *C hotels.

PALMYRA p. 162.

Name: The Latin and French forms are generally used in place of the official name of the commune: Tadmor, which is nonetheless earlier. Cananaean period, 11th to 1st centuries B.C.: Tadmor (city of dates). Hellenistic and Roman period: Palmyra, from palma (palms, oasis of palm-trees). Variant names: Tadmour, Tadmur.

Location and access: Homs governorate. Altitude 400 m. 155 km east of Homs, by asphalt road. 315 km north-east of Damascus, via Homs. 210 km by desert track (first 100 km from Damascus tarred, track passable for all vehicles thereafter). 210 km southwest of Deir-ez-Zor over a difficult track with no filling-station, hard-surfacing scheduled for 1978). Small aerodrome: fights intermittent or by special request.

Information: Official multilingual guides on application to the keeper of the ruins (Temple of Bel), at the museum and in the hotels. See plan of the ancient city, page 239.

Accommodation: Méridien (Air France hotel)****, opposite the ruins, south side, near the Afqa spring; under construction; opening scheduled for 1977. *Zanoubia***B, opposite the ruins, north side, between the museum and the Temple of Bel-Shamin, 15 rms, tel. 107.

THE ASSASSINS

In the 487th year of the Hegira (1094) the Fatimid Caliph died and his elder son was ousted by a younger brother. As had happened when Isma'il had died prematurely, in the 8th century, some of the Isma'ils of Syria, led by Hasan Sabbah, proclaimed their fidelity to the principle of primogeniture and refused to recognise the new Imam. These neo-Isma'ilis—the more gifted and vigorous who have been hailed as renaissance humanists—formed a new revolutionary movement. Their supporters in the Middle East were reputed to be takers of hashish. They did indeed use this drug—to induce ecstatic states or to stupefy themselves before committing the political outrages in which they specialized. They became known in the West as Assassins, users of hashish, and the word took on the meaning that it has in English and French today... For a long while they seemed invincible and it took the Mongols, under Genghiz Khan, to defeat them. Crushed by these conquering nomads, they survived only as a sect of minor importance.

JEAN-PAUL ROUX
"L'Islam au Proche-Orient"
(Payot, Paris, 1960)

palmyra

■ Advice to the visitor...
Get up before dawn. Leave your hotel and wander out into the ruins... It soon becomes quite a tricky business, walking over the uneven ground dotted with thistles; one stumbles over the pebbles with only the odd piece of marble paving to reflect the moonlight. Great shadows rise up suddenly, scattered blocks of stone take on fantastic shapes. Feeling the rough stone one makes out the sharp edge of a cornice or the curve of an acanthus-leaf.

Walk towards the great stone barrier, still shrouded in darkness but appearing to stretch in a straight line right across the horizon from east to west... Hundreds of columns continue the night-watch that has already lasted a thousand years. As one nears the first group the sky lightens, turns palest green, then pink, bringing out the details, the almost infinite perspective of the porticos, revealing the vastness of the plain, silent and littered with debris, like a battlefield. An icy breeze blows for a moment over Palmyra.

Before we have walked a third of the way down the main colonnaded street we suddenly see an ancient fortress, lit up by a by a beam of red sunlight, on the hillside straight ahead of us. Then everything speeds up. The tops of numberless columns are touched suddenly with fire. The wide spreading palm-leaf capitals light up. The pillars become for an instant flaring torches. The light hovers over the wide ledges of the consoles half-way up the columns, before bathing the whole dead city in sunshine... Within a minute the dogs are barking and people are about.

From all directions they come —navvies and masons, crane-drivers and architects, alone or in small groups, on foot, by cart or in a swaying lorry, to converge on the diggings that are under way down there to the west. Palmyra is awake. Palmyra is being re-born.

The ruins of Palmyra are impressive both by their extent and by their remarkable state of preservation. The ancient Arab city is gradually being restored in all its grandeur.

To be sure vast areas still await excavation, and there are no doubt many riches left to delight the archaeologists; but expeditions of experts of every nationality are at work all the time, making the stones speak again, and undertaking skilful and intelligent restoration, a contribution to the vast and splendid scheme of the Syrian Department of Antiquities to completely excavate the city.

A capital risen from the sand

The reddish colour of the limestone of the upper parts of the colonnades and buildings exposed to oxydization from the air over the centuries shows the depth of the sand (three or four metres sometimes) that had to be excavated. Some discoveries are relatively recent—the agora, the theatre, the baths, the Temple of Nabô amongst others—while the restoration of the great Temple of Bêl, one of the finest monuments in all the East, dates back to 1930. This latter operation involved a bold solution that no one would now disagree with. The inhabitants of Palmyra had used the Temple as the centre of their village and a whole new settlement had to to built for them outside the walls of the old city. Five thousand Syrians now live in this town and the Temple, freed now of all later accretions is the wonder and delight of experts and tourists alike.

Palmyra is one of those exceptional places where art and history have fused to produce a synthesis that will dazzle succeeding generations. It needs little commentary to understand its development; its general layout can be easily grasped by strolling around or climbing one of the nearby hills (see plan p. 238).

Palmyra is separated by some hundred and fifty kilometres of steppe from the lush valley of the Orontes, to the west. There are more than two hundred kilometres of desert to cross before you reach the fertile banks of the Euphrates, to the east. To both north and south there is nothing but sand and stones... But here at Palmyra a last fold of the Anti-Lebanon forms a kind of basin on the edge of which a spring rises out of a long underground channel whose depth has never been measured (near the "Méridien" hotel, to the right of the road coming in from Homs). This spring is called *Afqa* (or Ephka) in ancient inscriptions, an Aramaic word meaning "way out." Its clear blue, slightly sulphurous waters are said to have medicinal properties; they have fed an oasis here, with olives and date-palms and cotton and cereals. For generations this oasis was known as *Tadmor*.

A meeting-place for East and West

This remarkable site in the centre of the Syrian Desert became a necessary stopping-place for caravans taking the shortest route from the Persian Gulf to the Mediterranean, as well as for those taking the Silk Route and crossing the Tigris near Seleucis in Babylon. Tadmor is mentioned on tablets dating from the 19th century B.C. From the end of the second millenium Aramean was the language spoken there, this language persisted until the Byzantine period. Its distinctive written script was respected; later on there were few Greek inscriptions, still fewer Latin ones; Arabic script was very much influenced by the Palmyrene. The population consisted, from very early times, half of people of Aramean origin and half of Arab nomads of Nabatean extraction.

But it was from the 1st century B.C., when the Romans invaded Syria, that Tadmor (city of dates), now *Palmyra* (city of palm-trees), took full advantage of her geographical isolation, which gave her some protection against military coups, and her economic opportunity as a staging post between the Orient and the Mediterranean world. Both ships and pack-camels are to be found sculpted on the facades of her buildings.

For four hundred years the city enjoyed uninterrupted prosperity.

At the centre of the caravan traffic, Palmyra levied heavy taxes on goods in transit. A desert fortress she hired out her famous camel troops to the Roman armies. Jealous of her independence she negotiated skilfully with her powerful neighbours, the Romans and the Persians (cf. "Iran Today" in this series) whose expansionist policies were not the least of their faults.

In 129 the Emperor Hadrian visited the city. Breaking with his predecessors' dreams of hegemony he abandoned the Euphrates line and recognised Palmyra as a "Free city", only too pleased to put a buffer-state between the Persians and his Legions. In recognition the city adopted the name of *Adriana Palmyra* for a time. The main temples were built or enlarged during this period; the agora was made; the residential quarters grew up on both sides of the great colonnaded central avenues.

Luxury amid the desert

At the end of the first century, under the Emperor Severus, of African and Syrian origins, Palmyra enjoyed new favours. Moreover, her ancient rival Petra (in present-day Jordan) had disappeared from the scene. In 217 the Emperor Caracalla proclaimed Palmyra a "Roman colony"—a popular move amongst the merchants of the city for it freed them from taxes. Spices, perfumes, ivory and silks from the East, glassware, statues, and objets d'art from Phoenicia, all passed through Palmyra. The traffic was organised by the Palmyrenes; some of them even owned ships sailing the Indian Ocean.

Luxury came to Palmyra. Contemporary sculptures depict a wealthy bourgeoisie, bejewelled and splendidly dressed. Magistrates, merchants, citizens whom the city wished to honour, had their statues erected, inscribed, on consoles along the innumerable columns that lined the streets. The grand colonnade was extended eastwards and, at the same time another was built, at an angle to it, leading to the Temple of Bêl. In the Valley of the Tombs, to the east of the city, the "houses of the dead", veritable underground palaces, were decorated with particularly fine sculptures and frescoes.

The whole city reflected activity and great prosperity, but this in no way hampered cultural development nor did it restrict innovation in thought. Alongside the traditional worship of Bêl, a kind of Babylonian equivalent of Zeus, and his two acolytes Yarhibôl (the sun) and Aglibôl (the moon), and that of Bêl-Shemên, "a good and generous god", a tendency to monotheism very soon appeared—illustrated by dedications "to the one, single, merciful god", "to him whose name is everblessed", etc. From the 2nd century there is evidence of a Jewish colony and Christianity was already prevalent before the year 300, since a Palmyrene bishop played a leading role at the Council of Nicea.

The ambitious Arab Queen Zenobia

During the 3rd century the wars in which Rome was involved caused a slackening of trade between East and West. Persia once more became a major threat to the Roman world. In 260 the Emperor Valerian himself was captured by the Sassanid king, Shahpur I (cf. "Iran Today" in this series).

The confrontation of these two giants, and Rome's need to call more and more on the aid of her former subject peoples caused the leaders of Palmyra to come to the logical conclusion that the hour had perhaps come to liberate the whole of the Middle East from foreign domination, whether Roman or Persian. But ways had to be found to do this...

Impelled by an influential Arab family, Palmyra passed, in two or three stages, from being a merchant republic governed by a senate, to being a kingdom under a certain Odenathus the Younger awarded himself the Oriental title of "King of kings." To be sure, his brilliant military actions had earned him the gratitude of Rome: the Palmyrene armies had twice defeated the Persian armies and, in 267, Valerian had been liberated by Odenathus who was named "Corrector of the East" in return. The authority of Oriental Palmyra seemed destined to extend over a vast territory.

But at the end of 267, Odenathus and his son, the heir to the throne, were assassinated in mysterious circumstances. Rumour had it that the King's second wife, Zenobia, mother of a very young son, was in some way involved in the crime. At all events the Queen immediately revealed herself to be an exceptionally able monarch. She was boundlessly ambitious for herself, for her son and for her people. Within six years she had affected the whole life of Palmyra. Her dreams of unattainable glory and greatness had brought ill-fortune, ruin and death to the flourishing city.

In 270, the Queen, who claimed to be descended from Cleopatra, took possession of the whole of Syria, conquered Lower Egypt and sent her armies across Asia Minor as far as the Bosphorus.

In open defiance of Rome, Zenobia and her son took the title "August", and had coinage struck in this name, thus setting themselves up as rivals to Aurelian who was at that time having difficulties on the German borders of the Empire.

The death of a metropolis

They had acted rashly and too hastily. The Emperor Aurelian disengaged from the northern front, raised a new army, crossed Anatolia, hustled the Palmyrenes out of their positions at Emesa (Homs) and made straight for Palmyra which fell after a few weeks's siege. Zenobia managed to escape and fled east, mounted on a dromedary, hoping for help from the Sassanids. The Romans, fear lending them wings, recaptured her as she was crossing the Euphrates (in the autumn of 272). Zenobia was taken prisoner to Rome where she was forced to ride in Aurelian's "Triumph" in 274. She died soon afterwards, in comfortable exile at Tibur (Tivoli), but not before she had learned that a last revolt by her subjects against their Roman rulers had been bloodily put down, and that her splendid wealthy city had been pillaged and was due to be destroyed (273).

Palmyra was reduced from being a capital to a mere Syrian frontier stronghold. New walls were built, smaller than those in Zenobia's time, and under Diocletian (293-303), the Romans established a military camp to the west of the city, apparently on the site of the palace of Odenathus and Zenobia, which is said to have been demolished and of which archaeologists have so far discovered no trace. It is thought that important excavations, under way at the moment, should solve this mystery.

Palmyra never recovered her position. Aleppo, during the Byzantine period, and then Damascus, after 634, from the beginning of the Islamic, became, in their respective ways, equally important as centres of commerce and ideas. The temples of Palmyra were converted first into churches then into mosques. In the 12th century the walls around the shrine of Bêl itself were adapted for use as a fortress. At the beginning of the 17th century, the Emir Fakhr ad-Din was still using Palmyra as a place in which to excercise his police. However he was anxious to have greater security than that offered by the ruined city, so he had a castle built on the hillside overlooking it. Down below, the ruins soon sheltered only a few peasants.

THE PALMYRENE LANGUAGE, THE PALMYRENE SCRIPT

■ *The language of the inscriptions at Palmyra represents the last appearance of a major Aramaic dialect, distinguished under the name of "imperial Aramaic".*

As a written language Aramaic was widely used in the Middle East before being replaced by Arabic with the spread of Islam.

The Aramaic of Palmyra is characterized by the presence of a strong Arabic element in the vocabulary and in the names of people and places.

The Arabs of Palmyra formed a large proportion of the population. They gave the city its most powerful dynasty during the 3rd century. By using their own language, sometimes together with Greek, in official, religious or honorific inscriptions, the Palmyrenes were demonstrating their independance of Rome.

The Palmyrenes used an alphabet of twenty-two letters and wrote from right to left. This script evolved to point where it rivalled contemporary Greek script.

Two types of Palmyrene script can be distinguished.
Monumental script for engraving on stone. The most ancient inscription in this script goes back to 44 B.C. The most recent dates from 272 A.D.
The cursive script was written with a brush, a pen or a qalam, on papyrus or parchment. It was most often written from top to bottom of the page. "Syriac estrangula" is derived from it.

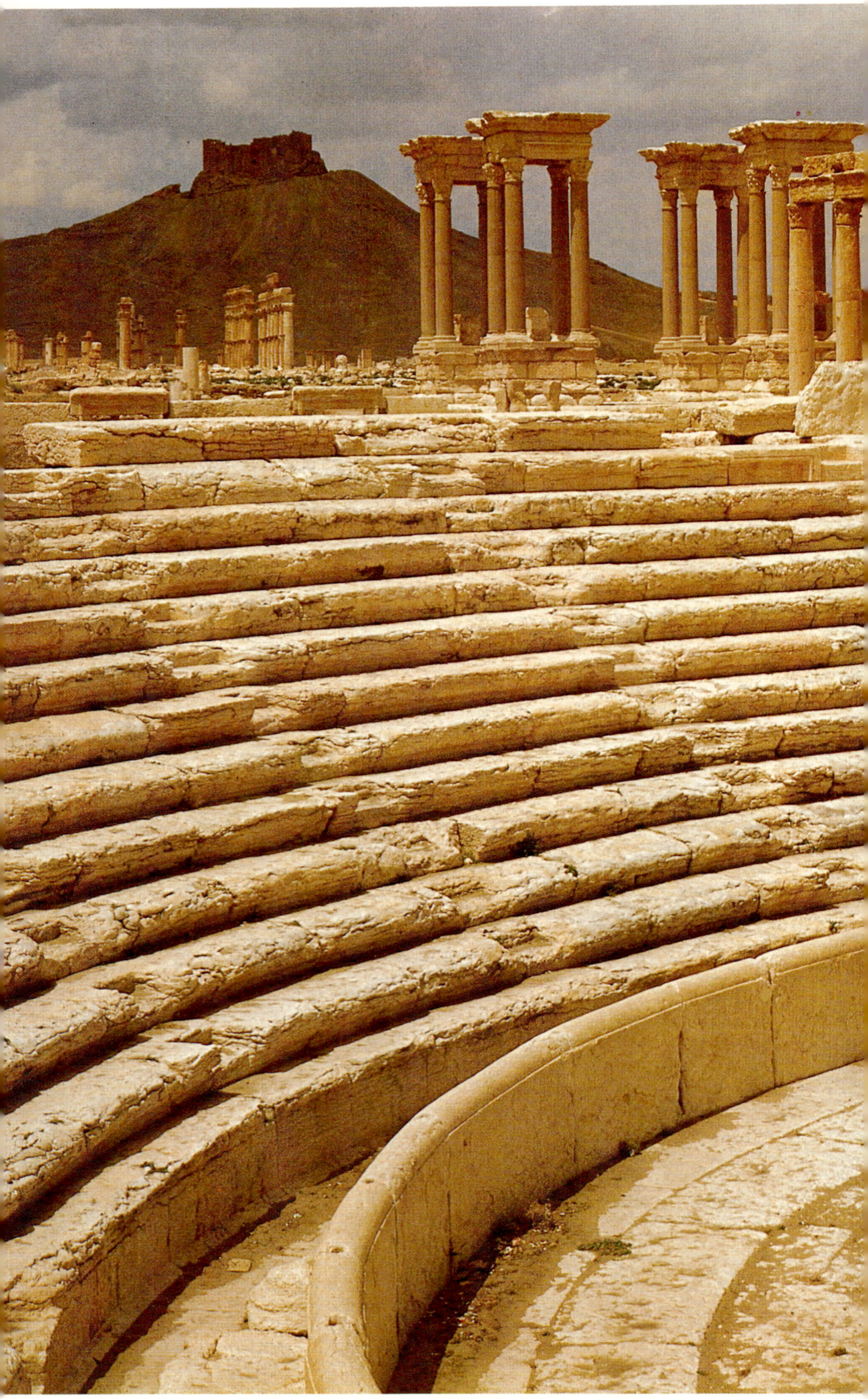

All still seems set for a performance in this theatre: symbol of the luxury of Queen Zenovia's capital. The stage wall looks more like the facade of a palace. Beyond stand the Colonnade, the Four Pilastered Arch and the Arab castle.

In 1751 Palmyra was visited by two English travellers, in the course of a long and difficult journey around the Orient. They brought back books of sketches which astounded the contemporary artistic and scientific world. The elegant and mysterious Palmyrene script was deciphered soon afterwards. However, it was not really until our own time, eighteen centuries after the dramatic end of the Arab Queen Zenobia's all-too-brief reign, that Palmyra finally re-emerged from oblivion.

Palmyra, now Tadmor once again, a peaceful township, lives from the produce of its gardens and palm-groves, still watered by the Afqa spring. The nomads are virtually extinct. No more do riches come by slow caravan from the East. But curiously the surrounding desert still continues to be an economic factor, since enormous deposits of phosphates have been found there. The ancient caravan trail is now a road along which lies the long green and yellow ribbon of an oil pipe line. Finally, and not the least of the signs of re-birth, are the visitors who come, sometimes from the ends of the earth, alone or in small groups, simply to have the pleasure of watching the sunrise over some magnificent ruins—silent witnesses to the will of a queen possessed by a mad dream of liberty and glory for her city.

A long but fascinating visit

It takes a long while to see all round Palmyra-Tadmor—a whole day is necessary—and it is quite an exhausting business because the site itself is so large: more than six square kilometres. There is a surfaced road, however, between the two furthest points, the Valley of the Tombs and the Museum, which also passes quite close to the great Temple of Bêl. There is a small entrance charge at the two latter buildings and one is taken round them by a guide. Photography is permitted. The weekly closing day is Tuesday. One is free to walk about over all the rest of the site, by day or by night (except, of course, where excavations are actually under way; here even photography is forbidden). The services of one of the two or three official guides may be found useful at first, especially in exploring the vaults in the Valley of the Dead.

The site divides naturally into four distinct areas which can be best visited perhaps in the following order. In the very early morning, the Great Colonnade and the monuments along its length; at the end of the morning, the museum; at the beginning of the afternoon, since the cella is located to the west, the great Temple of Bêl; at the end of the afternoon, the tombs and, if you still have the energy, the Arab Castle; the view over Palmyra from the high ground to the east is very fine at sunset.

The Plan of Palmyra, on page 238, makes it easy to situate the various monuments in relation to each other.

City of a thousand columns

Four tall columns that have been re-erected beside the modern road show the alignment of the roadway that used to link the Temple of Bêl with a great porticoed avenue. They are splendid in their isolation and form a magnificent foreground to the *Monumental Arch* which commands the main perspective.

This well-porportioned arch is made up of one central semi-circular opening, flanked by two smaller ones. It stands at a point where the central avenue makes a bend of thirty degrees. But its triangular base cleverly ensures that the perspective remains unbroken no matter from which side it is approached.

The *Great Colonnade* stretched for more than a thousand metres. Its porticos have been re-erected over about a third of this distance. The roadway, 11 metres wide, is bordered by raised lateral roadways, 6 metres wide, which used to be covered. The diameter of the columns, 0.95 metres, is one tenth of their height, 9.50 metres.

Pleasantly harmonious in style the columns are all crowned by wide Corinthian capitals.

The *moulded consoles*, half-way up the shafts of the columns, supported statues of public figures; only one of these survives and it has been put back in place. There are also some inscriptions commemorating the citizens who contributed to the costs of building the avenue itself. On both sides there were warehouses and the principal public buildings of the city.

On the right-hand side (going towards the centre of the city) four granite columns—unusual in this limestone region—indicate the site of *baths* dating from the later, Diocletian, period. The other public buildings are all on the left of the central colonnaded avenue. The first one we come to after the monumental arch is a *nymphaeum* (a sacred fountain). Then, immediately past the arch, there is the base of a temple, excavated in 1963-65; this excavation yielded many objects, frescoes, bas-reliefs and twenty-five texts hitherto unknown. The temple was dedicated to *Nabô* (variously Nebô, Nebû), a Babylonian divinity who enjoyed great popularity in Syria. "A good and generous god" Nabô directed the destinies of mortals and was also the scribe of the gods. Identified later with Hermes and Apollo, he was, like the latter, the god of oracles and wisdom.

Further on along the Great Colonnade is the outside wall of the *theatre*. Two perfect arches outlined against the sky form an entrance to the semi-circular road surrounding the hemicycle of the theatre itself. From the highest row of seats inside there is a fine view down over the orchestra pit, the stage and the wall behind which looks like the facade of a palace. Everything seems ready for a performance...

From the left-hand side of the theatre a short street, lined with the remains of shops and those of a more important building, the Senate House, leads to the *agora*, a great open space, almost a perfect square (84m by 71m), surrounded by porticos. Eleven passageways led into it, making it easy for crowds to gather here on market days or for public meetings. In the north-east corner stood the tribune from which speeches were made. There were public fountains at each end of the north portico. Statues of Septimus Severus and his (Syrian) family adorned the central gateway of the east portico. The laudatory inscriptions that went with statues, now lost, that stood on the consoles, have been either left where they were or laid out on the ground in the agora; they show that the north portico was for officials, the west for the military, the east for Senators and the south for leaders of caravans.

Near the west portico is the entrance to the *official banqueting hall* with its stone benches ranged round the walls on three sides. On the other wall there is a "pyrea" or altar at which incense was burned. As they entered the official guests would hand in a "tessera", a sort of token made of terracotta, usually depicting the god Bêl; several of these tesserae are displayed in the Museum.

We rejoin the Great Colonnade near a group of eight columns which look extremely slender by contrast with a colossal monument that stands at the intersection of the two main axes of the city. Two of these columns used to carry statues of King Odenathus and Queen Zenobia. The central monument, made up of four groups of four columns at the corners of a platform 18 metres square, is known as the *tetrapylon*. A statue used to stand in the centre of each of the pedestals. Only one of the great granite pylons is old, the others bear the signs of rather too hasty restoration.

The great porticoed avenue continues beyond the tetrapylon, but there are fewer and fewer columns still standing, or restored, the nearer we get to the portico frontal of a charming small temple built right in the centre of the roadway. This *funerary temple*, built during the 3rd century outside the city as it was in Palmyrene times, was included within the new city wall built by Diocletian, whose entrenched camp is not far away on the left. The gravestones from several tombs nearby were reused in the construction of the *ramparts*, with their bastions every thirty seven metres.

As has been already mentioned, Diocletian's camp is being intensively excavated at the moment, one of the aims being to discover whether the Romans did in fact build upon the foundations of Zenobia's palace.

The roads at right-angles to the Great Colonnade lead to quarters that have not yet been extensively excavated. The only buildings of any importance, in the northern sector, are two Byzantine churches and, specially, near the "Zénobie" hotel, the *Temple of Bêl-Shemên*, the "Master of the Heavens". The cella of this temple remains almost intact, with the six columns of the facade (pronaos), its pilastered side-walls and its open forecourt in front giving onto a main road that leads back to the Great Colonnade not far from the tetrapylon.

The Museum: history and folklore

A visit to the Museum which has been installed in a building specially built for it, will answer most of the questions the visitor has been asking himself as he walked around the ancient city. The items on display have been carefully chosen in order to cover every aspect of Palmyrene civilization throughout the ages; they are many but there is little repetition or duplication. There are informative labels in Arabic and French. Points of particular interest are illustrated by large charts.

There is thus little point in going into detail about the collections in this guide. A few landmarks will be sufficient.

The entrance hall is devoted to *pre-history*—depicted in a series of highly realistic dioramas.

The room to the right of the entrance shows the evolutions of the Palmyrene *script*.

In the next room there are *religious sculptures*. One of the most beautiful is a carved lintel on which the god Bêl-Shemên, god of the heavens, is depicted as an eagle with outstretched wings and smaller eagles by its side, each with an olive branch in its beak, also beside it are figures of the gods of the sun and moon with light beaming from their heads.

There is also a great model of the *Temple of Bêl* as it was when it was built.

In the third room there are sculptures mostly from public buildings. They depict *everyday life,* commerce, honours. In them people are dressed either in the local costume: a long gown under a wide cloak worn round the shoulders, or in Parthian dress: a tunic worn over trousers tucked into boots. The pack or army dromedaries wear harnass very similar to that used today.

The gallery that leads back to the entrance contains many representations of the various *gods of Palmyra*, notably of Yaribol, the sun god, dressed in Palmyrene costume.

The three rooms and gallery on the left of the entrance hall are occupied mainly by splendid *funerary sculptures*. The actual tomb chests in the hypogeia were sealed by limestone slabs on which the deceased was depicted, as if alive, in high relief, in an attitude of serenity. Various details reveal his social rank or symbolize traits of character. One hand is generally open, as a token of resignation in the face of death, while the other clasps some familiar object, to indicate attachment to life.

On the first floor there are many collections of objects, explanatory panels, and reconstructions—with life-size wax figures—which together constitute a veritable *museum of the Syrian desert.*

Certain scenes show everyday life in the oasis of Tadmor, others depict nomadic life which is gradually disappearing today. Family life is portrayed most realistically, with all the appropriate clothes, chests and tools, appropriately arranged, and models of men and women going about their household tasks. Elsewhere the range of Palmyrene craft-work is displayed—rugs, trays made of straw, leather and wickerwork. The production of turpentine is also shown, with the special press that is used. The turpentine tree, the rare plant much sought after by the Egyptians for the mummification of their dead, grows in abundance on the hills around Palmyra.

In other rooms, camels, Arab horses, tents, and the desert itself with the animals that live there—eagles, falcons, wolves, and hyenas—help to illustrate the life of the nomadic Bedouin, a people whose social structures, adapted over centuries to severe conditions of life, have been severely shaken by the development of the economy, by modern transport and by changes in customs and behaviour.

The great Temple of Bêl

The temple is surrounded by a great blank wall, 200 metres on each side, the walls of the fortress that replaced its ancient propylaea during the 12th century. This bleak exterior gives no hint of the magnificence of the building's internal layout.

There is an immense courtyard surfaced with smooth rock, which rises gently towards a majestic edifice at its highest point; this is the *cella,* the holy of holies, towards which the faithful used to crowd, where the sacrificial mysteries were celebrated. The wall surrounding it, lined with porticos whose columns are still standing for the most part, allows one to appreciate the vast proportions of the whole building, but at the same time emphasizes the enclosed nature of this shrine to the chief god of the city.

THE SILK ROUTE

■ *It was at Charax on the Gulf of Arabia that they used to unload the cotton goods, the spices and precious stones from India, and the silks and furs from China. The latter country was linked to Mesopotamia by a second route, the famous "Silk Route," which crossed the Sing Kiang plateau, Afghanistan and Iran. From about 70 A.D. it used to end at Vologesiade on the royal canal linking the Tigris and the Euphrates. Vologesiade served as a port to two neighbouring cities. Seleucis on the Tigris, the ancient Seleucid capital, and Ctesiphon, the Parthian capital, on the left bank of the Tigris. The caravans from Charax also passed through Vologesiade and continued up the Euphrates as far as Hit or even Doura-Europos. Following a series of watering places and caravanserais they reached Palmyra first of all, then went on to Emesa (Homs) and the Mediterranean ports. Damascus was also linked to Palmyra. Down the track that later became the Strata Diocletiana came incense and the products of Arabia which the Nabateans had taken up to Damascus. Glassware and fine china as well as Phoenecian purple cloth passed through Emesa and were stored in warehouses at Palmyra before being sent on to Volgesiade, Charax and India. This is a brief sketch of the double commercial traffic of which Palmyra was both the crossroads and the beneficiary.*

JEAN STARCKY
(adapted)
"Archeologia"

The layout of the temple corresponds to the arrangement of semitic sanctuaries. There are many points of similarity with the Temple at Jerusalem. Thus here there is, in front of the cella, the great sacrificial altar (corresponding to the "altar of the holocausts") and a ritual basin (the "sea of bronze") in which the priests performed their ablutions and in which ritual vessels were washed.

The *cella* was surrounded by a colonnade. Its capitals were made of bronze; only the stone cores remain. The limestone beams joining the colonnade to the wall behind show by their sculptures with what refinement and abundance the building was decorated. Their themes are floral, representations of the god and of processions. One particularly remarkable scene shows a camel carrying a statue of the god Bêl passing in front of people dressed in the local costume, a cloth draped and tied around its middle and followed by a group of veiled women, their heads bowed in reverence. The altar is shown loaded with gifts: pomegranates, pine cones, grapes and a kid. The two worshippers are in Parthian dress.

The interior of the *cella* consists of two open chapels facing each other with ceilings made from single slabs of stone, and richly decorated; the one on the left (as you enter) with signs of the zodiac, the one on the right with very fine geometric designs. The Palmyrene trinity (Bêl, Yarhibôl and Aglibôl) is also depicted. The arrangement of these two chapels, like two opposed niches, is enough to show how original this Palmyrene architecture is, typically Arab and Syrian. Other details noted by specialists have shown that, far from having been influenced by the Greeks and Romans, the civilisation of Palmyra, earlier than that of Rome itself, inspired both the architecture and the decoration practised by her invaders.

There are enormous cemeteries all around the city, but it is above all on the slopes of the hills to the east that the ancient tombs have furnished new evidence about Palmyrene civilisation. There are four types of burial place to be found here: the tomb-tower (a square structure with narrow windows), the house-tomb (the one that stands in the perspective from the Great Colonnade for example), the hypogeum-tower (a stairway linking a network of underground chambers inside a tomb-tower), and finally the hypogeum-tomb, built to receive the bodies of one family over a period of two centuries, a real underground house decorated with frescoes, each cell of which is sealed with a sculpture representing the deceased.

The Valley of the Tombs

There is a guided tour of the most remarkable of the tombs. These include: to the north of the city, beyond the ramparts, the so-called *Marôna* house-tomb; behind Diocletian's Camp the *Jamblique* tomb-tower, built in 83 A.D., and 500 metres further on, up the hill, the tomb-tower of the *Elahbel* family, 103 A.D. Near the latter, on the edge of the sandy road, is a hypogeum-tower, from the terrace of which, in the evening, there is a fine view over Palmyra. Near the top of the hillside there is an entrance, at ground level, to the *hypogeum of Atenatan* which was dug in 98.

But the most impressive of all the underground tombs is that known as the *Tomb of the Three Brothers* (at the beginning of the Valley of the Tombs), which countains some four hundred niches and whose walls are covered with frescoes in a remarkable state of preservation.

The Arab castles in the desert

If you climb the hill crowned by a 17th century for you will be rewarded by a magnificent general view of Palmyra—the ruins, the village, the oasis and the desert. The ruined castle itself is of no interest at all.

qalaat-najm

There is almost as little to say about two other fortresses some distance away in the desert sands. To the north-east of Palmyra there is *Qasr al-Hir ash-Sharqî* (15km by an indifferent track, turning off the Deir-ez-Zor road at the 99km post). To the south-west of Palmyra there is *Qasr al-Hîr al-Gharbî*, which is more accessible since it lies alongside the track, suitable for motor vehicles, from Damascus to Palmyra, some 40 kilometres from the road to Homs.

These buildings, both at the same time palaces and military camps, have the same square plan, with round towers at the corners and two semi-circular towers flanking the main entrance. They date from the time of the Umayyad Caliph Hicham, who also built a residence at Resafa (see entry), i.e. from about 688-9 (the 110th year of the Hegira).

The fortified gateway of Qasr al-Hîr al-Gharbî has been moved and re-erected in the National Museum in Damascus.

The remains of irrigation channels, ruined villages, and cisterns in the mountains nearby, all show that Palmyra was less isolated in years gone by than is generally thought. Recent excavations have shown, moreover, that the hill overlooking the Afqa spring was inhabited by the Amorites from the end of the 3rd millenium. The region has indeed a long and splendid history...

Information p. 161.

■ A ford or a bridge across a great river have often led to the growth of a town or the building of a fortress.

Here the river is the Euphrates, wide and heavy with mud from the Taurus, flowing between high cliff-like banks. The crossing was the one used on the ancient road from Aleppo to Harran—the traditional trade route across Northern Syria until the 15th or 16th century when a more reliable bridge was built at Birecik where the Euphrates flowed less strongly (on the other side of the present Syro-Turkish border).

The bridge at Qalaat Najm was destroyed by floods and the ford has been rendered impassible by the recent construction of a dam upstream, in Turkish territory. The flourishing towns on each bank are now reduced to humble mud-coloured villages housing a few fishermen, shepherds' families, and reed gatherers. There are now only a few poor gardens, narrow strips of green standing out against the mud-banks of the river and the dusty plateau.

The fortress remains, a brooding presence within its blank walls; it is a typical Arab citadel, with its great steep glacis up which winds an almost vertical path, its double range of ramparts with square tapering towers, and its solid entrance fortification.

Remnants of a fortress

From a distance the castle is impressive but inside Qalaat Najm is nothing but ruins. A gap in the base of the northern ramparts provides a way in. One has to pick one's way between great lumps of fallen masonry to reach the remnants of some vaulted rooms, now a refuge for eagles, owls and bats. Flights of beautifully paved steps give some idea of the care that went into the original building. Fine Arabic inscriptions in kufic script adorn the walls of what was once a mosque. The wind penetrates everywhere, whistling between the sections of wall still standing. Archways open on to the void and show what a vast panorama the castle once commanded. Down below the muddy Euphrates flows slowly south, towards Lake Al-Assad where men have contrived to hold it prisoner and bend its strength to their service (see under Al-Thaura).

No trace of the Syrian goddess

The road to Qalaat Najm, although the last part of it is difficult, is not devoid of interest.

Vines and flocks are almost the only resources of the region: carefully cultivated vineyards, patches of deep green here and there on the plateau; flocks of sheep and goats in great numbers, flocks of thirty or forty at least, sometimes as many as a hundred. On the outskirts of Aleppo there are vast walled enclosures with sinister black iron gates where the selected animals are marshalled for sale or slaughter.

There are several villages, consisting entirely of characteristically Syrian houses, mud-walled and with sugar-loaf roofs, well adapted to the climate; they are highly picturesque. The most typical is certainly *Al-Bab,* a sizeable township some 38 kilometres from Aleppo.

Forty-five kilometres beyond Al-Bab, *Manbij* (where you leave the road to Jarablûs for the track to Qalaat Najm) is quite a town, with its double lane boulevards and public gardens dotted with ancient remains. A few stelae and capitals are the only signs of the vanished splendours that the Greek writer Lucian delighted to describe during the 2nd century A.D. Dating back to Assyrian times Manbij was famous, when it was called *Hierapolis,* for its "Syrian goddess" —whom people came from far and near to worship. "Much money flows in from Arabia, Phoenicia and from Babylon," wrote Lucian. "Nowhere are there so many festivals and religious assemblies..." In the principal temple the writer saw many proofs of its foundation by Dionysius: barbarian costumes, precious stones from India, elephants' tusks brought here from Ethipia by Dionysus himself." What follows is even more astonishing since it indicates the presence—before the arrival of Christianity and two centuries before Saint Simon (see under Qalaat Samaân)—of local ascetics who sat on columns. To be sure, these columns were known as the "phalluses of Dionysus." Of the god of "the vine, wine and ecstatic delirium" nothing remains, at Manbij, but the vine...

QALAAT NAJM

Name: The citadel of Najm, name of the local deputy governor in the 9th century. Variant names: Nedjme, Nadjm.

Location and access: Aleppo governorate. Altitude about 400 m. 110 km north-east of Aleppo, left bank of the Euphrates. Leave Aleppo by the Raqqa motorway; about 600 m further on, make U-turn and then fork right before water-tower on to the tarmac Al-Bab, Manbij, Jarablûs road; in Manbij, tarmac road at the north-east end of the built-up area; 18 km from Mambij, the tarmac ends after a big village on the left; the broad, rutted track with potholes and ridges splinters off in several directions: keep bearing right in a mainly E.N.E. direction making for the cliffs and hills along the Euphrates valley: once round these cliffs, Qalaat Najm suddenly comes into view. Accessible in a good private car. Petrol at Mambij.

Accommodation: At Aleppo.

qalaat salah-ad-din

■ On 10 March 1957, the Minister of the Interior of the Syrian Arab Republic approved a decision by which the castle of Saône (still known as the castle of Sahyoun) would henceforth be called Qalaat Salah-ad-Din (the castle of Saladin), to commemorate the capture of the fortress, in 1188, by the great hero of Islam.

His exploit is well worth recalling. Saône, protected as it was by deep wild ravines, recognized as a masterpiece of military architecture, and defended by the Knights Hospitaller, was considered impregnable... It was taken in a hour! An Arab chronicler, Beha ad-Din, records that the ardour of the Muslim solidiers was such that they grabbed food that was being cooked in the houses and ate it without ceasing to fight. The population took refuge in the keep, and when the keep fell to Saladin they were liberated only on payment of ten gold pieces for each man, five for each woman, and two for each child...

Saône never fell into Crusader hands again. During the 14th century it was still in good order, a powerful citadel controlling one of the passages between the sea and the Orontes valley and an advance defence post for Antioch. The importance of the position had been exploited long before the Crusades. The site changed hands several times during the wars between Arabs and Byzantines throughout the 10th century. Towards the year 1000 the Byzantines heavily fortified this eagle's eyrie. The remains of their fortress with its triple ramparts are still visible. When the Franks occupied the region, around 1110, they drew on ancient techniques to build on the Byzantine foundations. Perhaps they only in fact completed a colossal feature of the castle to which it owed its reputation for impregnability—the east ditch.

Saône stands on a rocky spur whose vertical walls rise above the junction of two fast-flowing streams. As late as 1965 it was impossible to reach it except on foot or on horseback, by a difficult climb first down and then up again after having forded one of the streams. Today there is a bridge and a road which provide easy access to the foot of the eagle's nest.

Thick gorse and thorn-bushes fill the spaces between the greyish rocks and rocks and cover the base of the plateau, gradually burying arches and walls under greenery and flowers.

An island cut off from the world

The weak point of this triangular site was obviously on the far side where a narrow neck of land joined it to the plateau. The architects of Saône doubled and redoubled their defences on that side: three towers with walls 5 metres thick, a keep 24 metres high with no communication with the neighbouring buildings, a low narrow postern entrance, flanked by towers and bristling with defences... But, no doubt judging all this insufficient or too much the familiar pattern of defence, they adopted a radical solution: they would isolate the fortress completely by digging a deep ditch right through the connecting neck of land!

How many poor men—prisoners or slaves—must have worn themselves out cutting into the mountainside with pick-axes... a great gash 156 metres long, 15 to 18 metres wide, and 28 metres deep! Its vertical walls show a smooth, fine, yellowish rocksurface.

In the middle of the cutting a tall needle of rock, topped with a few blocks of masonry, rises level with the plateau and the entrance postern of the castle. It was merely a matter of raising a double drawbridge, which rested on the point of this needle, and the castle could be completely isolated from the rest of the world.

Visitors park their cars at the bottom of this remarkable ditch, opposite the horses' mangers and hitching holes carved out of the rock. There is a spring close by. A great cavern dug out of the rock wall, some distance up, served as a prison.

The present entrance to the fortress is by a double flight of steps which lead up to one of the towers on the north side.

Five hectares of defences

A passageway with a bend in it leads into the central courtyard. A mass of shrubs and bushes and yellow, mauve and blue flowers seem about to submerge the ruins, block up the entrances, prise up the paving on the stairs. From outside the Qalaat looked very impressive; inside we can see how it has been marked by time. Perhaps it would be enough to clear away the undergrowth and remove the heaps of rubble to restore some grandeur to these remnants. But they are certainly more moving in their present romantic abandon... The Keeper's explanations too, help us to see some order in this labyrinth.

Near the entrance there is a stairway on the outside of the tower which leads up to a rampart walk and to the upper level of the castle. The layout of the whole citadel can be grasped from here.

Diagonally opposite, a narrow passageway leads out onto the void overlooking the ditch. It is a pity that the drawbridge has not been restored, at least as far as the top of the needle—for from there the castle could be seen in all its strength, with its blank walls and its round towers rising sheer from the cliffs.

The keep, to the left as you leave the entrance postern, is a massive, almost cubic building, 25 metres square. A single opening, protected by a portcullis, leads into the lower hall, a dark room in which the vaulted ceiling is supported by an enormous square pillar. The upper room, reached by a staircase built within the thickness of the walls, has the same central pillar.

Adjoining the keep, but not in direct communication with it, is the largest hall in the whole castle. A service-room and stable (mangers have been carved out of the walls), it is divided into five aisles by four rows of heavy pillars. Through this room one can reach the round towers which overlook the ditch; it also communicates with a deep cistern with a round vaulted roof. A second, even bigger cistern (33 metres long, 10 wide and 16 deep), lies on the other side of the castle, across the courtyard.

Rather strangely the courtyard is crossed by the remains of a fairly tall wall, built of small stones, in front of the keep. This structure, quite different from those surrounding it, is a remnant of the previous Byzantine castle wall. Five similar ones, still quite easily made out, stretched right across the plateau. A square structure, a sort of keep, three-quarters ruined, stood in the centre of this fortification.

Another, rather jumbled, group of buildings lies opposite the medieval keep, level with the entrance tower and the second cistern. They include the remains of a mosque and Arab baths, whose water channels and marble tiling are still in place.

Thus this citadel—the Byzantine Sayoun, the Frankish Castle of Saône and the Arab qaalat now dedicated to Salah-ad-Dîn—played its part in Syria's history under three different and competing authorities, over three successive centuries.

QALAAT SALAH AD-DIN

Name: "The fortress of Saladin", a recent name (see text). Crusader period: Sahyoun (from the name of the nearby village), whence the French form Saône. Phoenician period: Sigon (?). In the 10th century: Sehone.

Location and access: Latakia governorate. Altitude 410 m. 35 km east of Latakia by the Haffe-Slenfe road (Fork left over the bridge, leaving Latakia on the south side by the Tartus road; at Haffe (21 km), narrow, winding, hilly, but fully surfaced road. The sharp descent and the no less steep climb across the gorge to the castle are also negotiable by car.

Accommodation: At Latakia, Homs or Tartus.

qalaat samaân

■ Forty-two years on top of a column... Forty-two years under the blazing sun, in the bitter cold, and exposed to all the mountain winds!

The man's name was Simon: a shepherd from Northern Syria he became a monk as the result of a revelation in a dream. It was not enough for him to live walled up in a cell, isolation as close as possible to the Heavens was his way of demonstrating his detachment from the world and his faith in God.

There is only a stump of the column left, some two or there metres high, such was the superstitious fervour of pilgrims over the centuries — each wanting to take away a piece, no matter how tiny, of the column which had been the scene of such a remarkable exploit.

It must be said that excellent arrangements were made for the veneration of the memory of the ascetic. Shortly after the death of the holy man the most beautiful church in the East was built on the ridge of the hill where he had taken up "residence". The lay-out, centring on the famous column, was original. Four basilicas, arranged in the shape of a cross, opened onto a sort of octagon covered by a dome; in the centre stood the sacred pillar.

The church orientated eastwards, and hence slightly out of alignment, was the one mainly used for worship. The three others sheltered the pilgrims, of whom there was always an enthusiastic crowd, hoping for a miracle. Women were admitted, but not allowed to approach close to the column. There were many candidates for baptism, anxiously awaiting admission to the baptistery nearby, in the narthex in front of the southern facade.

Monks and clergy were lodged in the vicinity, in a building several stories high, whilst visitors found their way down a splendid road lined with classical style triumphal arches, to the shops and hostelries at the foot of the hill. If a traveller were to die during his stay here, there was a special funerary chapel behind the basilica to receive him.

Over a thousand years later

Well over a thousand years have passed. Books, documents, sculptured stones (there are some in the Museum in Damascus) all tell of Simon, whom the Church soon declared to be a saint. But if we know the elements of the remarkable story we can read it for ourselves on the very spot where it took place.

More impressive even than the astonishing story itself, are the beautiful remnants that remain. Their simplicity and harmony combine to make the ruins of the Basilica of St. Simon one of the masterpieces of pre-Islamic art in Syria.

Its builders had absorbed much from classical antiquity but they expressed what they had learned in an original way. Preceded by a flight of seven steps, extending along its full length, the facade with its three porches is a model of architectural balance. The eight great arches which form the central octagon rest on a skilful arrangement of vaults, columns and pilasters. The apses, either flat or rounded and the lateral apsidal chapels, form a perfect contrast to the great round-headed windows open to a sky that is almost always intensely blue.

Everywhere the stone has taken on a warm golden tint, almost pinkish. The decoration was conceived so as to emphasize the purity of the main lines; there is a discreet plain moulding linking the openings; a frieze or band of delicately carved grapes and foliage emphasizing the arches or lintels; sober Corinthian capitals, but whose acanthus leaves seem sometimes strangely shaken by the wind...

Outside, the facade with its arches surmounted by a triangular front, but even more the east end of the church with its great apse of six bays flanked by small columns, anticipate by six centuries, the finest Romanesque churches of Europe.

Beyond the apse the funerary chapel still stands, well preserved, amid tombs carved out of the rock.

On the other side, the baptistery adjoins the ruins of another basilica. Its square external plan embraces an octagon formed by eight arches springing from pilasters or engaged columns. It was a halt on the processional route around the narrow plateau, where they were joined by the newly baptized Christians who then went with them to the great Basilica of St. Simon.

The setting is magnificent, with extensive views all around. Other "ghost towns" can be seen, even with the naked eye, on the nearby hilltops (see under Qalb Loza, Al-Bara, Maarat ann-Numaan). In the 10th century ramparts flanked by towers made the place into a fort, a "Qalaat", a citadel, the citadel of Simon. Down below the city gradually became deserted and fell into ruin. Some two and three storey facades still remain standing.

Shortly before the turning for Qalaat Samaân, approaching from Aleppo, the road to Antioch crosses a strange paved road built on a solid stone foundation. The structure is intact and modern cars can be driven quite safely down this road from another age. Usually Roman roads seem to consist of a few scattered blocks of paving: here there is a stretch of twelve hundred metres that might have been preserved expressly to delight the tourist.

There are other curiosities in this region, along the road to Qalaat Samaân and Aafrin.

Dâna, the first village to the right of the road after the crossroads near the Roman road, has a Roman tomb dug out of the rock, surmounted by a strange little building with four columns. (Not to be confused with the village of Al-Dâna near Maarat; see entry under that name) The country hereabouts was named "the bloody plain" after the bitter battle between the Muslim armies of the princes of Mosul and Aleppo and the Crusader troops of Roger of Salerno, prince of Antioch. A track leading off to the left of the main road as you come in sight of Qalaat Samaân, leads to the ghost towns of *Refadé (Rafad)* and *Qatura,* on the hill. There are several

The façade, apse, and many details of the church of St. Siméon, at Qalaat Samaan, foreshadow—six centuries before— some of Europe's finest Romanesque buildings. It was built shortly after the death of this original anchorite, who spent forty-two years here on top of his column.

qalb loza

monumental tombs to be seen there and others dug out of the rock with sculptured stelae on the rock face itself. These sites are not accessible for light vehicles.

Although not indicated on most maps, the asphalt road continues north beyond Deir Samaân, the village below Qalaat Samaân. The sparse cultivation of the karstic uplands, as poor in arable land as they are in water, is soon succeeded by a fertile zone watered by the river Aafrine. It flows brimming between its banks at the bottom of a wide valley whose slopes have recently been planted with fruit-trees. Some distance away there is a cone-shaped hill dotted with the white houses of the village of *Ayn Dara*. Here one feels very far from the "ghost towns" and their nightmares... This valley has remained a source of life. As early as the 7th century B.C. civilisation flourished on these banks, as is shown by the magnificient stone lions (now in the Museum at Aleppo) that were discovered in a tell, 8 kilometres to the north of the village. One of them remains on the site and is easy to find.

Passing through *Aafrin,* a township on a crossroads to the north of Ayn Dara, a good road leads back to Aleppo, 60 kilometres away. The complete round trip—Aleppo, Dâna, Qalaat Samaân, Ayn Dara, Aafrîn, with a few diversions, —adds up to about 170 kilometres and takes a whole day. A visit to Qalaat Samaân alone (going both ways via Dâna) can be made in half a day.

Another extremely interesting archaeological site, lies far to the north of Aafrine. This is the ancient city of *Cyrrhus*, near the present *Turkish* frontier. Many Roman monuments, notably a theatre 110 metres in diameter, in a remarkable state of preservation, indicate the importance of this former garrison town.

Unfortunately it is still difficult to reach Cyrrhus; there are two tracks, both long and neither of them good —one via *Aazaz* and the other via *Bûlbûl.*

Information p. 181

■ The road confronts the mountain head-on, rising steeply. The climb takes only a few minutes. Four or five-tree, a host of small boys, and a few humble houses—stones among stones. Another fifty metres... And there, braving the winds and the centuries, splendid and incongruous, stands a cathedral!

Of course the basilica at Qalb Loza isn't, and never was, a cathedral. Its powerful, somewhat squat, shape gives it more the appearance of a large country church. But in this wild solitary setting it seems like a challenge. With its three big rounded arches at the front, its apse behind, it has survived twelve or thirteen centuries of oblivion. And now it is being restored, there are scaffoldings on the facade, the towers and the lintels are being re-built, by men of another faith...

The church is laid out as a three-aisled basilica with a narthex in front. The external wall of the left-hand aisle is in ruins, so that, even before entering the building, one has a glimpse of the harmonious rhythm of the central nave. The sunshine streams in, touching the coppery stone with fire. The vaulting falls in perfect curves to join the short columns with their generous capitals. The central columns have square-cut niches with wide mouldings. The great blocks of masonry are so beautifully cut and set that this alone suffices to decorate the walls and the inside of the apse. Ornament is happily limited to finely-chiselled mouldings which emphasize the curves of the bays and the doorframes.

The great absidal arch, one of the doorways on the south side and the porch linking the narthex and the body of the church, are certainly amongst the finest examples of Syrian art of the Byzantine period.

The architectural quality and beautiful decoration of Qalb Loza are present even in the smaller details. Thus the small windows of the upper storey of the nave have square openings but, on the outside, a finely-cut double fluting prolongs these square frames in graceful half-circles. Such simple and delicate touches relieve any coarseness that a building built of such big blocks of stone (the roof blocks are five metres long) might otherwise have.

The abandoned town of Kirk Biza

Less than fifteen hundred metres from Qalb Loza and on the other side of the road that leads back into the valley, the village of Kirk Biza, built of grey stone quarried from the mountain, seems to await the return of its menfolk gone off to work in the fields. Tobacco plantations and, down below in the plain, the chequerboard of crops and orchards, add to the impression.

But alas! Kirk Biza is another of the many "ghost towns" of Northern Syria.

A closer look helps us to understand; the tobacco plantations are in fact pitifully small. They are tributes to the infinite patience of a few peasants who cling to these desolate heights. The least little remnant of soil trapped between two outcrops of rock is used and the small patches of red soil here and there have actually been gathered from these pockets... A thousand years and more of wind and rain have left the uplands quite bare. So life has left Kirk Biza.

The town contracted in on itself and you have to climb over heaps of rubble to get into it. There are quite a few single and two-storey houses still standing. The door lintels are often decorated with geometrical designs or with bunches of grapes.

The tiny church is said to date from the end of the 3rd or the beginning of the 4th century and thus is one of the first to be built in Syria. There are many carved stones. A stone seat, its back decorated with rosettes, standing on a raised platform, no doubt was used by the superior of the community or by a bishop. Blocks of stone, decorated and with holes in them, may have contained relics of early martyrs now forgotten.

There are many "ghost towns" like this one, elsewhere on the jebel (see under Al-Bara, Maarat ann-Numan, Qalaat Semaân). Kirk Biza has the advantage of being easily accessible. But other discoveries are always possible. With a pair of binoculars one can make out other ruins, but roads are bad, the climate is harsh, and there are no facilities of any kind...

However, the whole region is not just stone and desolation. Just a quarter of an hour by car from Qalb Loza brings us to the lush orchards around Harim (on the road to Jisr ash-Shughur), and very little more to reach the shady streams of the "summer resorts" of *Sheykh Obed* and *Salqîn* (10 and 15 km to the west of Harim, respectively; see entries for Idlib and Jisr ash-Shughur).

QALB LOZA

Name: Variant names: Qalb Lauzah, Kalb Lauzeh, Kalb Lozé. Ancient site attached to the village of Biza.

Location and access: Idlib governorate. Altitude 600 m. About 65 km west of Aleppo along the Bab al-Hawa-Antakya road turning left on to the Harim road (3 km beyond the turning to Samaâm); follow the Harim road for about 12 km, then turn left along a narrow, but surfaced side-road which cuts through a valley between two stony hillsides; 4 km further on, steep ascent to the right up to Qalb Loza. The whole route, including the last section, is completely asphlated contrary to the information given in some "guides".

Accommodation: At Aleppo. Possibly at the summer resort of Salqîn, *Casino***A.

QALAAT SAMAAN, p. 177

Name: Monastery (resembling a citadel) of St. Siméon. Variant names: Semaan, Semân, Sma'an, Simân.

Location and access: Aleppo governorate. Altitude 900 m. 60 km north-east of Aleppo, by the Bab al-Hawa-Antakya road until the right fork 700 m beyond the Roman road (see text); Dana road, Afrine by Aavaz road, Afrine, then left, Ayn Dara road. 90 km. Total distance 150 km.

Accommodation: At Aleppo. Cafeteria near St. Siméon's Basilica (information from the keeper).

qamishli

■ Cotton and wheat, wheat and cotton. These are the dominant colours of this far north-east corner of Syria, a distant region stretching from the Tigris to the Euphrates, which is not merely the granary of the country but its store of energy as well since oil has begun to flow from wells near *Qaratchok* (100 km east of Qamishli).

The capital of the governorate is *Hassaké*, an agricultural market centre on the middle reaches of the Khabûr. The basin of this smaller version of the Euphrates is the scene of many considerable development schemes that will continue under the fourth and fifth Economic Plans. The town is expanding rapidly, but there is little there to interest the tourist.

Qamishli (or Qamishliyé), a frontier town, a rail and road halt on the way to Mosul, is more attractive. A mass of green and lots of flowers, a river that is almost a torrent, a decent hotel and, on the northern horizon, the first outlines of the Taurus Mountains, make it a pleasant place in which to stay. Moreover, one can visit from Qamishli various archaeological sites, of secondary interest admittedly, though there are more than a hundred historic tells in the neighbourhood.

Tall Halaf, near *Ras al-Ayn* (120 km west of Qamishli), on the Ganzana, has yielded Assyrian texts. At *Tall Brak* (half-way between Qamishli and Hassaké, on the right bank of the Jaghjagh), six archaeological layers have been uncovered, ranging from the 4th to the mid-2nd millenium B.C. At *Tall Shakar Bazar* (South West of Qamishli), fifteen levels have been identified, six prehistoric and five ranging from 3000 to 1600 B.C.

It is more difficult to get to the Tigris, whose right bank is Syrian territory for some 50 kilometres. The river winds down at the bottom of a valley overlooked by cliffs. The remains of a massive three-arched bridge (only one—15 metres high is visible—as well as a great pile) mark the site of *Ayn Diwar*, a military post situated in the extreme north-east corner of Syria. We are closer here to the Russian frontier than we are to the Mediterranean.

The inhabitants of these far-flung regions are often very distinct types —Kurds, Mesopotamians, Assyrians. The women are particularly pretty, but also very wild and it is better not to try to take photographs of them on the sly...

QAMISHLI

Name: Variant names: Qamishliye, Kamichlie, Qâmichliye, Al-Kamishly.

Location and access: Hassaké governorate. Altitude 900 m. Syrian-Turkish frontier post on the main Ankara, Mossoul, Baghdad road. 260 km north-east of Deir-ez-Zor, via Hassaké (83 km). 87 km north-west of Tall Kijak (Syrian-Iraq frontier) and 200 km from Al-Mosul (Mossoul) 600 km from Baghdad. Aérodrome: Intermittent flights to and from Aleppo. Railway lines to Aleppo, Turkey, Baghdad.

Accommodation: Hadaia**B, al-Soak al-Jadid, tel. 10141. *Semiramis***B, al-Jisrein street, tel. 10185. Plus about ten * establishments.

QANAWAT, p. 183

Name: Variant names: Kanawat, Kanawath, Qanouate. Nabatean period: Nobah (after the chief of a tribe). Roman period (1st century): Qanatha (Kanatha, Canatha); under Septimus Severus (2nd century): Septima Kanotha, then Qenat.

Location and access: Suwayda governorate. Altitude 900 m. 8 km north-east of Suwayda.

Accommodation: At Damascus.

SAFITA p. 191.

Name: Safitha, Qalaat Safita, literally "White Castle", from the Frankish period.

Location and access: Tartus governorate. Altitude 380 m. 40 km south-east of Tartus by the old Homs road (turning on the Tripoli road, 2 km south of Tartus, to the left). 53 km south-west of Masyaf.

Accommodation: At Tartus, Hama, Homs, Latakia.

qanawât

■ Apart from the ones at Bosra (see entry), the monuments at Qanawât are the most impressive and richly decorated in this region of the jebel al-Arab (see under Sûwayda) where so many ancient stones are strewn on the ground or built into the fabric of present-day dwellings, or else soar up sometimes as haughty columns, all cracked and broken, and yet superb! The site where Qanawât stands enhances the interest of the ruins.

The town lies stretched along the crest of a hill and straggles off down the side of a valley where trees have been planted, gardens cultivated and meadows kept. After crossing the Bâshân plateau, all black and bare, the relief of the land here and the green are like a touch of coquetry. High stone walls bound each piece of land, rough enclosures made from blocks of basalt gathered round about, and amongst the blocks here and there the drum of a column, a Corinthian capital or a finely chiselled architrave piled together at random, some straight, some slanting, some up-turned... Who cares? And why should anyone care?

The first town of the province

Named Qenat or Nobah in the Bible and Canatha in Nabatean and Roman times, ancient Qanawât was the most important city in the land. In the sixties B.C. it belonged to the Decapolis League of merchant cities, all situated in Transjordan, of which Damascus was for a time the chief, and which survived until the end of the 2nd century. This past importance explains the wide spread of the remains. The ruins fall into three main groups.

At the entrance to the present village, coming from Sûwayda, in the hollow of the valley on the left, a cluster of columns rises from the bushes; they belong to a 2nd-century temple dedicated to Helios. A little further on, the village square certainly stands on the spot where the ancient agora (or forum) stood. Old paving-stones still cover part of the ground and remnants of columns are built into the facades of the houses. The street that climbs up the hillside, over a long stretch follows the track of an ancient pathway. It leads up to the principal edifices: the Temple of Zeus (2nd century) and the group known as "the serail" or "Es-sérail".

The temple occupied a spur with a view over the whole valley. Mulberries and other fruit trees provide a foil to the half dozen columns that still stand capped by magnificent Corinthian capitals with broad entablatures, whose shafts a third of the way up bear consoles (as at Palmyra) which are also finely chiselled. Other capitals and fragments of architraves left where they lie on the pavement allow one to look more closely at the work of the forgotten sculptor whose skilful hand carved these scrolls of acanthus and vine out of the hard basalt. The big monumental group known as "the serail" stands on the highest point in Qanawât. A big clump of trees marks the spot, a little wall surrounds it and a closed gate is supposed to keep visitors out when the keeper is not there.

It is an interesting collection of Roman and Christian buildings. The columns with console of a temple can still be seen. One of the walls of the temple was used in the 4th or 5th century to support a of the Christian building, by its elegance, is evidence of very great refinement. This flowery style is found elsewhere on other parts of the building and on many of the fragments lying on the ground, whereas other stones from the same sanctuary have a highly geometrical design: key-patterns or stars.

The right slope of the valley also has some interesting ruins: A few steps of a small theatre or odeon, the remains of a nymphaeum and of an aqueduct, the foundations of a square tower and of a big round tower, etc.

Going up the valley, a winding path leads 4 km south-east to the isolated ruins of ancient *Sia*: thermae, paved terraces, temples built in the period from the 1st century B.C. to the 2nd century A.D.

qnaytra

■ "Mister Visitor, Sir, look at this town, and judge for yourself!" This injunction scribbled in French on a chunk of tumbledown wall at the entrance to what was once Qnaytra, soon seems superfluous.

In June 1967, a smiling town of 37,000 inhabitants, living happily in the freshness of the winds blowing from over the snows of the jabal ash Cheikh (Mount Hermon), amongst its fruit trees, its vines, its wheat, its poultry and its oxen.

Today Qnaytra is no more than the ghost of a town. On either side of streets that are still in one piece the houses lie fallen, dismantled, and gutted, as if blown down by some giant hurricane. Three or four cracked minarets and the two towers of a church, with gaping holes in them, point symbolically towards the sky. Some way off, a building that was once a modern hospital with three-hundred beds is rent with holes. Five or six houses, alone in the centre, form a small unscathed island... Built as they are of volcanic rock (the rest of the town was concrete) the bulldozers could not shift them!

For the tragedy of Qnaytra is not that it was, like so many other towns in the world, alas, ponded by artillery and flattened by air forces; there was practically no fighting here. Qnaytra was "totally and systematically" destroyed. All the international experts have affirmed that the destruction was "deliberate". No need to be an expert to spot the effects of deliberate dynamiting, in conjunction with the work of machines normally used in building rather than in warfare. The buildings have not been blown up; they just caved in, as the supporting pillars were knocked away. The destructive fury of the occupying forces, which in June 1974 were suddenly forced to evacuate the Syrian town they had held since 1967, is shown by any number of other details: electricity and telephone poles sawn up; mosques, churches and cemetery sacked; removal of commemorative plaques from the Monument to the Dead; theft of sanitary equipment, of the town pumps and even the precious tiles that covered the Khaled Ibn Walid Mosque, etc.

Moreover there are a few witnesses here to tell how and when the horrors happened: Mrs. Widad Nassif, for one, who speaks four or five languages fluently and humorously. She was manageress of a small spa in the Golan and was evacuated to Qnaytra, where she stayed throughout the seven years' occupation. She still lives here, in the shade of her climbing vines and surrounded by her farm-yard. She has made a vow never to go back to Damascus until her homeland has been set free.

QNAYTRA

Name: Variant anmes: Qouneitra, Kunietra, Quneitra, Qunaytra, Qenaitrâ.

Location and access: Principal town of governorate. Altitude 1,000 m. 70 km south-west of Damascus. No access at present without authorization from the military authorities, easily granted.

RAS AL-BASSIT p. 188.

Name: Variant names: Ras el-Bassit, el-Bassite, al-Bassit.

Location and access: Latakia governorate. Seaside. 60 km north of Latakia, by Antakya road for 42 km, then left along tarmac road climbing through the forest. For Kassab, continue along the Antakya road for another 16 km coming close to the frontier, then turn left.

Accommodation: Camping possible beneath the pine-trees along the edge of the beach. Permission and supplies from the open-air cafés at various points around the bay. Plans are being prepared for a large holiday centre (see text).
At the summer resorts (altitude 600 m to 8)) m): *At Qastal Al-Moâf, Verte Montagne**B, 25 rms., tel. 4; *At Kassab, Ar-Rawda**B, 71 beds, tel. 8; *Ramsis**B, 45 beds, tel. 6; *Semiramis**C, 65 beds, tel. 16; *Amira**C, tel. 28; *Spiro* Restaurant, tel. 17 and *Restaurant-Casino* of the Municipality, tel. 24. *At Nabheim, Montana*, 53 beds.

raqqa

■ Two bridges, a stone one and a more recent suspension bridge, lead across the river to Raqqa, which stands on the left bank of the Euphrates.

The river, tamed since the building of the great dam, flows along a number of separate arms bordered with vegetation, leaving long stretches of pebbly and sandy beaches.

The town, which is the principal town of the governorate, is the only urban centre in an immense area: to the south, steppe on the edge of the desert proper; to the north (on either side of the River Balikh and as far as the Turkish frontier) a plain with arable and pasture-land. The whole area is expecting to reap benefit from the improvements resulting from the creation of Lake Al-Assad (see under Al-Thaura). The town of Raqqa, which is already on a railway line, will see its activities considerably enlarged as it gives up its age-old function as a bridge-head at one of the world's frontiers and gradually takes up a new one as a modern regional capital in a new agricultural and industrial Syria.

On the route to China

From this viewpoint, it matters little that the vestiges of past glory are few and far between, and of minor interest.

Nothing remains of the "Nicephorion" of Alexander the Great or of the "Callinicos" of the Romans. As the Persians several times fought the Byzantines here, nothing has come down to us of Christian Raqqa. In 772, the Abbassid Caliph Al-Mansour founded a new city, *Al-Rafiqa*, which quickly eclipsed ancient Raqqa, but in the 18th century, the Mongols laid waste the rich city. Brick, the frailest of all building materials, cannot stand up to the ravages of time...

Digging about in the clay, the eternal treasure-seekers end by toppling what remains of palaces and mosques. The countless "shell holes" gouged in the ground are the work of these diggers, sometimes well-intentioned, sometimes not, but it is only fair to say that thanks to these same "archeologists" the Damascus Museum is today in a position to exhibit, in a room specially devoted to Raqqa, one or two pieces of glass and ceramic of great beauty, including a wonderful horseman in Chinese porcelain to attest to the fact that one of the great "roads" between the Occident and the Orient did indeed pass this way.

For its part, the Syrian department of Antiquities has started to uncover the remains of the palaces which were among the favourite residences of the Abbassids in the 9th century. The principal remains are to the south-east of the present-day town, more or less on a line with the downstream bridge. A huge quadrilateral area, forming a shaded walk, bounds an ancient mosque which is revealed by a succession of archways and by a cylindrical minaret built of brick standing on a base of ancient stones. A few hundred yards further on, ramparts flanked by a big corner tower trace the shape of a horseshoe, illustrating the avowed intention of Al-Mansour to build Al-Rafiqa on the pattern of the circular plan of Baghdad. A copy also of the architecture then common in Baghdad, with a monumental doorway in baked brick surmounted by a series of small columns and niches with iwâns, decorated in a very simple manner by staggering the positions of the bricks in relation to one another. All the rest round about is nothing but shapeless ruins.

RAQQA

Name: Variant names: Er Raqqâ, Rakka. At the time of Alexander: Nicephorion; Roman period: Callinicos (the philosopher of that name was killed here); Arab period (8th century): Er Râfiqa, then Raqqa.

Location and access: Principal town of governorate. Altitude 000 m. Crossing of the Euphrates, 60 km downriver from Al-Thaura (big dam); 130 km upriver from Deir-ez-Zor. Temporary terminus of the newly built railway from Aleppo.

Accommodation: Tourist'Hôtel (Al-Syaha)**B, Kuwatli street, tel. 20725. Plus 7 *C establishments.

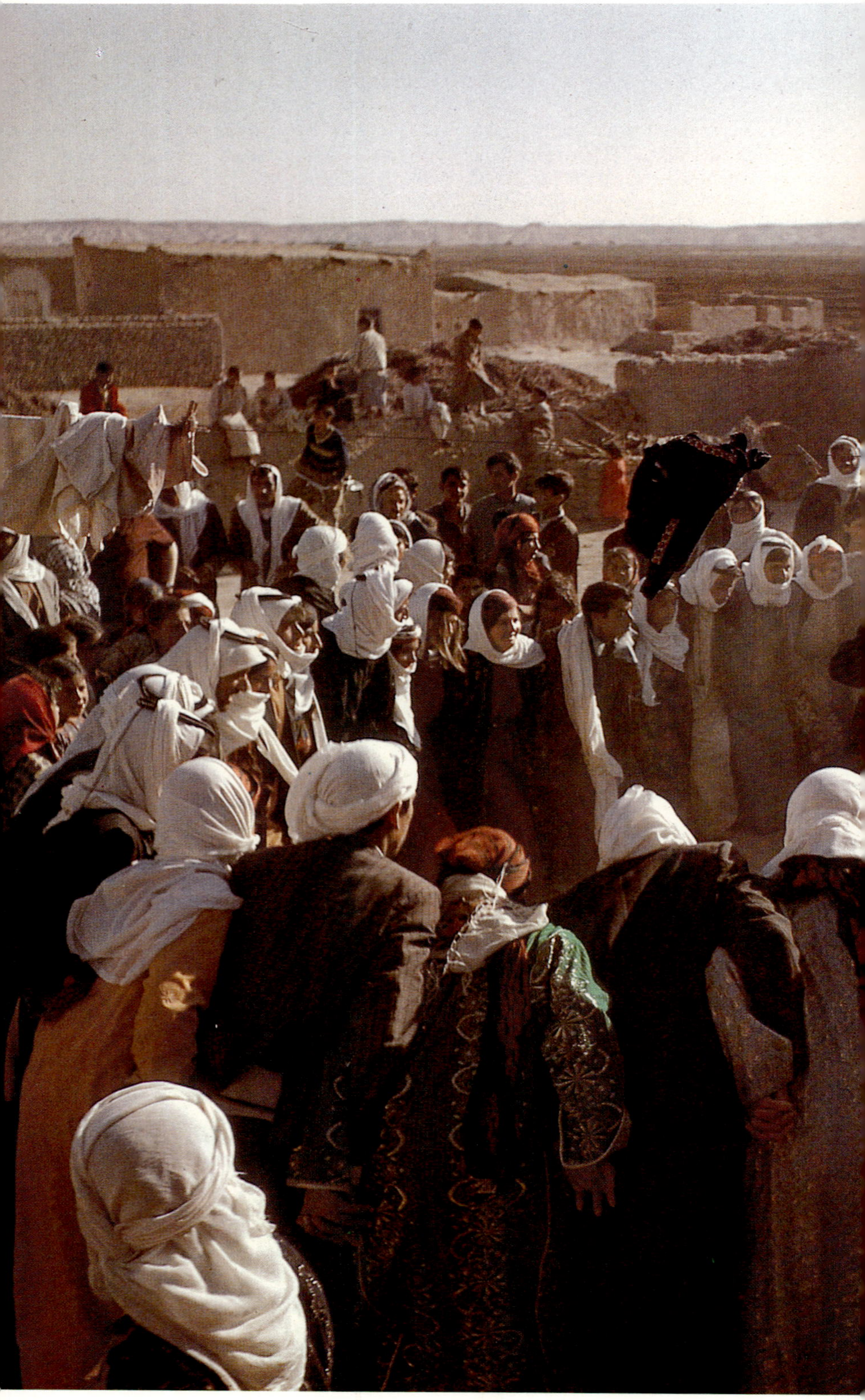

*Traditions are still upheld by the Bedouin
and the shepherds of the steppe—
as in this frenzied, joyful dancing
at a wedding in a village near Rasafa.
(Photo Th. Vogel, Explorer.)*

ras-al-bassit

■ The name of this cape (ras), often missed out on the maps, ought in a few years' time to be well-known to tourists and travel agencies who are always on the lookout for fresh, pleasant and peaceful sites along the Mediterranean. Ras al-Bassit is to become the great, popular, and at the same time international, sea-side resort still lacking on the Syrian coast.

A thorough study, called for by the Ministry of Tourism, has brought to light the many advantages of the place: a beautiful setting, possibilities for bathing and sailing, ease of access, interesting excursions into the nearby mountains, convenience for the building of various kinds of facilities.

The setting: a large, almost perfectly semi-circular, bay surrounded by high mountains, the highest in Syria, covered with vegetation. No pollution, either in the sea or on the land. Scattered dwellings: fishermen's cottages and, now, a few camp sites and holiday villages (Casino of the Workers' Union) in the shade of the oak-and pine-woods that come right down to the shore.

The beach is black sand mixed with pebbles, and this is certainly the least agreable thing about Ras al-Bassit. But the shore is wide for the Mediterranean and slopes gently down. There is a slight tide. The expanse of water, usually calm in the hollow of this conch facing north-west, is well-suited for water-skiing and regattas.

The access road from Latakia is a delight in itself. After driving through some forty kilometres of rich plantations rising in two or three terraces from the roadside, carefully kept and ingeniously irrigated, the traveller enters the area of forests. "Oh! so you're going north... There are the forests up there!". This is the envious exclamation you hear everywhere from Syrians from the middle of the country.

Yes, indeed, real forests, forests of sea pines and... Aleppo pines, but real mountains, too. Once over a small pass, the Ras al-Bassit road suddenly opens out on to an unexpected, and very pleasant landscape: the forest all at once gives place to fields of cereal crops enclosing a vast expanse of water, a deep blue lake like a precious stone mounted in a setting of green and gold.

After the lake, the road drops rapidly through a valley of oleanders and comes to a stop at the water's edge. On the left, a sandy path leads off towards the headland of the cape; on the right a similar path leads to the camp sites and the refreshment bars along the beach but does not follow the north shore of the bay: it goes off to connect the bathing resort with the summer resort of Kassab.

1770 metres... it's not the Caucasus! But when it is the altitude of a mountain that virtually overlooks the sea, and when that mountain has a whole line of peaks in its train, and when the steep slopes are covered with a forest, albeit, of conifers, but of a density rare in this country where trees are often a luxury, then one may well be allowed to describe the landscape as exceptional.

The mountain is *Mount Cassius*, very close to the Turkish frontier. The panorama it affords over the jebels as well as over the coast is very fine. The short climb starts from the "summer resort" of *Kassab*, a village inhabited mainly by Armenians, which has several small hotels and restaurants. The white houses, with their flat roofs overhanging on to a peristyle, are ranged on the hillside. Apart from a few cypresses, the vegetation is rather sparse, but a bit higher up, the dense *Forest of Ferelloq* begins, with its sturdy trees.

Five kilometres from Kassab, the locality of *Nabheim* offers an inn, "la Verte Montagne" (the Green Mountain), whose name speaks for itself. An identical setting surrounds the village of *Qastal Moâf*, which also boasts a modest hotel, situated near the fork where the minor road to Kassab branches off the Latakia-Antakya international highway.

The complete circuit Latakia, Kassab, Ras al-Basit, Latakia covers a distance of some 150 kilometres.

Information p. 184

rasafa

■ A continuous line of ramparts, marking out a quadrangle 300m wide by 500m long in the hard soil of the steppe at the edge of the desert, is something of an archeological common-place in Syria, above all on the approaches to the Euphrates, where so many ruins lie, so many vainglorious monuments returning to dust... The ruins of Rasafa do, however, deserve special attention and more than make up for the thirty bumpy kilometres along a miserable track.

Time and again in this narrow perimeter flanked by towers, destruction and reconstruction, victory and defeat have come and gone. Potentates reigned until they fell, men suffered for their faith, pilgrims came to pay respect to their memory, treasure was amassed, only to be plundered...

Sergiopolis becomes an Umayyad city

It was thus, in particular, that a grandiose basilica came to be dedicated to Saint Sergius, a Roman officer stationed on the Euphrates, who died for refusing to deny Christ: that was in 305, under Diocletian. When Islam had overcome Christianity, one of the first caliphs, the Umayyad Hisham, came to live in Rasafa, after he had had palatial summer residences built there, which in their riches were compared with the palaces in Baghdad. But less than six years after his death in 743, the Abbassids desecrated the sepulchre of their brother enemy and destroyed every one of the buildings and the monuments he had erected.

Then the city fell prey to exhaustion. It survived for a few centuries more living off the toil of the weaving mills that wove the wool of the countless sheep that were the sole wealth of the stony wastes around.

Rasafa is now nothing but ruins, but the sheep are still here. Their wool goes to supply mills at Raqqa or Aleppo. The Bedouin nomads still water their flocks with the brackish water from the open well at the north-west tip of the rampart. What a colourful sight it is to see the swollen water skin drawn up, hauled by a mule or a camel to the accompanying sounds of plashing water, squeaking pulleys and children's cries! The rope, more than 40 metres long, shows how deep the well is.

A city of crystal

Four fortified gates give access to the town, one in the middle of each side of the rampart. The north gate, though half buried in the sand, is the most imposing and the most finely decorated. The five arches of which it is made up rest on columns with lavish Corinthian capitals. Friezes of fine sculptures follow the lines of the architecture. An impression of richness, almost of luxuriance is created using very sober means. The method is typically Syrian; it is to be found in almost all the "ghost towns" of Northern Syria and is used with even more finesse at Qalb Loza and at Qalaat Samaân in particular (see articles under these names). The exceptional interest of Rasafa lies elsewhere, therefore. Although the north face, always in the shade, has not revealed it, the smallest stone exposed to the sun will draw the visitor's attention: the city shines with a thousand lights!

The chipped cornices, the edges of the acanthuses or of the sculpted rosettes, the carved or broken blocks, all have the glint of rose crystal. Rasafa was built out of a rose-coloured marble encrusted with gypsum; the countless fragments of the shattered city catch the light like so many pieces of quartz-crystal.

Strong buttresses support the defensive wall on the inside. Made of big blocks well bonded together, they allow room for a vaulted passage to serve as a curtain. The row of arches creates an effect of alternating light and shade and the whole is bathed in an astonishing rose-coloured glow.

Of the city itself, there remain only two or three buildings that can be identified and deserve the attention of the ordinary visitor. All around is desolation; the bare and upturned land is pitted with craters as if it had come under heavy artillery fire, whereas all that has really happened, are acts of vandalism and all these thousands of holes are the work of generations of shameless treasure-seekers...

From the north gate, the *Via Recta* formed the main thoroughfare of the city. It is now no more than a pathway overgrown with grass, but lining it on either side there are still blocks of marble, the broken stumps of pillars and chunks of wall from the past. The street leads to a first building of some size: the *martyrium*, a church where, at an early date, the bodies of Saint Sergius and his companions Bacchus and Julia were laid to rest. It is a basilican church with an apse. The floor and walls are made of gypsum stone found in Rasafa and the great monolithic columns are of rose-coloured marble. The absidal chapels are well preserved; the capitals and the archway carved like lace. Unfortunately, the whole structure seems to stand only by a miracle; the keystone has already slipped more than half its height. Clearing, restoration and strengthening is urgently needed if this relic from one of the great periods of Syrian art is not to become a scatter of stones forgotten in the sand.

A hundred metres east of the martyrium stands a larger and more majestic replica of the first church, the great basilica dedicated to Saint Sergius. It has the same logical layout, the same shapeliness, the same pretty decoration and, of course, the same great beauty of the building material. Here, fortunately, some restoration work has already been begun.

Built on to the north wall of the basilica, and perhaps taken from a lateral nave of the Christian building, is a big rectangular, colonnaded hall used as a mosque in the 13th or 14th century. Two alcoves made in the church wall became mihrabs. There are both Byzantine and Arab writings which confirm that the two religions, Christianity and Islam, lived side by side at Rasafa right into the Middle Ages.

Close to the great basilica, a breach in the south-east corner of the rampart leads outside the walls to a knoll on which Caliph Hisham built his palace, with a square layout and with all the rooms opening on to a vast inner courtyard. Unfortunately, the destruction wreaked by the hatred of the Abbassids for the Umayyads and centuries of erosion of the brick have left little here to fire the imagination.

Returning to the inside of the walls, the visitor will again be delighted at the sight of the crystalline stone, just as remarkable even when reduced to pieces of debris strewn on the ground. Taking a bearing on the tall silhouette of the martyrium, he will then set off towards the south-west district of the city.

Behind the martyrium, several vaulted rooms are to be seen in a building with a central courtyard. This was a pilgrims' inn. One of the walls bears an enigmatic inscription.

A little further on at ground level are the entrances to two huge cisterns hollowed out of the rock with transverse rib vaults and walls still covered with water-tight cement. Their capacity gives a good idea of the population of Rasafa, Rasafa which is now nothing more than a tiny fragment of crystal glittering in the dreary desert.

RASAFA

Name: Variant names: Ressafe, Resafé, Rûssafa, Resapa, Rosapha. In the 4th century: Sergiopolis (Saint Sergius, martyred in 305). In the 5th century: Anastoshopolis (Anastasius, Byzantine Emperor).

Location and access: Raqqa governorate. Altitude 300 m. Archeological site about 170 km south-east of Aleppo, approximately 90 km from Al-Thaura: turning 90 km along the Aleppo-Raqqa road, then broad, well-marked track with sometimes deep pot-holes: Ressafe is 30 km to the south. Another track running from north-east to south-west connects Raqqa directly with the Ressafe ruins, but it is less clearly marked and for light vehicles there is a risk of getting stuck in the sand. No filling-station.

Accommodation: At Aleppo or Raqqa.

safitâ

■ The road climbs, undulating over hill after hill and winding its way through the olive groves. All of a sudden a pink and white town comes into view in the midst of the greenery and the flowers, huddled on the top of a small hillock above which rises a proud-looking square tower.

These are the houses of Safita, houses built of good stone, some of them covered with a terrace, others with a roof of tile. And there, standing quite upright, is one of those sturdy keeps which the Frankish conquerors erected at vantage points everywhere, thinking, in their vanity, that in this way they would shelter the annexed lands from surprise attack.

This keep fell, together with its neighbours, Chastel Rouge (Qalaat Yahmûr) and Arima (Qalaat al-Arayme), for the first time under the assault of Nur ad-Din, and then finally in February 1271, just before Sultan Beybars laid siege to Crac des Chevaliers (see entry).

The present-day township stands on the site of the fortress, which was surrounded by a double wall, the first of them almost perfectly oval in shape. It is therefore no surprise as you walk about the streets to come upon some vestiges of medieval architecture: remains of towers, part of a glacis, a vaulted room...

The keep, 28 metres high, is a two-storey structure: on the ground floor, a fortified church; above it, a large room 26 metres by 12 divided into two parts by a line of three pillars. For defence purposes, deep arrow slits are cut into the walls. A stairway leads up to the terrace, which is still partly crenellated. The view carries far into the distance. From this watch tower, the defenders could communicate by fire or signal with the other castles and even with Crac which is as much as 15 kilometres away as the crow flies.

One exceptional point worthy of note: the castle chapel has never been deconsecrated or converted into a mosque: the majority of the population have remained Christians of the Greek Orthodox faith and nowadays services are still held here.

Draykich (or Dreykich, 10 km north of Safita on the Masyaf road) is a biggish market town whose name will soon be familiar to all travellers in Syria now that water, renowned for its virtues and its purity, flowing from abundant springs here, is being bottled and marketed.

Hosn es-Sleiman (14 km beyond Draykich, in the direction of Masyaf; to the right of the road) is the Arabic name for the site of the ancient *Baetocece*. In the heart of wild mountains cut through by ravines, the inhabitants of Aradus (the present Isle of Arwad see under Tartus) had built a temple to Baal and Astarte.

South of Safitâ, two sites bring the tourist back to Crusader times again.

Arima, today *Qalaat al-Arayma* (15 km south-west of Safitâ), a forward strong-point for Chastel Blanc and for Crac, was a fortress of lesser importance, though situated on a spur at the confluence of two waterways. The walls are almost completely in ruins. Only two towers half eaten away by the shrubbery conjure up the combats of the 12th and 13th centuries. At the time of Nur ad-Din's lightning reconquest, the place fell in 1149. The lord of the castle, a certain Bertrand, was carried off into captivity together with his sister, but the sister's charms must have been great, for the fierce emir could not resist them. He married the lady from Toulouse, and she shortly bore him a son. Recaptured by the Templars, the Arima fortress was finally liberated during the decisive battles of 1271.

Chastel Rouge or *Castrum Rubrum,* today *Qalaat Yahmûr* (20 km west of Safitâ on the Tartus road, then 1km to the left), had a history very similar to that of Arima. Like Arima, Chastel Rouge was a quite small fortress, but the 15-metre high keep, placed in the centre of an enclosure 34 metres long on each side, is still impressive. The site is certainly an ancient one. Tombs dating from Roman times have been discovered not far from the castle...

Information p. 182

shahba

■ Coming from Damascus, Shahba is the first of the towns, near the Jebel al-Arab, that are sometimes incorrectly referred to as "the ghost towns of the south". Whereas "the ghost towns of the north", Qalaat Semaân, Al Bara, Kalb Loza, etc., have indeed lost almost all their inhabitants, Shahba, Kanawat and Suwayda still shelter many families, living off the produce of their gardens, and off their flocks and their vines (the Druzes distil a remarkable "arak"). In the north, the villages grew up in the valleys, leaving the skeletons of the cities isolated up on the hill-tops; here, the people have built their humble homes in the midst of the ruins or else they have quite simply set up house inside the ancient dwellings, temples, basilicas or palaces. A habit to be deplored, no doubt from an archeological point of view, but one which is of some interest to the passing tourist to whom some moustachioed and turbaned patriarch, by way of welcome, offers a draught of green coffee in the bottom of a minute cup, under vaults two thousand years old...

Philip the Arab, Emperor, was Born Here

From 232 to 237, an Arab from Syria reigned in Rome. He was a native of Shahba, an insignificant little township. During his short reign, he found time to do favour to his home town, which took the name of Philippopolis. The town was rebuilt in the Roman manner: square walls, two main thoroughfares with a tetrapylon (monument composed of four pilasters) standing at the point where they crossed in the middle, buildings in a uniform style: palace, theatre, thermae and a temple erected by the Emperor to the memory of his father. Notables and townsmen had sumptuous villas, decorated with mosaics, built for themselves.

From this past era, many fragments still remain, but they are few and far between and often spoiled despite all the efforts of the Department of Antiquities. Thus, a hideous iron railing, painted green, hits the eye as it is drawn towards four magnificent Corinthian columns, the remains of the *portico* which lined the *cardo* (still paved). Not far from here, on the left, the "*philippeion*", the temple of Philip, still has a roof over it, but reminds one more of a barn than a sacred edifice. By contrast, the *theatre* nearby has been well cleared and skilfully, though not excessively, restored and it seems all ready for some kind of festival. It is noticeable that there is practically no decoration whatsoever, since the hard basalt is an intransigent material for the sculptor's chisel; only one or two fish in relief on the lower part of the walls pointing the way for the public towards the tiers of the amphitheatre. Near the central cross-roads, there were some baths supplied by an aqueduct, some of the arches of which are still standing.

In the south-east of the town, a covered building has been put up specially to protect six big mosaics that were found here; subjects: Dionysus (the area has always produced reputable wines and spirits), Aphrodite, Orpheus, the seasons... Other mosaics are on display in the National Museum in Damascus. The keeper-guide of this small museum is very ready to talk about the area: "the fertile zone"; and about the inhabitants who, it is thought, came originally from the Yemen, fiercely individualistic; he will also let you taste his own aqua vite and ask you to buy *dolls* in traditional costume made by his wife and his daughters.

Nine kilometres north-east of Shahba, along a small tarmac road with witchbacks, is Shaka, which is not built, as its neighbour is, according to the strict Roman pattern. The houses cling to the rock on the side of a hill. The remains of ramparts and a few towers stand guard over the place.

Almost in the centre is an imposing building of heavy black stone, known as *Qaisarieh*, which was probably the Roman officers' residence when the town was promoted to the rank of "Roman colony". The main room, lit by narrow openings, has a

shaizar

stone roof made of long, heavy flags supported by corbels and wide-based semi-circular vaults, a typical feature of the local architecture. Today, the notables of the town gather here; seated on stone slabs, they hold interminable discussions. The visitor is received here, and it is here, too, that he is offered the traditional cup of green coffee. In the adjacent courtyard, the women hang their washing up to dry, the children squabble and the hens cluck.

All over the village, trunks of columns, sculpted lintels and other ancient debris are to be seen lying around on the ground or used here and there as building material.

South of the town stands an isolated edifice, known as *ad Deir*, "the convent", which consists of a three-storey tower dating from the year 176, a ruined church and some dwellings. In the northern part of the town, narrow passageways lead to a small building at the end of a courtyard, consisting of four small chambers beyond which is a larger room; a domed ceiling supported on four columns is ornamented with grapes and scrolls of leaves; finally there is a more spacious room with a ceiling of stone flags supported by a huge transverse rib arch decorated with a sort of crown: it is here that the Druzes meet to hold mysterious debates.

SHAHBA

Name: Variant names: Chahba. Around 245, as a tribute to the Emperor Philip the Arab, who was born here: Philippopolis.

Location and access: Suwayda governorate. Altitude 1,000 m. 20 km north of Suwayda. 90 km south-east of Damascus.

Information and guides: At the museum.

Accommodation: At Damascus.

SHAIZAR

Name: Variant names: Qalaat Seidjar, Shayzar, Sheizar, Cheizar. Roman period: Caesarea.

Location and access: Hama governorate. Altitude 300 m. Right bank of the Orontes. 23 km north of Hama; 30 km south-east of Apamea, by good road.

Accommodation: At Hama.

■ The Orontes, which from Hama has flowed broad and calm towards the north-west, suddenly runs up against a high reddish cliff and, as if exhausted by the shock, wanders off in several separate streams before gathering itself together again to go on and bring fertility to the Ghab Plain.

To cross the streams and connect the islands, an old hump-backed bridge, baked in the sun, spans the river on twelve piles of bricks packed round with stone to protect them from floods and earth tremors.

From the top of the cliff, a "qalaat" (a fortress) carved out of the red earth still seems, though in ruins, to dominate the valley and to stand on the lookout for the enemy to emerge from the folds of the barrier of the Coastal Chain which blocks the horizon in the west.

The site is in fact virtually impregnable. The citadel occupies a narrow spur detached from the nearby plateau and the ridge that connected it to the plateau has been dug away by human hand so as to make its isolation complete (like the Qalaat Salah ad-Din: see entry under that name). Entry, in the Middle Ages, was across a draw-bridge spanning the ravine and resting on two arched platforms; later, it was replaced by a narrow steeply sloping stone bridge. A great vaulted entrance, bearing a long inscription in Arabic above it and formerly equipped with a portcullis, leads though to a great square tower. The whole fortress makes a very impressive sight.

The interior of the citadel is obviously very delapidated, since the present-day inhabitants of Shaizar live down below in the valley. A tall keep towers over the defence works. Its flat roof looks out over an immense panorama. The knights ensconced here must have had a boundless sense of power.

But, a sign of the times, at the foot of the cliff, the bucolic charm is broken by the presence of a hydroelectric power station and, a few kilometres further upstream, the *Mhardé* dam.

sûwayda

■ The southern tip of Syria is black basalt country. The eruptive rocks that litter the ground give the landscape a very special appearance: black are the stones, black the monuments, black also are the sculptures and the ornaments.

This rather gloomy colour of the countryside is not very noticeable on either side of the international highway from Damascus through Deraâ and Hamman, since the immense expanse of the Huarân Plateau, right up until July, is a sea of ears of corn swelled by the drying wind.

But for anyone who takes the old caravan road, the one that heads off to the south-east on leaving Damascus towards Bosra (see entry), the volcanic nature of the hills outlined against the horizon is soon plain to see. Approaching Shabba (see entry), less than 90km from the capital, one can properly speak no longer of hills, but of small mountains with the characteristic shape of extinct volcanoes, together forming a range: the *jabal al-Arab* (on old maps still called jebel Druze).

Although the summits rise to between 1,500 and 1,700 metres (highest point Tell al-Kine, 1,850 m), the relief appears relatively even, for the land rises gradually and the places round about are all situated at over 1,000 metres. Westward the countryside is free of natural obstacles and a certain amount of humidity reaches the jebel al-Arab from the Mediterranean; the rainfall here is quite exceptional for Syria: 600 millimetres a year on the average, and there are a good number of springs.

Suwayda, principal town of the governorate

In the middle of this sparsely populated country with so few villages, Suwayda, the principal town, has all the appearance of a city. The many white-plastered houses and administrative buildings are almost a luxury in this land of lava. The thoroughfares are lined with trees and gardens. Schools and barracks help to create an atmosphere of lively activity.

Unfortunately, the developments that have occurred in the town over the last fifty years or so, have been to the detriment of the ancient monuments. All that is left of a temple to Dusares, the Nabatean god (1st century), are four Corinthian columns; and of a great 6th century basilica, part of the apse and a few pillars.

To limit the damage, the Department of Antiquities is having inventories made and is doing strengthening work throughout the governorate where the need is most urgent, but the profusion of ruins so widely scattered and so difficult to reach make effective conservation a rather haphazard business.

A welcome museum

The most constructive piece of initiative was the foundation of the *Suwayda Museum* (in an outbuilding of the serail, the town hall) in an endeavour to prevent the dispersion and disappearance of local finds...the finest pieces still too often slip away to Damascus!

A collection of very fine mosaics discovered in 1962 constitute the most interesting curiosity in the museum: Artemis, the goddess of chastity, surrounded by nymphs, is surprised by a hunter while bathing, a piece of Roman work of the 4th century, full of life and richly coloured; a birth of Venus, rather more heavy-handed; Neptune and the sea monsters; the wedding of Thetis and Peleus; Gaea, goddess of the Earth offering the fruits of the four seasons to Bacchus and Ariadne...

Cruder as pieces of art, but how much more strange, are the statues carved in the hard basalt: a representation of a Pantheon showing a mingling of Arab (Nabatean), Hellenistic (after the conquest of Alexander), Roman (Suwayda was one of the chief towns of the Roman province of Arabia), and Byzantine (the town was the seat of a bishopric in the 5th century) influences. Dusares rubs shoulders with Athene and Venus; Nabatean inscriptions are found close to slabs bearing the cross of Christ. An eagle, wings spread (Nabatean deity), and small but agressive female busts take on an extraordinary force when carved in the reddish rock.

A long circuit and awkward excursions

As in the case of Bosra (see entry), it is sad that there is no modern place to stay at Suwayda, which would make it easier to visit properly the sites in the region. At present, a rapid trip round the chief among the places of interest is only feasible by making an early start from Damascus and it takes a full day. Halts should be planned at Shahba and Shaka, some twenty kilometres north of Suwayda (see article on Shahba); at Suwayda, Kanawât (7km to the north-east), and Ezraâ (35km to the east), returning to Damascus by the international highway.

This route leaves out Bosra which can be given a day to itself (Kanawât and Ezraâ are covered in special entries). A quick visit to Bosra, and to Ezraâ (on the way back via Deraâ) can be fitted into one single day by sticking to the essential sights. The complete tour adds up to about 300 kilometres, from Damascus and back to Damascus.

Any detour along the tracks leading to those many small villages in the jebel al-Arab that possess some vestiges of the past, such as, *Tafha, Mûshannaf, Sâlé, Miyamas, Sahouet al-Kader,* is out of the question.

The sights would also be worth the journey in this countryside still lacking in any tourist facilities: villages perched on the slopes of volcanoes, springs watering genuine oases, cliffs of lava, the immensity of the oriental desert, *al-Hamad,* where the golden sand mingles with the black slabs of volcanic debris. With experienced and suitable vehicles a journey across al-Hamad is conceivable between Suwayda and Sabaa Biâ on the Damascus-Baghdad road, after first crossing another volcanic range, the *jabal Siss* well-known to archeologists for the many rock graffiti drawn by generations of nomadic shepherds in the early centuries of the Christian era, the inscriptions being written in a dialect close to Arabic.

SUWAYDA

Name: Variant names: Soueida, Sowaida, Es Suweidiya. Nabatean period: Soada, "little blackie" (the town is built of volcanic rock). Roman period (3rd century): Dionysias (the region produces a very good grape).

Location and access: Principal town of governorate. Altitude 900 m. 90 km south-east of Damascus, by direct route, via Shahba, asphalted; 125 km by Deraâ road (wide, but worsened by heavy lorry traffic), as far as Shaykh Miskin (80 km from Damascus), then turning left for Ezraa.

Information: At the museum.

Accommodation: At Damascus. On the spot, three *B establishments.

TARTUS, p. 196

Name: Variant name: Tartous (French name very often used). Phoenician period: Antaradus (facing Aradus island, today Arwad). Byzantine period: Constantia. Crusader period: Tortose.

Location and access: Principal town of governorate. Port on the Mediterranean. 95 km west of Homs. 90 km south of Latakia, by coast road, well maintained but carrying heavy traffic. 55 km north of the Syrian-Lebanese frontier post at Arida. 80 km from Tripoli; 170 km from Beirut.

Information: Tourist Bureau in the new Municipal Building.

Accommodation: The New Damascus**B, 10 rms, tel. 20910; Danyal*A, Abdel Azir street, 23 rms., tel. 20581; Al-Sufara*A, Tarik Ibn Ziad street, tel. 20183. Renting of chalets with kitchenette, water-closet and refrigerator, on the beaches near Tartus: Al-Jazireh; The New Chalets, near Masbah Al-Jazireh; Al-Shate-Al-Akhdar, at Tartus-Al-Bousayra. On the Isle of Arwad, at present no tourist accommodation, but many restaurants, cafés.

tartûs

Large, big-bellied and brightly painted boats sail back and forth between the city of Tartus (Tartûs) and the Isle of Arwad, lying flat on the blue surface of the sea a few miles off shore.

The boats leave from the fishermen's harbour where what seem to be old Mediteraenan tartanes to have appear been left behind. From out at sea, the honey-coloured town, huddled in the centre between the ruins of ramparts on the sea-front, appears to be pulled towards the north where the shapes of industrial developments are a sign of its newly acquired status as an oil port. To the south is a flat sandy coast that looks like an unbroken beach. In the background, green hills roll away towards the distant peaks of the Ansariya.

At the end of the short forty-minute crossing, the scene changes, but is no less appealing to the visitor. The Isle of Arwad, round and tightly-packed like a bee-hive, consists of a conglomeration of houses and of strongholds. The sea beats up against the foot of the walls. There is no tree and not a single piece of vegetation in sight. There is only one open space, and a rather confined one at that, which serves both as quayside, wharf and forum, and which looks on to the busy harbour full of sailing-boats and fishing-smacks of all colours. Souvenir-sellers add to the bustle, and restaurants built out on piles overlook the little port. Some way off on the other side of a jetty lies another, deeper harbour to take the decked vessels. A maze of narrow streets lead up to the highest point on the island where a 13th century stronghold raises its crenellated walls.

Unparalleled in the eastern Mediterranean

Arwad is a lively and colourful place whose picturesqueness is quite without artifice. Tartus itself is also worth more than just a quick visit. Together, the two places could well look forward to a tourist future that would make them among the best-known resorts on the eastern Mediterranean.

It would not take much: some cash, certainly, to put up one or two good class hotels (the island's old fort would make a marvellous "parador"), but above all a bit of imagination from the municipal authorities and a bit of concern from the local people for the attractiveness of the places where they live.

Priority has rightly been given to the industrial development of Tartus. The port was fitted out with loading installations in record time to enable it to cope with the flow of oil along a new pipe-line 650 kilometres long from Qaratchok. Might not this kind of vigorous approach be used in other spheres as well? Some of the work done, such as the (as yet incomplete) clearing of the sea fromt and the remarkable conversion of the Crusader cathedral into a museum give cause for hope.

The greatest period in the history of *Antaradus,* as Phoenician port on the mainland, annexed to the active island base of *Aradus* (the present Isle of Arwad), occurred in Byzantinetimes. The name gradually changed into *Tortosa.* Crowds of Christians used to come here on pilgramage to pray in a chapel which was said to have been dedicated to the Virgin Mary by Saint Peter, when the Father of the Apostles was on his way from Jerusalem to Antioch. An ikon was placed here, so they say, by Saint Luke the Evangelist, the same ikon that the Covent of Said Naya today claims to possess (see article under Mâloulâa).

Muslim, then Byzantine again around the year 1000, Tortosa was to become one of the main supply ports for the Crusades and a military base of considerable importance, held by the Templars.

In 1188, Salah ad-Din reconquered the town, but could not capture the keep, surrounded as it was by a broad ditch, equipped with advanced engines of war and defended by the best knights of the Order. Tortosa was to remain in the hands of the Franks until 1291. The struggle was then an unequal one, and the last defenders had to flee in a pitiful manner through a postern-gate which can still be seen at the foot of the keep leading straight down to the sea. Rwad Island (Arwad) was not liberated until 1302.

The few remains of the medieval fortress and its double wall are lost in the midst of the present-day town and little is left to stir the imagination. The town itself, however, with its tiny streets and narrow passageways, does convey something of the atmosphere of the medieval city, while the square foundations of several towers are to be seen on the sea front, a pointed-arch gate-way at the north entrance to the town and some fragment of arrises and some sculpted consoles on one side of a square that corresponds to the great hall where the Chapter of the Templars gathered. Not very much in view of the past importance of Tortosa.

The cathedral, a jewel of Romanesque art

Fortunately, the cathedral at least has been saved from damage. Skilful maintenance has brought it down to us intact. The conversion of it into a museum (it was converted into a mosque in the last century) will safeguard it from any future deterioration.

Purity of line allied with sober materials, giving an architectural strength itself the symbol of a living faith, is not this a definition of medieval Christian art? It fits the Cathedral of Notre-Dame de Tortose perfectly. Even the main door way, which is a piece of reconstruction, blends in fully with the whole building. Five windows with broad embrasures, emphasised by fine colonnettes, are the sole and sufficient ornament of a facade of otherwise military austerity. There is indeed, moreover, something of the fortress about this solid, squat edifice flanked by very salient buttresses and leaning against two towers whose walls are pierced by narrow arrow slits.

The interior is in marked contrast. The medieval rigour is now relaxed. The high central nave divides into four pointed vaults. The side-aisles with their rib-vaults follow the same pattern. The stone-work of the three apses is done with the greatest of care. The Mediterranean light streams in through the triple window in the facade and through the choir windows on to the delicate pink stone. The capitals are an imitation of the Corinthian type, but with great variety in the leaf patterns: broad curling leaves, crockets opening out into graceful eglantines, central rosettes with sometimes a small human head in their place...

One of the curious features of the church is found on the second pillar on the left-hand side of the nave. Its base is lodged in a cubical piece of masonry pierced by a low vault. This is probably the entrance to the old Byzantine chapel through which the pilgrims passed in the 4th or 5th century to make their devotions to the ikon of the Virgin and take communion at the altar of Saint Peter.

The museum that has now been arranged inside the cathedral is of recent design and gives a careful display of a selection of objects found locally or at the great sites along the Syrian coast: in the right aisle, remote antiquity; in the central nave, the Islamic period; in the left aisle, recent folklore.

Antiquity and folklore

Antiquity: Ugarit-Ras-Shamra show-case (site near Latakia (see entry for Latakia); Tell Soukas show-case (see entry for Jable); bigger show-cases for finds made at Amrit (the site is attached to Tartus): lamps, small statues, human figures from the 4th century B.C.; prettily draped busts, Venus in terracotta, bronzes, surgical instruments of the Graeco-Roman period, etc. In the central apse, a monumental sarcophagus ornamented with rose gar-

TARTUS

*The Isle of Arwad with its huddle of houses
and forts is picturesque without seeming contrived.
Closely linked with historic and modern Tartous
it could become a major tourist resort.
Plans for this are under consideration.*

lands, pine-needles, and representations of Eros, dating from the 2nd century A.D. (rather crude craftsmanship).

Islam: porcelain, faiences, terracotta, glassware, mosaics. Chiefly floral decoration with the pomegranate as the predominant motif.

Christianity: In the left apse, a medieval fresco found in the chapel of the Crac des Chevaliers.

Folklore: In this area with a seafaring tradition, the objects collected here are mainly to do with the sea, fishing and navigation: shells, madrepores, fish, models of ships and sailing boats, fishing-nets and fishermen's clothing; there is an earthenware crater 1.20 metres tall used for carrying wine. There are posters describing the importance of the Isle of Aradus (Arwad) for trade and transport in Cananaean times. As a self-governing kingdom, the island also provided a place of refuge for the peoples of the coast at the time of the Assyrian invasions and the refugees were made responsible for keeping the people of Aradus supplied with drinking water. The port and the city that were thus in close relation with the island, did not in fact stand on the site of the present Tartus, but occupied a section of the coast 10 kilometres further south; they have gone down in history by the name of Amrit in Cananaean times and later, under Greek influence: Marathos.

Amrit-Marathos, a dependency of Arwad

Several coastal towns served as "mainland suburbs" for the Aradians on their island stronghold: Paltos (Arab al Mulq, between Jable and Baniyas), Balanea (Baniyas), Carne (Al Qarneine, south of Baniyas), Antaradus (Tartus), Enhydra (Tell Qhamqa, near the present Lebanese frontier). The most prosperous, perhaps because closest to the tiny, but powerful metropolis, was *Amrit-Marathos*. In the 3rd century B.C., under the Seleucids, the colony made an attempt to free itself from the domination of the Aradians, but the people of Aradus had no hesitation in destroying the town which had served them for more than a thousand years.

Finely decorated cups, elegantly shaped vases, bronze tools and, above all, admirable figurines, whose smile expresses pleasure in life and untrammeled intelligence, testify to the degree of civilisation attained at Marathos-Amrit. These souvenirs are assembled (apart from the showcase in the Tartus Museum) in one of the rooms of the Syrian National Museum in Damascus.

Outside the museum, a necropolis and a temple are all that appears to remain of the vanished town.

Seven kilometres south of Tartus (Homs-Tripoli road, then track suitable for motor vehicles to the right), two strange monuments stand on the summit of a tell, overgrown by the heath and adjacent to some military installations (photography forbidden in that direction); they are sorts of towers or landmarks, one of them pyramid-shaped, the other phallic. The local people call them "*Maghazel*", the spindles. The cylindrical one stands on a base flanked by four lions, unfortunately now rather dilapidated. An indented double crown sits on the top. The other is entirely without ornament. At the foot of these monuments and round about, tombs and burial vaults have been carved out of the rock. The biggest of them p 'ably belonged to the kings of Aradus (Arwad) and to the rich families of Amrit.

The temple that has been uncovered 1,500 metres or so to the north is no less intriguing. Like the "spindles", it is thought to date from the 5th century B.C. It consists of a vast sunken area (about 50 metres by 40 metres, and 3 metres deep) in the centre of which stands a naos, the central part of the temple, resting on a rock pedestal. The sanctuary was dedicated to some aquatic deity and was surrounded by water from a sacred spring gushing from an open grotto in the east side of the temple.

Information p. 195.

thaura (al)

■ There is something rather pathetic about seeing a new town rise up out of the sand. And when it is an administrative and industrial town that must be "operational", as they say, even before it is finished, there is little point in dwelling upon aesthetic issues: it has all beeen aligned by surveyors, and concrete reigns supreme. But one can already feel life beginning to take hold of the anonymous blocks, to flow through the oversized arteries and along the brand new railway line.

Al-Thaura, "the Revolution", is the capital of the Dam.

Here, when people talk about "the Dam", they do not only mean the huge dike that holds back the Euphrates: 4,500 metres long, 60 metres high, 512 metres wide at the base, 41 million cubic metres of rock, earth and clay. The Dam is also the lake, Al-Assad: 80 kilometres long, 12 billion cubic metres of water; and the hydroelectric power-station: 800,000 kwh today, 1,100,000 tomorrow; and the 640,000 hectares of agricultural land brought under cultivation. The Dam means the whole social life of the peoples of the Euphrates Basin, which is destined to undergo the most sweeping changes in less than a generation.

Gone already are the fears of devastating floods. Experimental farms and agricultural colleges are pointing the way to the future.

The plain is scattered with new villages. Over here, the houses are single-storey blocks, white as dominoes placed on the sand; over there, other dwellings built of the traditional clay are built in the "sugar-loaf" shape so ideally suited to the climate of the area. Sometimes the two designs are intermingled. There are several of these new housing areas to be seen between the Aleppo-Raqqa road and the lake.

A problem of a different kind raised by the filling of the reservoir was satisfactorily solved thanks to effective international action, called for by the Syrian Government and coordinated by Unesco, backed by the experience gained in saving the monuments of Nubia. Inventories were drawn up and a number of archaeological sites along the banks of the Euphrates were excavated and surveyed before they were finally submerged, and a number of interesting monuments from the reservoir zone were rescued, either by protecting them or by transplanting them. This exemplary exercise, and the remarkable results achieved between 1967 and 1974, are illustrated in one of the rooms of the Aleppo Museum.

Out in the field, the visitor can see at leisure three typical edifices that have been quite literally saved from drowning: the citadel of Jabar, the Maskana minaret and the minaret of Abû Hurayra.

From the top of the dam, in the distance, on the other bank, a pink fortress can be seen with its reflection in the blue water of the lake. It is the *Qalaat Jabar,* surrounded by two walls broken by thirty-five towers of different shapes: four-, five-, six-, eight- sided or half-moon shaped. Today it stands on an islet joined to architecture, dating from the time of Nur ad-Din (12th century) is unique of its kind. The facades of the towers are richly decorated with ornamentation and inscriptions. The citadel, which has been cleared, strengthened, restored and protected from damp from the lake, is to be made into a tourist centre. There will be a museum here where objects found in the region of the lake will be displayed.

The *Maskana minaret* is a brick tower 27 metres high. It was first scaffolded up by the department of Antiquities and then cut into segments which were transported to the edge of a cliff overlooking the lake, near the new village of Maskana, at an altitude of 345 metres; there the segments were reassembled.

The same exercise was undertaken for a similar minaret, this time only 18 metres high, which was transported from the place called *Abû Hârayra,* near the village of Krein, to the centre of the new town of Al-Thaura, thus establishing a link between a rich past and a promising future.

Information p. 208.

ugarit

■ The keeper of the site offers visitors (apart from a very well produced explanatory leaflet) a "souvenir" which some will regard as the most original one can bring back from Syria: a little rod of clay as big as your finger moulded simply and engraved with cuneiform signs... The signs are letters and in a row they make up the alphabet: *the oldest alphabet in the world*.

The alphabet, an invention of genius

The original of this "document" is exhibited under triple glass in the Damascus Museum. It is recognised as dating from the 14th century B.C. There is some controversy as to whether this alphabet of thirty cuneiform letters is earlier or slightly later than a linear alphabet found at Byblos, the letters of which are based directly on Egyptian hieroglyphs. Be that as it may, the order of the letters is identical and proves the kinship between the two. Carried by the Phoenicians, the alphabet was to be adopted by the Greeks, the Etruscans and the Romans; and it is this alphabet which is used today by a large number of the peoples of the world.

The invention of the alphabet was at least as important for mankind as the invention of printing was to be, three thousand years later. Before the alphabet, writing was the privilege of a caste: the "scribes", who were the only ones who knew how to use hieroglyphs and ideograms and to mix them in learned combinations to reflect the meanderings of the mind. The inspired idea of using only a limited number of signs, no longer representing entities, but sounds, and of grouping these signs together in an unchanging order, made it possible, almost from one day to the next, for anyone whoever he might be, king, merchant or village yokel, freely to put down and convey his thoughts, in short, to write.

Though this little finger of dried loam is the most exciting discovery for the mind made at Ugarit, it is not the only one. The rooms devoted to this site in the Damascus and Aleppo Museums (and at the Louvre in Paris) are evidence of the activity and richness of this ancient port whose origin is lost in the mists of prehistory. The golden age of Ugarit came between the 16th and the 13th century B.C. The town was in constant relation with Egypt, Cyprus, the islands in the Aegean Sea, Mycenae... Gold ornaments, bronze weapons and ceramic vases were discovered, laid as offerings, in cellars directly under the subsoil of the houses. The royal palace consisted of ninety rooms laid out around eight inner courtyards. Thousands of engraved tablets were collected in the archives, in two private libraries and in two religious libraries.

The documents discovered exhibit great variety: diplomatic, legal, economic, administrative, scholastic and religious texts.

Twenty tablets have likewise yielded us a set of mythological poems of great poetic beauty. Older than the Illiad and the Odyssey, they must henceforth be numbered among the most ancient literary monuments known today.

Even so the site is not very evocative for the unschooled visitor. It needs the eyes of an expert to pick a way through the labyrinth of stones three-quarters buried beneath the brambles and the thistles cropping up through the bumpy surface of the immense mound. Furthermore, at every step one could easily break one's neck in the ground-level openings to funeral vaults, the entrance stairways of which have very often disappeared.

This thirty-letter alphabet, found at Ugarit, is considered to be the most ancient in the world. Links have been established between these signs and the alphabets most widely used today. (Photo Ministry of Tourism.)

ALPHABET D'UGARIT

UGARIT	Alph. Latin	Alph. Arabe	UGARIT	Alph. Latin	Alph. Arabe
⪫⪪	A	أ	⋎	ḏ =	ذ
⪫⪪⋎	B	ب	⪫⪫⪫	N	ن
⋎	G	ج	⪫⋎	ẓ =	ظ
⋎	ḫ =	خ	⋎	S	س
⪫⪫⪫	D	د	◊	' =	ع
⪫	H	ه	⪫	P (F)	ف
⪫⋎	W	و	⋎⋎	ṣ =	ص
⋎	Z	ز	⪫⋎	Q	ق
⋎⋎◊	ḥ =	ح	⪫⋎⋎	R	ر
⪫⋎◊	ṭ =	ط	⋎	ṯ =	ث
⋎⋎⋎	Y	ي	⋎	ġ =	غ
⪫⪫	K	ك	⪫	T	ت
◊⋎⋎	š =	ش	⪫	I	إ
⋎⋎⋎	L	ل	⪫⋎	U	ؤ
⋎	M	م	⋎⋎	(S)	(س)

204 UGARIT

The town, built on a natural hill, was girdled about with defences. A *fortified postern* gave access to it, and this structure, though it faces the present car-park and has been reproduced time and again in photographs and post-cards, may go unnoticed by many visitors, who, without the slightest ill-will, may well mistake it for a gully-hole... What an astonishing piece of architecture this vaulted passage is, however, built in a zigzag, opening out on to ditches where the frogs croak, with its arched section following the line of the 45° slope that served as the glacis of the citadel. The remains of a tower show the defensive purpose of these buildings.

Whether you make way into the town through the old postern or, more simply, by the path leading to the house of the keeper and seller of entrance tickets, you all the same end up on a path overgrown with brushwood, which corresponds to the main street.

To the right of the main street, and therefore immediately behind the fortified postern, stood the *royal palace,* whose somewhat confused layout is rather difficult to make out. Ugarit was an independant kingdom from the 18th century B.C. Its military and economic history, as well as the names of its kings, have been revealed in detail by the tablets found in the archives of the palace.

It was thus learned that the excellent relations existing between Ugarit and Egypt endured even after the conquest of Syria by the Pharaoh Thutmose III in the 15th century. Ugarit as a State, was not however to survive the invasion of the Philistines, the tribes that came down from the north, sometimes called the Sea Peoples, and overwhelmed the country at the end of the 13th century B.C. This hill overlooking a sandy bay was henceforth no more than a stage and a periodic refuge for the Greek fishermen. The stables and outbuildings of the palace were aranged on the left of the palace, while behind it was the residential district, where the layouts of vast, rich dwellings can be seen on the ground. Weapons and works of art were found here, as well as the library of a diplomat named Rapanou. This Rapanou must have had an encyclopaedic mind, since he preserved, apart from his official correspondence, sorts of dictionaries containing lists of animals and deities, and of weights and measures then in use, and even an account of the way to treat sick horses...and still more precious for philologists, a comparative lexicon of Sumerian, Hurrian, Babylonian and Ugaritic words.

Under the protection of El, Baal and Dagôn

By climbing through the brush to the highest point on the tell, the visitor can gain a better idea of the general layout of the town: palaces and fortresses face south, the landward side, the side for relations with the peoples from inland; on the slope going down towards the sea, the commercial and harbour districts (the shore has now sanded up and receded a good hundred metres); opposite, quite compact, popular districts traversed by narrow streets; up here, on this sort of acropolis, the part for the gods, the temples.

One temple was dedicated to Bâal, supreme god of the Cananaean, Phoenician and Aramean pantheon. In poems found at Ugarit, Bâal won kingship among the gods with the help of his sister, Anat. Their father, El, is the father of the gods and of men.

A second temple was dedicated to Dagôn (or Dagan), the god of fertility, the god of wheat, particularly honoured by the Amorites, a nomadic people from Upper Syria, of whom Hamurabi, at Babylon, was the most famous king.

The priests' houses and the funerary vaults stood between the two temples. Treasures buried in hiding-places and hundreds of engraved tablets have been discovered. A high priest, who no doubt practised divination, kept terracotta pebbles in his library, shaped like livers or lungs, after having first engraved on them

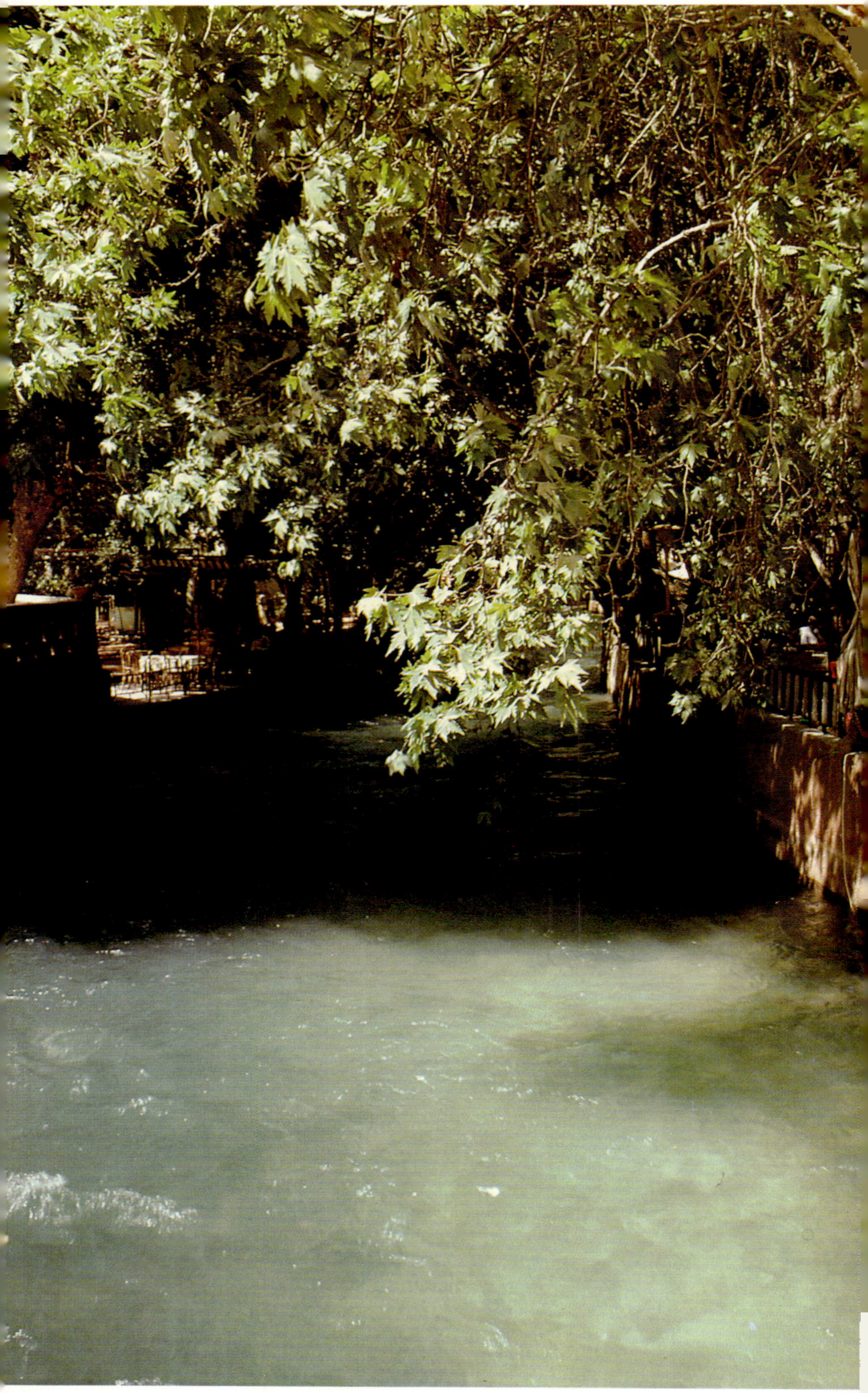

*The life-giving waters of the Barada spring
from an underground source near Zabadani.
Its short but fertile and delightful valley is a popular resort
of the Damascenes on Fridays and throughout the summer.
(Above, photo Jacques Guillard.)*

zabadani

the answers to questions put to him by his clients.

These examples go to show that no visit to the site of Ugarit can yield its full meaning unless it is supplemented by visits to the Tartus, Damascus and Aleppo Museums, where fine examples of the rich treasures unearthed here are expertly displayed.

Returning from the temple area towards the exit (and the cafeteria near the keeper's house), the visitor walks along the side of a dig being made by the archeologists to study a deep stratigraphic cross-section. Another section has also been cut in the main courtyard of the royal palace. These soundings have produced firm evidence of the occupation of the site since the Neolithic Era towards the beginning of the fourth and perhaps even into the fifth millenium. Out at sea, the cargo-boats sail by, heading for the port of Latakia...

UGARIT (RAS SHAMRA)

Name: The name Ugarit appears in a text dating from the 18th century B.C. found at Mari.

Location and access: Latakia governorate. Hillock by the sea, near the village of Minet al-Beida, 16 km north of Latakia, either by the coast road as far as Blue Beach, then turn right, or by the Antakya road for 15 km and then turn left.

Information: Keeper on the spot. Admission fee.

Accommodation: At Latakia. Cafeteria on the spot.

THAURA (AL) p. 201

Name: "The Revolution", name officially adopted at the wish of the dam workers, in 1974. Previously: Tabka, Tabqa.

Location and access: Raqqa governorate. Altitude 1,100 m. New town in the immediate vicinity of the dam and Lake Assad. 140 km east of Aleppo on an excellent road. 60 km west of Raqqa; 190 km north-west of Deir-ez-Zor; Trains twice a day to Aleppo.

Information: Permission to visit, take photographs or stay: Ministry of the Euphrates, Public Relations Department, on the spot or in Damascus, ave. Adnan al-Malky. Brochures in several languages.

Accommodation: At Aleppo. On the spot, with permission, in one of several newly built hotels.

■ Every Friday, and quite often on summer evenings too, a continuous line of cars and coaches leaves Damascus by the Beirut road and, once up on the plateau some thirty kilometres away, turns right in the direction of Blûdân and Zabadani. Other Damascenes crowd onto the narrow-gauge train that puffs its way up the valley of the Barada. All these people are off in search of fresh air, (relative) coolness and green. There is no lack of water, running water, at that.

Zabadani, its houses widely scattered over the countryside, stands in the centre of a broad valley dominated by high ridges. Poplars everywhere sing in the wind. Everywhere fruit trees, vegetable plots and gardens flourish. Small detached houses, looking gay in their brightly coloured coats of pebble-dash, lie scattered on the slopes up to an altitude of about 1,500 metres, where the greenery gives place to orange-coloured rock.

Evocative names, such as "the Vine", "Paradise", or "The Green Plain", are painted over pleasantly situated restaurants, beside which are playgrounds for children and adults.

Half way up the slope stands the recently renovated "Grand Hôtel de Blûdân"; it offers the advantage both of being very comfortable and of having a pleasant and magnificently situated park, not to mention its reputation for excellent cuisine. Games and a swimming-pool make it an ideal place for tourists, equally suitable for a few hours' relaxation or for a longer stay.

Dozens of small streams come cascading down from the numerous springs at the upper end of the village of Blûdân. One of them, the *Bokkein* spring, is famed for its curative virtues and for its agreable taste, and its waters are tapped off into bottles and sold as table water. It is the second source of marketed mineral water in Syria, the other being located at Draykich, near Safitâ (see article under the latter name).

The Barada is the rushing stream of clear water to which the Ghouta at Damascus owes its fertility, and Damascus, quite simply, owes its life.

Before flowing away along channels and irrigation ditches finally to peter out in the sands the Barada lingers for a while on the plateau of Zabadani, and it is to this that Zabadani owes its smiling features.

The cheerful springs of the Barada

The main source of the Barada is one of the local beauty spots. A Vauclusian spring, it provides a vast pool of deep, clear water full to the brim at all seasons of the year, and therefore an ideal place for canoeing, bathing and picnicking. (5 km before reaching the centre of Zabadani, take the road to the left for about 3 km. The site is signposted).

The Barada leaves the gentle valley of Zabadani on a level with the village of *Takiye,* crouching on a spur enveloped in greenery and loud with the song of birds. In earlier times the waters have hollowed a deep, narrow furrow out of the ochre limestone. The cliffs are being quarried and you can find sepulchral grottoes in them, while at the bottom of the fresh and wooded ravine the stream is lined with wayside cafés. There is hardly room for the railway and the road to pass. The village houses are ranged on steep slopes.

Abel's tomb, a magnificent vantage point

At the town of *Ayn al-Fijeh* buried amongst the trees, there is another spring, a permanent one, more abundant than the Barada itself, which is now in capitiviy, since its particularly clear water is reserved for the Damascus water-supply, Damascus which soon makes its presence felt, through the dust from the cement works at *Doummar* seven kilometres from the centre of the city.

A hundred and fifty metres to the right of the Beirut road, Zabadani road crossroads, a stony track starts to climb up towards the top of the hills. Several paths branch off to the right. One should keep on bearing left up towards the summit. After 6.5 kilometres or so, a white-washed dome comes into view, set as it were, curiously, in a blockhouse of plain concrete. Nothing can be seen of the inside, for the windows and doors are boarded up with sheets of metal and iron bars. It matters little, though. All that counts is the view. The site rises above the Barada and one of its small tributaries and one looks down into the fault through which the river winds its way like a slender furrow of vegetation and of life, overhung by cliffs that are golden, white or purplish-blue depending on the way the light falls. The range of greys is infinite.

As for the monument, it is said very humbly to be the "tomb of Abel", Abel himself, the second son of Adam and Eve, murdered by the wicked Cain! At least, that is the claim of members of a certain sect, who come here every year on a pilgrimage.

ZABADANI

Name: Variant names: Zebedani, Zbadani, Zebdani.

Location and access: Damascus governorate. Altitude 1,100 m. 50 km north-west of Damascus along the Beirut road for 25 km then right on to the Takiyé road, or by the Beirut road for only 10 km, then taking the Ayn al-Fijé road through the Barada valley. Railway service on Fridays and Holidays.

Accommodation: Around Zabadani: *Al-Kindi***A, tel. 1437. *Tourist'Hôtel* (Al-Syahawal Istiaf)**B, tel. 1149; *Al-Zafraan**C, tel. 1609; *Ksar Al-Omara**A, tel. 1070. Plus three another establishments. At *Blûdân* (1,500 m. commanding position above Zabadani) *Grand Hotel* (Blûdân Al-Kabir)****L, extended and completely renovated, very comfortable, outstanding situation, swimming pool, garden, tennis court, renowned for its cuisine, 101 rms., tel. 1551; *Nadaff***A, tel. 1345; *Al-Sahle Al-Akhdar***B, tel. 1566; *Ramsis***B, tel. 1352. Plus 7 * establishments.

Restaurants: Many cafés and restaurants in the valley and at Blûdân, pleasantly situated by waterfalls or under the tress.

the syrian journey

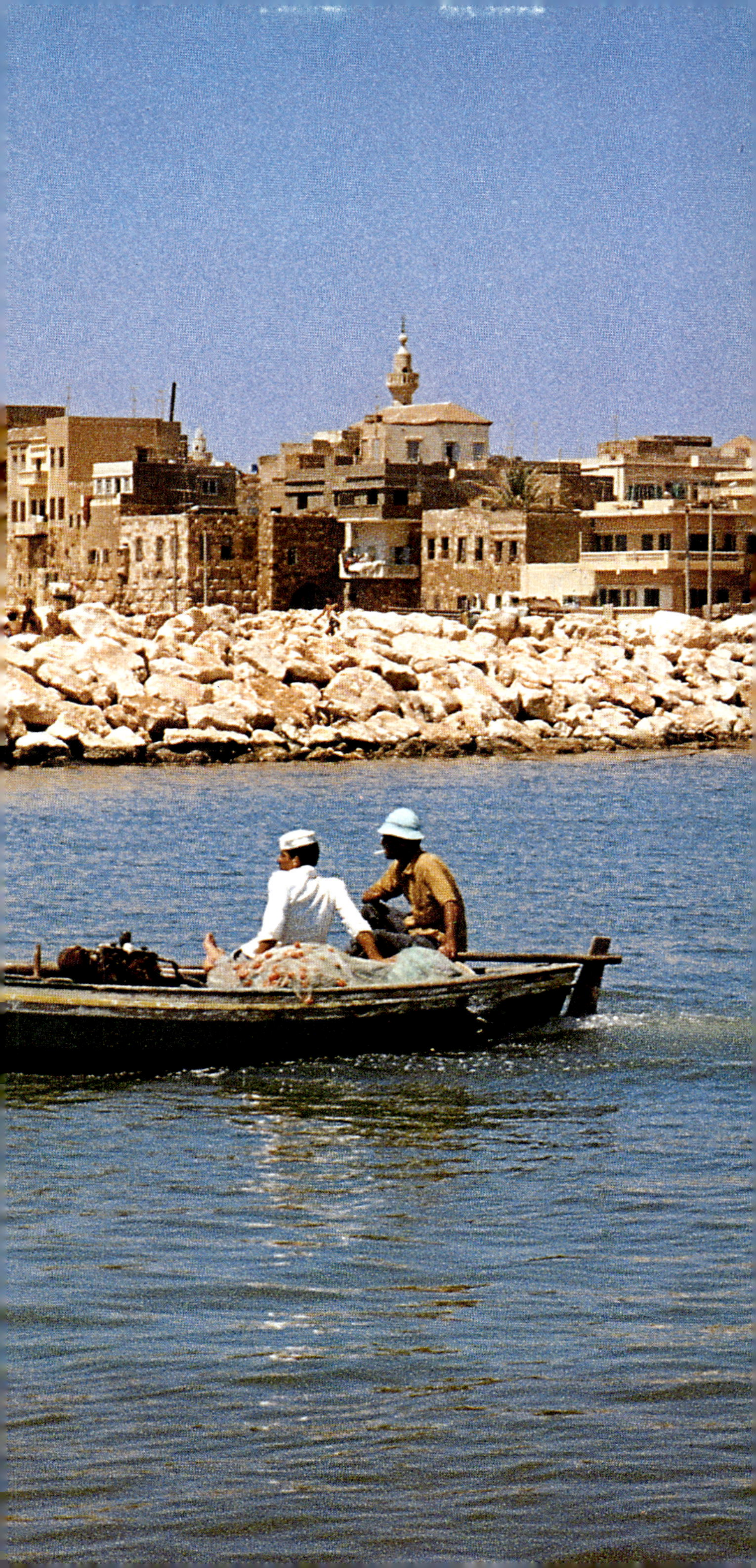

getting to syria

See map p. 226

By air

Damascus International Airport is becoming a major junction for the Near East. The national airline *Syrian Air* (still widely known as *Syrian Arab Lines*) has extended its network in Europe to Paris, London, Berlin and Moscow; in Asia to Delhi, Dubai, Sanaa and Beirut; in Africa to Cairo. Its fleet consists of Caravelles and Boeings 727 and 747. International airlines of all three continents, as well as Panam from the United States, fly to Damascus and maintain offices there.

The flying time from Paris to Damascus, by 747, is 4hrs 35 min.

Damascus time is three hours ahead of G.M.T.

Tourist excursion fares (the YE tariff) are available for visits of more than ten days but less than a month.

By road

The E.5 international highway, starting from London, crosses Yougoslavia, forks at Nis for Sofia (but an alternative route via Thessaloniki avoids the need for a Bulgarian visa) and reaches Asia via the Bosphorus Bridge at Istanbul. It then crosses Turkey via Ankara, Adana and Iskenderun. Syria can be entered either at Bab al-Hawa, for Aleppo; or at Kassab, for Latakia.

It is a long, often monotonous, journey; but the roads are good and quite fast. From London, Paris, Amsterdam or Frankfurt it takes five or six days—even with good driving. But it is so important to have one's own transport in Syria itself that this double journey is more or less inevitable—providing one has the time. By combining road and sea (see under Car Ferries) the journey can be made much pleasanter, if not much shorter.

For Western Europeans no visa is necessary for any country entered on the journey, except for Bulgaria, where a three-day transit visa can be obtained at the frontier. Green Card motor insurance is similarly valid for the journey, but it is not yet accepted in Syria.

To enter Syria with a car a *Customs Certificate* must be produced; it is obtainable from Automobile Clubs and Touring Clubs against a deposit of quarter of the current market value of the vehicle. The same organizations issue an *International Driving Licence* (on production of a national licence) which is technically obligatory in all countries where the Latin alphabet is not used—Greece, Yugoslavia, Arab countries.

Approaching from the East, the Teheran-Baghdad-Damascus highway is excellent; the road up through Jordon, from Akaba on the Red Sea (the terminus of the E.5), is good, with stretches of motorway.

By rail

This is somewhat lengthy trip but one that will appeal to railway enthusiasts. The Orient Express (the term alas, is no longer technically correct) links Paris and Teheran. By changing at Ankara, Kayseri, or Adana, in Turkey, Aleppo can be reached, by the "Taurus Express."

By sea

There are as yet no car ferries to Latak. Beirut, however, used to be served—from Greece, Cyprus and Alexandria—and Damascus could then be reached in a couple of hours by road.

An attractive alternative is to take a ferry either in Italy (Venice, Ancona, Brindisi) or in Greece (Piraeus) and go as far as Turkey (Izmir, Kusadasi or Bodrum). From any of these ports it is easy to join the main road south via Aydin (after at least a glance at Ephesus and Pamukale), Dinar, Antalya, and the steep rugged coast through Alanya, Anamur, Mersin, Tarsus (home of St. Paul whom we will meet again at Damascus...) Iskenderun, Antakya, to Aleppo or Latakia. Three days should be allowed for the sea cros-

Previous pages: Tartous.
A little restoration and improvement
would make the waterfront of this old maritime city,
last stronghold of the Crusaders, an attractive shop
window for Syrian tourism.

sing and another three for the drive. Certain lines offer a mixture of cruise and car-ferry; the return journey could be made via Bodrum, Rhodes, Heraklion, Santorin and Piraeus.

These cruise-ferries are organized by Italian, Greek, Turkish and Cypriot companies and their programmes vary year by year. A good travel agent should be able to supply details.

Information and formalities

Where to enquire:
At Consulates and Embassies of the Syrian Arab Republic.
In Paris: 22 Boulevard Suchet, 75016, tél. 504.33.36; office open from 10 am to 3 pm.
In Syria:
Tourist Information Bureaux are open every day, including Fridays and holidays from 8 aun to 8 pur.
— in Damascus: at the International Airport and in the town centre, rue du 29 Mai;
— in Aleppo, rue Baron, opposite the Museum;
— in Latakia, in the town centre, place Sheikh-Daher;
— in Homs, in the town centre, place du Serail;
— in Hama, in the town centre, route d'Alep, behind the public gardens.

The offices of the *Ministry of Tourism* in Damascus are close to the place Merje and not far from Syrian Air, tel. 114.918.

The Ministry has organised a *Tourist Police Force*—young men and women who speak several languages and whose job it is to help foreign visitors at the airports and at the main sights. They can also be reached by telephoning Damascus 447.160. (The Police Emergency number is 93.)

At all the tourist sites there are official guides who come under the Ministry of Tourism; their tariff is regulated.

Police formalities

Nationals of other countries must have a valid passport and a *visa* obtainable (usually at 48 hours' notice) at the Consulate or Embassy of the S.A.R. in their country of origin. A visa (for which a cash payment is required) can also be obtained without difficulty at Damascus International Airport or at one of the land frontier posts. For group travel (at least ten persons) a collective visa suffices, but each member of the group must be in possession of a valid passport.

The entry visa is valid for six months and for an unlimited number of entries during that time.

Under the new "Tourism Pact" with Jordan a Syria visa is valid in Jordan and a Jordanian one in Syria.

If he is *staying longer than two weeks* the visitor must register with the passport division of the Sûreté authorities—this can be done either through his hotel or through the Tourist Police.

An *airport tax* of £Syr 10 is payable on leaving the country, before passing through passport control; this is payable in special stamps obtainable from a desk in the airport.

The visitor will see no policemen apart from the traffic police (all-too-few: see below). As is normal in other countries there are strictly controlled military areas where it is forbidden to take photographs of bridges, engineering works, airport installations etc.

Customs formalities

At Damascus Airport the normal system of red and green gates is in force. If the visitor has "nothing to declare" he walks through the green gate, if he has goods to declare he walks through the red one.

Goods admitted free of duty are virtually the same as in most western countries—personal effects, 200 ci-

syria by road, rail, air

garettes, a quarter of a litre of spirits, a camera, a transistor radio for personal use, etc. In order to avoid complications later on it is advisable to have the customs officer enter on the last page of one's passport, in Arabic, a list of any objects that could prove contentious—a second camera, jewellery, etc.

Motor vehicles (see above p. 212). An international driving licence and triptych or customs certificate are required. Once thus admitted the vehicle may remain in the country for a total of 180 days. Non-Arab nationals without such documents can obtain an "Entry Card" (valid for two weeks and renewable for a further two) at the frontier posts.

Arab nationals are exempt from the preceding conditions; they are issued with a "Special Passage Permit" at the frontier.

Insurance is not compulsory for visitors' vehicles. The Green Card is not recognized. A policy can be taken out at the frontier post.

Currency and cash. Foreign currency and travellers' cheques may be taken into Syria but Syrian currency may be brought in only up to a limit of £Syr25 for a Syrian resident, and £Syr100 for a non-Syrian resident. Non-residents may take foreign currency out of Syria, but only up to the amount brought in and declared. Travellers are therefore required to fill in a declaration of currency, at the customs post on arrival; this permits them to take out part or the whole of the sum when they leave. Credit cards are recognized in Syria, but they are not yet widely used.

Health formalities

There are none. A certificate of vaccination against smallpox (within the last three years) is required by western health authorities on the traveller's return.

Vaccination against cholera (within the last six months) is not required, unless the traveller comes from a contaminated country.

Roads and motorways

The north-south axis Aleppo-Damascus-Deraa has many sections of motorway (termed "autostrades" in Syria: "autoroutes" are highways, wide but with two-way traffic). In 1990 the motorway network (autostrades) will link Homs-Beirut, Latakia-Tartous, Latakia-Aleppo, Aleppo-Turkey; as well as Damascus-Beirut and Damascus-Amman, on which work is already under way.

Before 1980 one of the last "trails" will have been replaced by a modern highway—from Palmyra to Deir-ez-Zor and from Palmyra to Damascus via the desert.

The most comprehensive *map of Syria,* though the 1971 edition does not include the new motorways, is the one prepared by the Ministry of Communications and published by the Ministry of Tourism. The scale is 1/1,000,000 (10 cm = 100 km). It is on sale in bookshops and at hotel kiosks. Road maps published in Europe and covering Syria are usually sketchy, vague and inaccurate.

Road signs on the main roads are bi-lingual (Arabic-French), but they are too few and many tourist sites off the main roads are not signposted at all. Fortunately the helpfulness of the local inhabitants makes up for this.

Speeds are restricted only where there are signs to that effect. No one takes any notice of them.

Petrol stations are to be found mainly in the environs of the larger towns. Two qualities of petrol are sold, normal and premium; the latter is about 80 octane.

Thus the basic facilities are good and travel by road, even to the most distant and inaccessible areas, would present no problems if the liberties that Syrian drivers take with their Highway Code did not oblige motorists to be doubly on the alert. Excessive speed, acrobatic overtaking, overtaking on corners, systematic disregard of white lines—these are all too common. Indeed it is not rare to see vehicles being driven in the wrong direction on motorways! And one mustn't forget the hazards of carts, sheep, goats, camels and wandering donkeys. Victory goes to the driver with the loudest horn! Traffic police do exist, and they are well-equipped and competent, but they cannot be everywhere at once.

Taxis and collective hire-cars

Since there is not yet sufficient demand, a system of *selfdrive hire cars* will not be introduced in Syria until 1980. The traveller without his own car thus has to rely on taxis or on public transport. Regular bus services link many parts of the country but they are difficult to use without some knowledge of written or spoken Arabic. *Long-distance taxis*, which one can hire individually or by joining a group, are common. They are comfortable fast cars and can be used to travel from one large town to another. They are recognizable by their red number plates; the largest taxi company has painted its vehicles a distinctive shade of yellow. Rather than attempting to negotiate directly with the driver (although many speak some French or English) it is better to arrange them through one's hotel or one of the many *travel agencies* in Damascus, Aleppo and Latakia. In the towns *taxis* are the only practical and cheap form of transport.

Railways

Unfortunately the trains are slow and old-fashioned and connections are often poor, so the railways do not offer the tourist an ideal way of getting about. Nevertheless the recently-opened lines: Aleppo-Al-Thaura (Euphrates Dam) and Aleppo-Latakia, are well served by pleasant modern trains.

HOW THE SOUKS EVOLVED

At the beginning of the 6th century, some streets—which had become narrower with the building of pavements at the base of the colonnades—changed character completely in places and became what we would call pedestrian precincts. They were isolated from the traffic, which now flowed only east-west, by short flights of steps. Pedestrians now abandoned the arcades in favour of the pavements and the former were gradually used by merchants to display their goods, the various trades congregating together. This was the first step in the evolution of the souks—which J. Sauvaget the great historian of Syria has shown to derive from the great colonnaded streets of Antiquity.

JEAN-CH. BALT
(adapted)
Head of Mission at Apamea

essential information

Currency and exchange

The unit of currency is the *Syrian pound,* which is divided into 100 piastres.

There are 5, 10, 25 and 50 piastre coins, and notes for 1, 5, 10, 25, 50 and 100 pounds. The values of coins are marked in Arabic numerals only, the notes are printed in both Arabic and Roman.

Foreign currency and travellers' cheques can be freely exchanged, on presentation of passport, at Damascus Airport, at the frontier posts, in the larger hotels, and at banks (normally open from 8-30 am to 1 pm. In Damascus a Bureau de Change is open all day, every day, opposite the station, near the Orient hotel.

Days and times

Friday is the normal rest day, but some businesses run by Christians close on Sundays. In the resorts shops are open throughout the week during the season.

Government offices are open from 8 am to 2-30 pm. Private businesses often close during the day from 2 or 3 pm to 5 or 5-30 pm.

Museums are open every day, *except Tuesday,* at the following times: from 8 am to 1 pm and from 4 to 7 pm in summer (1 May to 30 September) and from 8 am to 1 pm and from 2 to 4 pm during the rest of the year.

Meals are served quite late: lunch from 1 to 3.30 pm and dinner from 8 to 11 pm.

Freedom and Communication

The foreign visitor is free to go anywhere at any time, *the language* is the only drawback, for those who don't speak Arabic. Fortunately there are many Syrians who understand English and French which they often speak perfectly. At all events their basic friendliness and hospitality is freely offered to the stranger who may be lost or in difficulty.

Sunbathing is quite in order on beaches and at swimming pools, and light clothing is accepted everywhere provided decency is observed; vulgarity and bohemian behaviour is not looked on favourably. Suitable clothes are required for visiting holy places. Shoes must of course be removed before entering a mosque and it is forbidden to pass beyond the ikonostasis in an Orthodox church.

In this Arab country where all religious beliefs are at home it is not surprising that there is a *spirit of tolerance* and respect. The Syrian merely expects this to be reciprocal. On this understanding all kinds of discussion are possible; the visitor will soon realise that he has much to learn...

The *Syrian press,* radio and television are entirely Arab language media (with the exception of a few publications in Armenian). The main French, English, German, Italian —and Chinese—newspapers are on sale in the main bookshops in Damascus.

Foodstuffs and goods of all kinds are freely available and in good supply. Cafes and restaurants are open to all but they do not all serve alcoholic drinks.

Climate and health

The coastal region enjoys a Mediterranean climate; the heat is never excessive, there is usually some breeze and humidity; March and April are often cloudy, even rainy months.

The inland region enjoys a Continental climate in which the midsummer heat is only made bearable due to the low humidity. Nights are often cool throughout the year. There are sometimes high winds and duststorms on the central uplands.

The Damascus region and some of the high valleys in the Sharqi and the coastal range (Bludan or Safita for example) enjoy an equable climate. Things are very different in the

Euphrates and Khabur basins where winters are severe and summers extremely hot.

Recommendations: The visitor should not be without sunglasses and some form of protective headgear, but he should also bring a few warmer clothes. In summer it is adivsable to carry some remedy for digestive upsets caused by the heat, and sodium and potassium tablets to prevent dehydration if he proposes to visit the desert areas or the eastern parts of the country.

Syria is a healthy country. In both large and small towns the water is clean, pure and safe to drink. There are numerous chemists and no shortage of medicines—their quality and prices are regulated by the Ministry of Health. There are both government hospitals and private clinics. With a doctor for every 2,500 inhabitants, Syria is better provided than any other Middle Eastern country as far as health is concerned.

Festival and fairs

Every year there are many artistic, economic and sporting events:
— in April, in Damascus, a Drama Festival; in Latakia, a Flower Festival;
— in May, in Damascus, the International Floralies (Flower Festival), and the Sculpture Salon;
— in July, in Suwayda, the Festival of the Vine; in Aleppo, the Industrial and Agricultural Exhibition;
— in the last two weeks of July and the beginning of August, in Damascus, the International Fair;
— in September, in Aleppo, the Cotton Festival
— in November, in Aleppo, the Sculpture Salon.

Throughout the year there are sporting events in the splendid new stadiums at Aleppo and Damascus.

The Cultural Centres (see Panorama: Human Syria) organize events and exhibitions all over the country.

THE (GOOD) RESTAURANTS OF DAMASCUS

The restaurant of the hotel Damascus International, *tel. 112.400*
Toledo, *rue Khalil Mardam Bey, tel. 333.810*
Al-Chark, *cité de la Foire, tel. 116.397*
Caves du Roi, *rue Ahmed Moureywed, tel. 330.093*
Blue Up, *rue Zahra, tel. 112.111*
Abu Kamal, *rue 29-Ayyar, tel. 115.216*
Cafetéria Etoile, *rue Mayssaloun tel. 332.286*
Ali Baba, *rue Fardoss, tel. 119.881*

IN THE BARADA VALLEY

The Green Valley, *at Rabouch, tel. 111.580*
Toledo, *at Abu-Roumanch, tel. 333.810*
Versailles (Al-Fersan), *at Abu-Roumanch, tel. 225.434*
Piccadilly (Cordoba), *at Abu-Roumanch, tel. 332.949*
Le Vendôme (Al-Bustan), *at Abu-Roumanch, tél. 338.362*
International Casino, *on the Beirut road, tel. 336.717*
Al-Kasr, *at Doummar, tel. 221.420*
Tivoly (Le Bois), *at Doummar, tel. 221.420*
Fardoss al-Jadid, *at Doummar, tel. 118.628*
Kasa al-Hir (Belvedere), *at Sahra, tel. 44*
Al-Sahl al-Akhdar, *at Zabadani*
and, said to be the best of them all,
the restaurant of the Grand Hôtel de Blûdan, *at Blûdan, tel. 15.51.*

a thousand souvenirs

■ It has already been noted (in the "Panorama" and in the entry for Damascus) how ancient crafts are far from dying out in Syria. Indeed, thanks to encouragment by the authorities, they are flourishing. Characterized mainly by originality of design, elegant decoration and fine workmanship craft products offer a thousand temptations to visitors. The following is not a list, merely an indication of the variety of materials and the forms they take.

Ancient crafts and handiwork

Textiles. The most essentially Syrian products of all are *brocades*—made from natural silk, and gold and silver thread, on looms worked by hand. The silk comes from the Homs region. The designs are called damasco, aghabani, dima, cashmere, etc. Incredibly tough, brocade is uncreasable no matter how it is folded or twisted. It is an ideal material for luxury ties and haute couture dress. Less dense materials, silks and cottons woven by machine, are embroidered with arabesques in *gold and silver thread*. Beautiful reversible tablecloths are made in this way. Cotton *stoles* are also decorated with designs in gold.

Carpets are not a particularly Syrian product; but in Aleppo there are craftsmen who specialise in rugs, usually on a red ground with symbolic geometric patterns.

Metals. Damascening—as the name indicates—is a very ancient Syrian craft. Steel, for *weapons,* and copper, for *trays,* are finely chased and inlaid with gold and silver wire. The same technique is applied to *ivory.* Gold and silver *jewellery,* often decorated with turquoise, is less authentically Syrian.

Wood. Marquetry boxes, chess-boards, and furniture are almost as fine as damascened work. Ebony, thuya, lemonwood, rosewood, pearl shell and ivory are all used.

Less fine *woodwork* is painted in bright colours in geometric or floral patterns. Chests, cupboards, bed and wooden wall decorations are treated in this way.

Simple domestic utensils: *spoons,* cake or butter-moulds, turned in the souks on primitive lathes, make cheap and attractive souvenirs.

Plaited straw. There is a wide range of baskets, mats. and seats—all at reasonable prices.

Fired wares. Pottery and earthenware are not outstanding. There is a great variety of *blown glassware,* however. Vases, flasks, lamps... in blues and greens and golds and flame colours. *Stained glass windows* too are coming back into fashion.

Stone. Several artists have rediscovered *mosaic,* while others perpetuate the typically Islamic art of geometric decoration on plaster and stucco.

Last, but by no means least, the art of fine decorative *calligraphy* is being revived.

cooking and food

■ Syrian cooking may appear to lack great variety but the dishes are always appetizing, colourful and beutifully served.

Innumerable hors d'œuvres

A special place must be reserved for the *mezza*, or hors d'œuvres, which are served in little bowls and dishes—so many that they cover the whole table. There may be as many as forty of them. One takes one's pick of radishes, celeriac, baby turnips, beans, peppers, cucumber, olives, vine leaves, lettuce hearts; green white and yellow purees, bathed in golden oil, offer flavours unknown to western palates: *hommos*, a puree of chick peas with lemon juice and sesame oil; *toum*, garlic with milk and olive oil (often served with chicken); *baba ghanouge*, a puree of aubergines with oil and lemon; *mutabal*, the same but with yoghurt... All sorts of green things are served with these dishes—parsley, chives, herbs one has never heard of, and, always, fragrant mint.

The popular national food is *burgol;* it is made of wheat that has been boiled, dried, and crushed (it is rather like semolina), it is used in many dishes. Most often it is rolled into large balls which are stuffed with minced meat, onion, nuts and pine kernels. *Tabbouleh* is another dish in which balls of burgol are served with parsley, potato, onion, oil and lemon.

Chicken is one of the favourite meats. The *farouge* is a little roast chicken, cut in two and served flat. *Poussins* are grilled and served with onions and mushrooms. *Shish taouk* is chicken on a skewer with truffles or mushrooms. More popular dishes are *kibbe mechwiye*, minced meat mixed with crushed wheat and grilled over charcoal; *kafta antakiye*, minced meat cooked on a skewer with parsley and lemon; *shish kabab*, lamb cooked on a skewer with tomato, onion and peppers. *Chawarma* consists of large pieces of meat (usually mutton) heaped one above the other on a vertical spit and roasted in front of a coal fire.

Fresh carrots, peas, broad beans, French beans, courgettes, aubergines and little gherkins called "ladies' fingers" are served with the meats and accompanied with sweetish or very spicy sauces. Potatoes are not common whilst tomatoes are served with everything. Rice is being more and more widely eaten. Mint and many other herbs unknown to us are used to flavour the vegetables.

Fish and shellfish are served almost only on the coast; they are succulent, served grilled or baked, with herbs and lemon.

Bread is made in large flat "loaves" using little yeast; it often tastes undercooked. It is better in the country—where it is baked in wood-fired ovens—than it is the towns. It is torn off in long strips which can then be used to scoop up purees, sauces and yaghurt.

Yoghurt is served in the morning. Mixed with iced water it makes a refreshing drink in the heat. Dried and salted it becomes almost the only Syrian cheese.

"All kinds of *fruit*, just about all the year round" This could be a Syrian slogan. Oranges, grapefruit, pears, apricots, figs, olives, plums, greengages, grapes, pistachios, walnuts, hazelnuts, and fresh or dried almonds—they are all offered for sale at the roadside, heaped up on the greengrocers' carts, a feature of every table. Melons are also much eaten—big *watermelons* and the smaller yellow ones.

Preserved fruits (particularly apricots) are a speciality of Damascus; Aleppo is noted for its almond paste. Great apricot *gâteaux*, and others stuffed with pistachios and dripping with honey, beckon from the windows of the many cakeshops in the capital.

Drinks

Since 1976 the pure spring waters of *Buqqayn* (near Bludan) and *Draikich* (near Safita) have been on sale

accommodation

in one and a half litre plastic bottles. They are light, contain few mineral salts and are a pleasant-tasting aid to digestion.

The vine-growing areas (Aleppo, Homs, Jabal al-Arab, Maalula and others) produce white, rosé and red wines which are often full-bodied and fruity with a pleasant bouquet. *Arak,* an aniseed-flavoured brandy, comes from the same districts.

"Stella" the national brand of *beer* is not without flavour, although it is non-alcoholic. It is pleasantly refreshing. Imported mineral waters, aperitifs, wines and beers are of course obtainable in the main hotels.

Sparkling fruit juices are gaining in popularity at the expense of the "colas." True fruit juices are drunk on the pavements, outside the little shops that specialise in preparing and mixing to order delicious cocktails of citrus fruits, cherries, carrots, bananas—all fresh and served ice-cold.

Turkish coffee (sweetish) and *tea* (strong, served in little glasses) are served at the slightest excuse throughout the day. They are often accompanied by a glass of iced water, which is welcome as they are served boiling hot.

■ The following exhaustive list was compiled at the end of 1976. The construction of many more hotels, guest houses, and tourist villages is planned during the next ten years (see Panorama: Tourism). Until this programme gets well under way it is advisable to book several weeks in advance if possible.

Hotels have been graded according to the "star system"—from 4 (luxury) to 1.

Hotel charges are controlled and hoteliers are obliged to display them at the reception desk and in the rooms. They are appreciably lower than in most other countries.

Hotel restaurants, where charges are also moderate, are uneven in quality. The so-called "international cuisine" figures more often on their menus than, do characteristic local dishes.

For the younger visitors

Holders of an international Youth Hostels card are welcome to use the Youth Hostels at Damascus, Zabadani, Homs, Aleppo, Idlib, Deraa, and Bosra. It is advisable to book at least a month in advance.

Students can also stay at the Cités Universitaires which become Youth Hotels during the summer vacation (July and August): at Damascus there are 320 beds (in two buildings, for men and women); at Aleppo there are 200 beds. Book a month in advance through the University secretariats.

Camping and caravaning

There are two camp sites near Damascus: one 3 km out, on the road to Aleppo; the second 10 km out on the road to Amman. Aleppo also has an official camp site. Elsewhere camping is permitted near the resorts.

hotels in syria

GOVERNORATE (mouhafazat), altitude, situation NAME OF HOTEL (adress, details)	Cate- gory	No. of rooms	Tel.
ALEPPO (HALAB, ALEP)			
Meridien (Air France Hotels), west quarter, near university, view over town, swimming-pool, night-club	****A		
Tourisme (Al-Syaha), Saad alah-Al-Djabri street (opp. public gardens), night-club, rooms for parties and meetings	****B	95	101.56
Baron, Baron str., next to Air France offices, nice atmosphere	***B	46	108.80
Ambassador, (Assûfara) Baron str.	**A	18	102.31
Granada, Baron str.	**A	30	249.59
Heliopolis, Bab Faraj	**A	45	171.04
Semiramis, Kouatli str.	**A	36	199.90
Omaya Jadid (New Omayyade), Al-Chahbandar	**A	38	141.04
Phenicia, (Venicia), Al-Masaben	**A	17	259.09
Ramsis, Baron str.	**B	34	167.00
Al Yarmuk, Al-Maari str.	*A	33	175.10
Al Syaha (Touriste), Kul-Ab str.	*A	17	165.83
Palmyra, Baron str.	*A	10	247.78
Al-Arabi Al-Kabir (Grand), Bab Al-Faraj	*B	27	113.75
Al-Hamra Al Jadid, Bab Al-Faraj	*B	17	269.34
Al-Raghdan, Kul Ab str.	*B	24	100.57
Az-Zahraa, Al-Maari str.	*B	19	201.84
Ar Lubnan, Al-Masaben	*B	22	210.93
Barada, Kul Ab square	*B	14	202.44
Ishbilia, Kul Ab str.	*B	27	218.30
Qanat Al Sueis (Canal de Suez), Al-Maari str.	*B	11	175.64
Syria, Al-Maari str.	*B	45	197.60
Wadi Al-Nile (Le Nil), Kul Ab square	*B	19	116.24
Plus many *C hotels and 34 guesthouses			
Youth Hostel, on the railway station square			
AR-RIHA (Idlib), 10 km s. of Idlib, on road to Latkia	**A	4	
Jebel Al-Arbaien			
Ar-Riha al Jadid, Lattaquié str.	**A		
BANIYAS (Tartous), by the sea			
Homs, Kuwatli str.	*B	10	408
BLUDAN (Damascus), alt. 1,500 m, 55 km n.w. of Damascus			
Grand Hotel (Blûdân Al Kabir) enlarged and renovated, splendidly situated, swimming-pool, amusements, tennis, noted for its restaurant	****L	101	1551
Nadaff	**A	38	1345
Al-Sahle Al-Akhdar	**B	11	1566
Ramsis	**B	15	1352
Plus 7 *hotels			

SYRIAN JOURNEY 221

DEIR EZ-ZOR, alt. 600 m, 320 km s. of Aleppo

Al-Arabi Al-Kabir, Grande-Rue	*A	2070
Al-Jamia Al-Arabia, Grande-Rue	*A	1371
Al-Riad, Grande-Rue	*A	1287
Omayyad, Grande-Rue	*A	1220
Semiramis, Grande-Rue	*A	1127
Al-Ragbdan, Al-Nahir str.	*B	2053

Plus 16 *C hotels

DIMASHQ (Damascus, Damas)

Damascus Airport and Casino (Al-Matar), opp. new International Airport, 25 km from city centre by motorway. Roulette, baccarat, blackjack and other games. Noted for its bar and cuisine. Cables: Airportotel-Damas	****L	44	225.402
Méridien (Air France hotel), Choukry Kouatly av. (opp. International Fair, very comfortable, amusements. Telex 11379	****L	372	222.856
Sheraton (international chain), Omayyades sq., very comfortable, amusements	****L	336	
Damascus International (Al-Dawli), Bahsa str., city centre, renovated quarter. Very comfortable. Pleasant atmosphere. Noted for its cuisine. Telex 11062	****A	133	112.400
Malki (Frantel), under construction (opening 1979)	****A	192	
Kattan, Jamhourieh str.	***A	64	112.513
The New Omayyad, Bresil str.	***A	66	117.700
New Semiramis, Jamourieh str., near Air France office, corner av. S. El-Jabry. Pleasant atmosphere. Night-club. Bazaar	***A	95	116.797
Samir, Shuhada sq. (ex-Merje) city centre	***B	70	119.502
Venezia, Bahsa str., city centre, renovated quarter. Opened in 1975	**A	100	117.031
L'Orient Palace (Al-Shark), Mousalam al-Baroudy sq. (opposite the railway station), city centre	**A	70	111.510 / 220.510
Atlas, Sanjakdar-Nasri	**A	25	228.547
Grand (Al-Kabir), Shuhada sq. (ex-Merje), city centre	**A	43	111.666
Tourist Hotel (Al-Syaha), place Shuhada (ex-Merje)	**A	47	114.772
Ramsis, place Shuhada (ex-Merje) city centre	**A	37	116.702
Imad, Faycal str.	**B	30	225.704
Al-Akhdar, Fakhri Al-Baroudi str.	**B	21	111.920
Al-Karnak, Al-Nasr str.	**B	33	116.490
Al-Sufara, Bresil str.	**B	34	221.111
Amal, Izzat Al-Abed str.	**B	31	115.880
Basman, Abi Firas str.	**B	42	118.003
Granada, Rami str.	**B	24	119.586

Plus many *hotels

Youth Hostel, Salah Al-Ali str., Al-Mazraah quarter	118.200

DRAYKISH (Tartus), 34 km e. of Tartus

Dray kish Al-Syaki	**A	27	
Al-Burje-Al-Fiddi	*B	15	43
Ras Al-Ain Al-Kabir	*B	27	6

HAMA, alt. 308 m, 140 km s. of Aleppo

Basman, Choukri al-Kouatli str.	**B	18	128.38
Cairo, Choukri al-Kouatli str.	*A	10	120.96
Al-Riad, Choukri al-Kouatli str.	*A	10	128.43
Al-Kasr Al-Arabi, Al-Sheikh Alwan str.	*A	10	123.10
Assyaha, Choukri al-Kouatli str.	*A	10	216.65

Plus 3 *B hotels

HASSAKEH, 175 km n.e. of Deir-ez-Zor

Al-Nadi Al-Ziraie, Kuwatli str.	**A	207.61
Jule Jamal, Al-Nahda str.	*A	206.47
Ksar Al-Hamra, Al-Andalous str.	*A	217.74

Plus 8 *B and *C hotels

HOMS, alt. 495 m, 160 km n. of Damascus

Qasr Raghdan, Kuwatli str.	**B	30	252.11
Basman Al-Jadid, Al-Sham str.	**B	15	269.77
Basman al-Kabir, Al-Maari str.	*A	20	257.00
Semiramis, Kuwatli str.	*A	12	218.37

Plus 20 *B and *C hotels

IDLIB, 55 km s.w. of Aleppo

Al-Kabir al-Syahi (Tourist Hotel), Malki str.	**A	209.70

Plus 3 *C hotels

JIRJANIEH (Damascus), alt. 1,275 m, 45 km n.w. of Damascus

Phoenicia	**A	35	1046
Al-Fardos	**A	13	

JISR ASH SHUGHUR (Idlib), on the Orontes, 75 km n.e. of Latakia

Al-Uruba, on the Aleppo-Latakia road	*A

Plus 4 *B and *C hotels

KASSAB (Latakia), alt. 800 m, 65 km n. of Latakia, wooded countryside, summer holiday resort

Ar-Rawda, Yussef Al-Azmé str.	*B	35	8
Ramsis, Yussef Al-Azmé str.	*B	24	6

Plus 2 *C hotels

LADHIQIYA (Latakia), by the sea, Hotels in the town

Méridien (Air France hotel), on the coast n. of the town, under construction. Opening 1978	****A

Tourist'Hotel and Casino (Al-Syaha), Andalous str., near public gardens, terrace overlooking the sea	**A	32	134.00
Gondole (Al Gandûl), Andalous str., facing the sea	**B	34	138.89
Venice (Venitia, Phénicie), Al-Azmé str.	**B	28	116.72
Khayyam, Shuhada sq.	*A	19	221.24
Ramita, Yussef Al-Azmé str.	*A	12	121.99
Ambassadeurs (Al-Sufura), Andalous str.	*B	14	137.60
Al-Mûkhtar, Yussef Al-Azmé str.	*B	24	128.49
Nahas, Hanano str.	*B	23	217.37
Plus 25 *A, *B, and *C hotels			
Youth Hostel, Al-Laghein str.			

LADHIQIYA (Latakia), on the coast to the n. of the town			
Méridien (see above)			
Casino Aphamia, bungalows on the beach, 4 km			3330
Casino Jules Jamal, bungalows on the beach, 6 km			4176
Florida, bungalows on the beach, 6 km			1830
Casa Rivage Bleu (Blue Beach), bungalows on the beach, restaurant with extensive views, gaming, boat hire, 7 km, near turning to Ugarit			1144
Club Ras Shamra, 8 km, near Ugarit			

MAARAT ANN NUMAN (Idlib), 60 km n. of Hama			
Abi Al-Alaal	*A		

MALKIYE (Hassaké), 95 km e. of Qamishli			
Semiramis, Al-Nasr str.	*A		

NABAHIN (or Ikki Zuluk) (Latakia) alt. 800 m, summer resort 5 km from Kassab			
Montana, open all the year	**B	28	6

PALMYRA (Tadmor) (Homs) alt. 400 m, 155 km e. of Homs			
Méridien (Air France hotel), facing the ruins, s. side, on the Homs road, near the Efqa spring. Under construction, due to open 1978	****A		
Zanoubia, facing the ruins, n. side, between the Museum and the Temple of Bel	**B	15	107
Tadmor, in the village	**C	20	156

QAMISHLI (Hassaké), 260 km n.e. of Deir ez-Zor			
Hadaia, Al-Soak/al Jadid str.	**B		101.41
Semiramis, Al-Jisrein str.	**B		101.85
Plus 10 *A and *B hotels			

QASTAL AL-MOAF (Latakia), alt. 800 m summer resort, 40 km n. of Latakia			
Verte Montagne, open all the year	*B	25	4

RAQQA, 200 km s. of Aleppo

Tourist'hôtel (Al-Sy aha), Kuwatli str.	**B	10	207.25

Plus 7 *C hotels

SALQIN (Idlib), summer resort, 40 km n.w. of Idlib

Casino, Al-Dawar str., swimming-pool, garden	**A		
Al-Zahra, Al-Bazar	*A		78

SLENFE (Latakia), alt. 1,100 m, summer resort, 50 km e. of Latakia

Tourist'hôtel (Al-Syaha wal Istiaf), country setting in woods	**B	50	6/14
Valley View (Al-Wadi)	*B	13	15

SUWEIDA, 90 km s.e. of Damascus

Rawdal Al-Jahal, Shuhada sq.	*B		118
Dar Al-Abrar, Al-Seir sq.	*B		184
The New Damascus, Salah ad-Din str.	**B	10	209.10
Danyak, Abdel Aziz str.	*A	23	205.81
Al-Sufara, Tarik-Ibn-Ziad str.	*A	20	201.83
Rafook, Minshied str.	*B	10	206.16

TARTUS, coast outside the town

Al-Jazireh, bungalows on the beach			
The New Chalets, near Masbah al-Jazireh			
Al-Shate Al-Akhdar, at Al-Bousayra	**B		

THAURA (Al) (Raqqa), new town near the dam
Several hotels under construction

ZABADANI (Damascus), alt. 1 100 m, summer resort, 50 km n.w. of Damascus

Al-Kindi	**A		1437
Tourist'hôtel (Al-Syaha wal Istiaf)	**B	16	1149
Qasr Al-Zafraan	*C	14	1609
Qasr Al-Omara Al-Kabir	*A	26	1070

N.B. For the many hotels under construction or planned, see Panorama, p. 39

TO SYRIA
FROM EUROPE, FROM THE EAST, FROM AFRICA

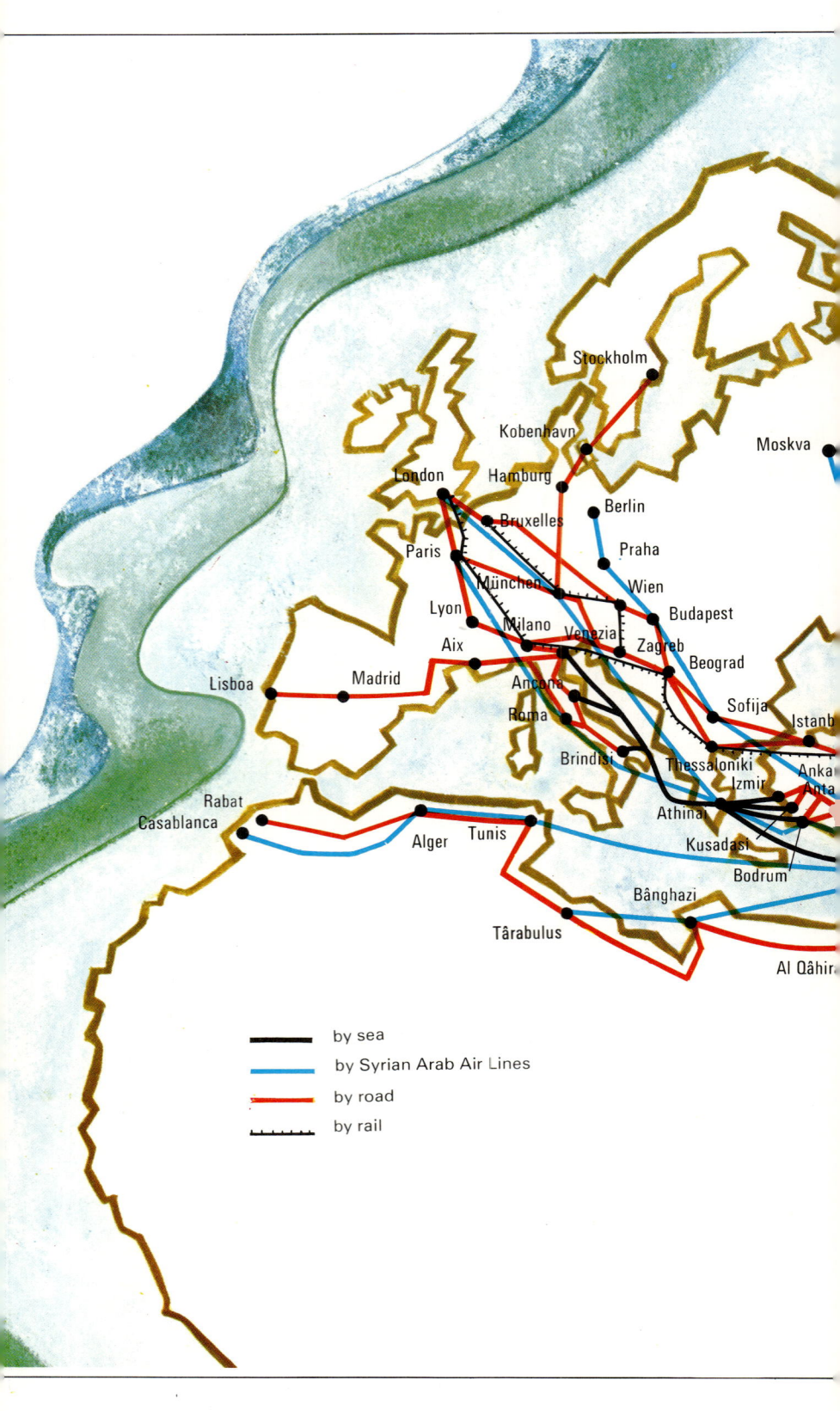

226 SYRIAN JOURNEY

SYRIAN JOURNEY 227

MEANS OF COMMUNICATIONS AND ADMINISTRATIVE DIVISIONS

*Province of Alexandretta/Iskenderun, detached from Syria following the Franco-Turkish Agreement of 23 June 11939

228 SYRIAN JOURNEY

SYRIAN JOURNEY 229

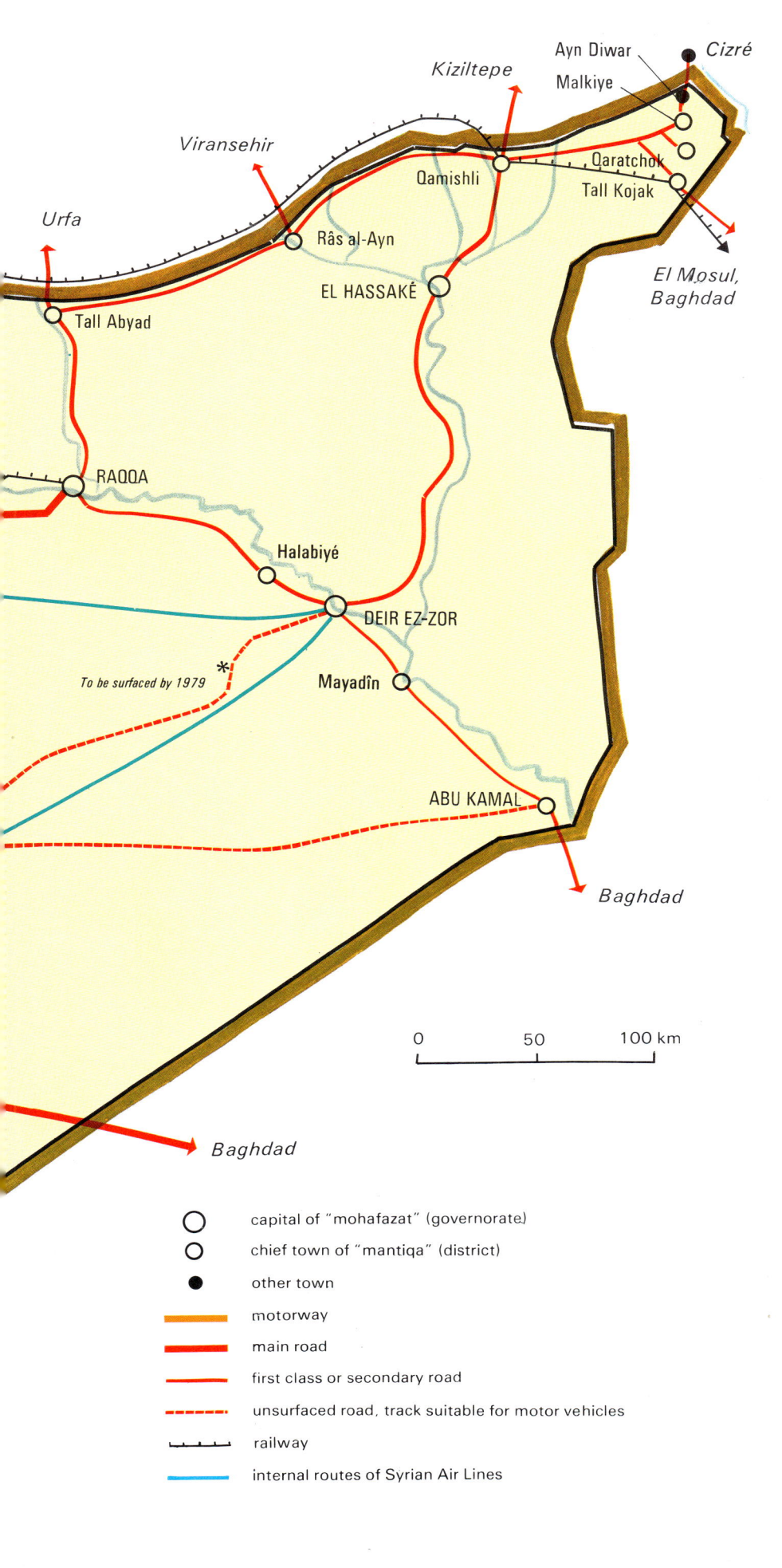

TOURIST SYRIA AND NATURAL DIVISIONS

*Province of Alexandretta/Iskenderun, detached from Syria following the Franco-Turkish Agreement of 23 June 1939

Map

Cities and sites:
- Malkiye
- Qamishli
- Tall Kojak
- Ras al-Ayn
- Al Hasseke
- Tall Abyad
- jabal abd al Aaziz ▲810 ▲920
- jabal Sinjar
- Raqqa
- Halabiyé ★
- ★ Zalabiyé
- Deir ez-Zor
- ★ Bûssayra
- jabal al Bichri 867 856
- ★ Qasr al-Hîr ash Sharqi
- Mayadîn
- Rajmaine
- Tell Hariri (Mari) ★
- Salhiyé (Doura Europos) ★
- Abu Kamal
- ▲ 783
- jabal Tenf ▲ 818

Rivers / regions:
- Jila (Tigris)
- Balikh
- Al Khabûr
- Al Furât (Euphrates)
- DJEZIREH
- FURAT
- ASH SHAM

Legend:
- ★ ● centre or sight of great interest
- ★ • other interesting centres and sights
- ▲ Mount
- **GHAB** major natural division

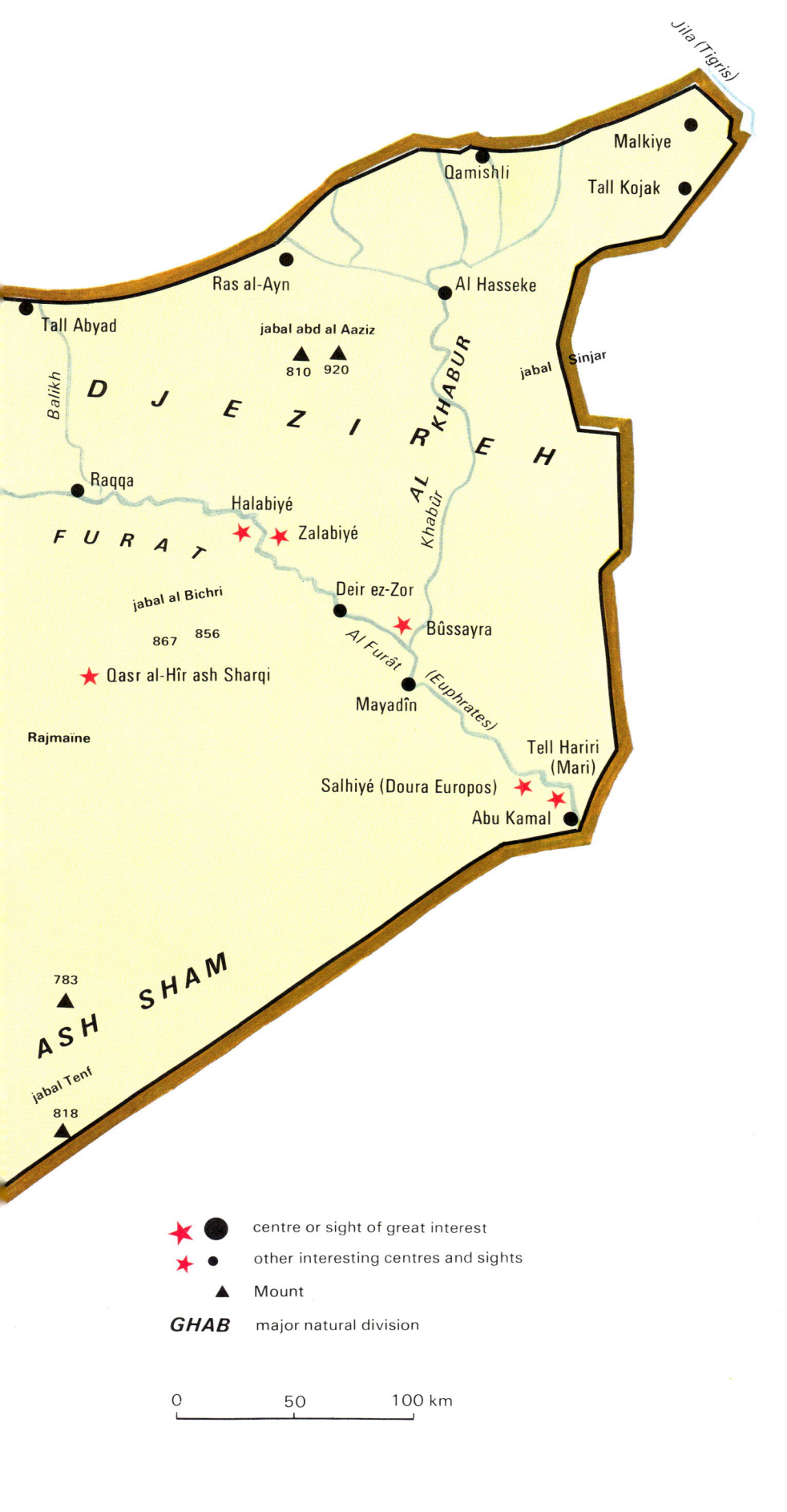

0 — 50 — 100 km

SYRIAN JOURNEY 231

SYRIA ARCHAEOLOGICAL AND HISTORICAL

232 SYRIAN JOURNEY

Map of Eastern Syria — Archaeological Sites

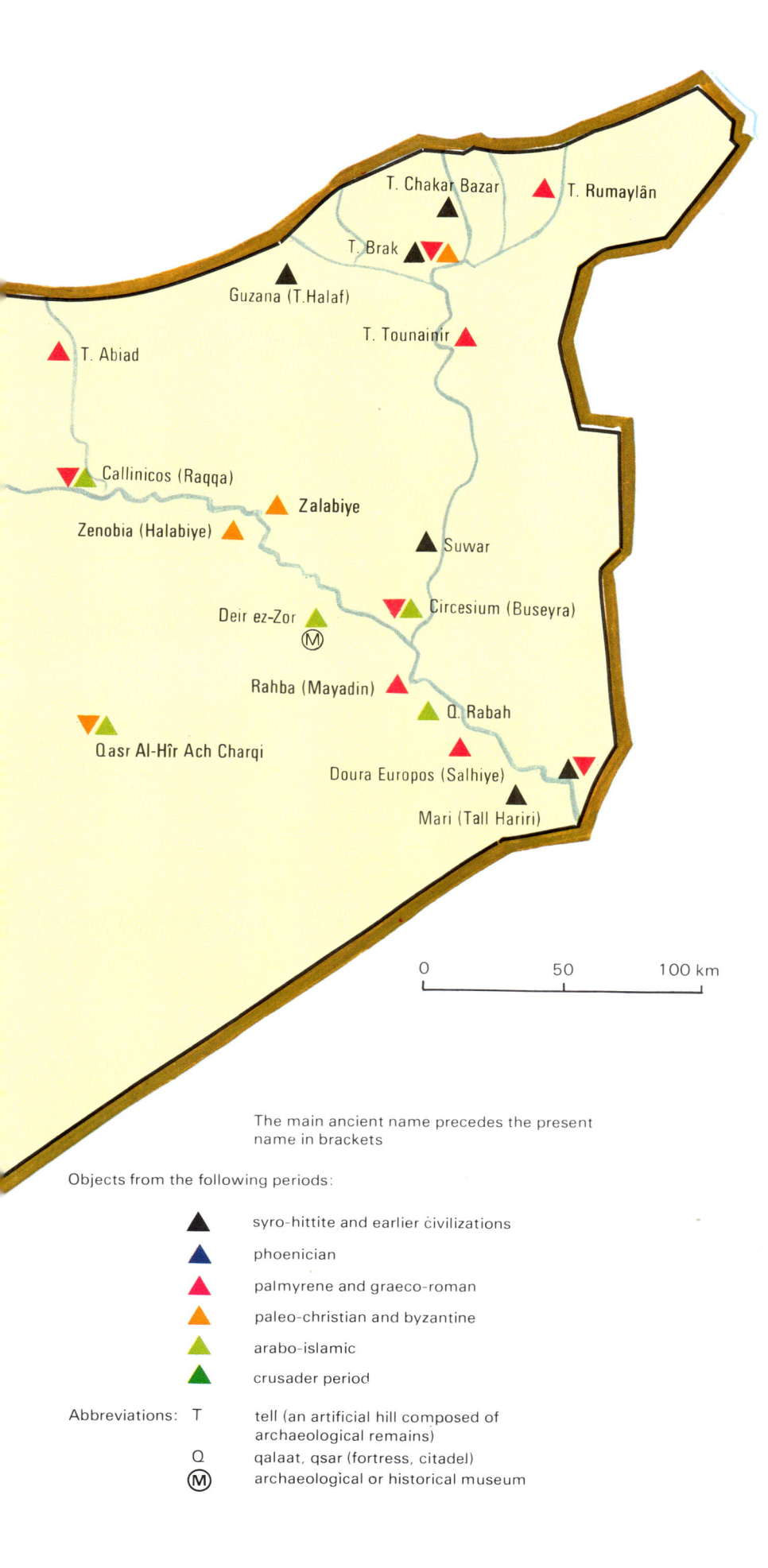

Sites shown:
- T. Chakar Bazar
- T. Rumaylān
- T. Brak
- Guzana (T. Halaf)
- T. Tounainir
- T. Abiad
- Callinicos (Raqqa)
- Zalabiye
- Zenobia (Halabiye)
- Suwar
- Deir ez-Zor (M)
- Circesium (Buseyra)
- Rahba (Mayadin)
- Q. Rabah
- Qasr Al-Hîr Ach Charqi
- Doura Europos (Salhiye)
- Mari (Tall Hariri)

Scale: 0 — 50 — 100 km

The main ancient name precedes the present name in brackets

Objects from the following periods:

- ▲ syro-hittite and earlier civilizations (black)
- ▲ phoenician (blue)
- ▲ palmyrene and graeco-roman (red)
- ▲ paleo-christian and byzantine (orange)
- ▲ arabo-islamic (light green)
- ▲ crusader period (dark green)

Abbreviations:
- T — tell (an artificial hill composed of archaeological remains)
- Q — qalaat, qsar (fortress, citadel)
- Ⓜ — archaeological or historical museum

SYRIAN JOURNEY 233

SYRIA IN 8 DAYS FROM DAMASCUS TO DAMASCUS

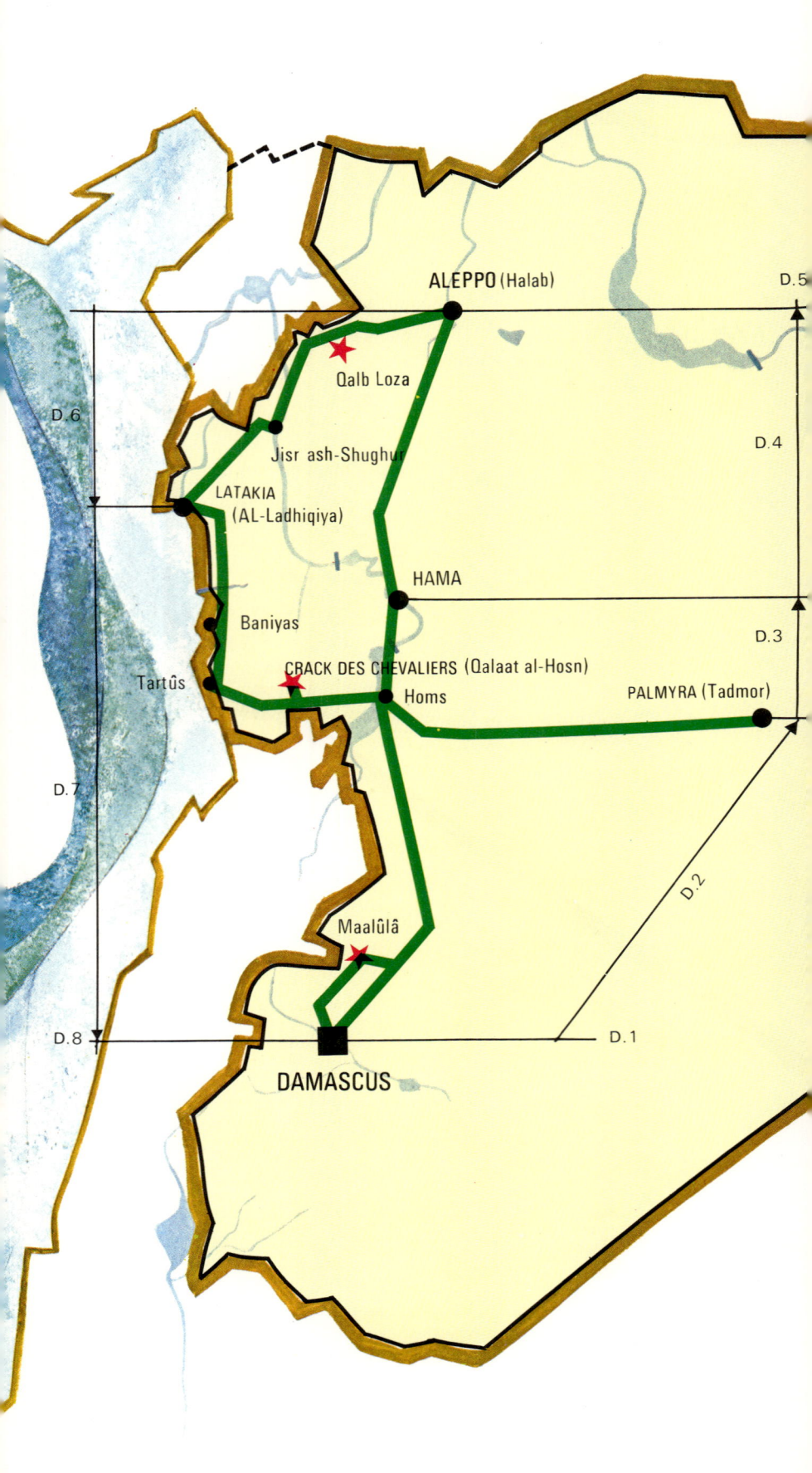

234 SYRIAN JOURNEY

SYRIA IN 15 DAYS FROM LATAKIA TO ALEPPO

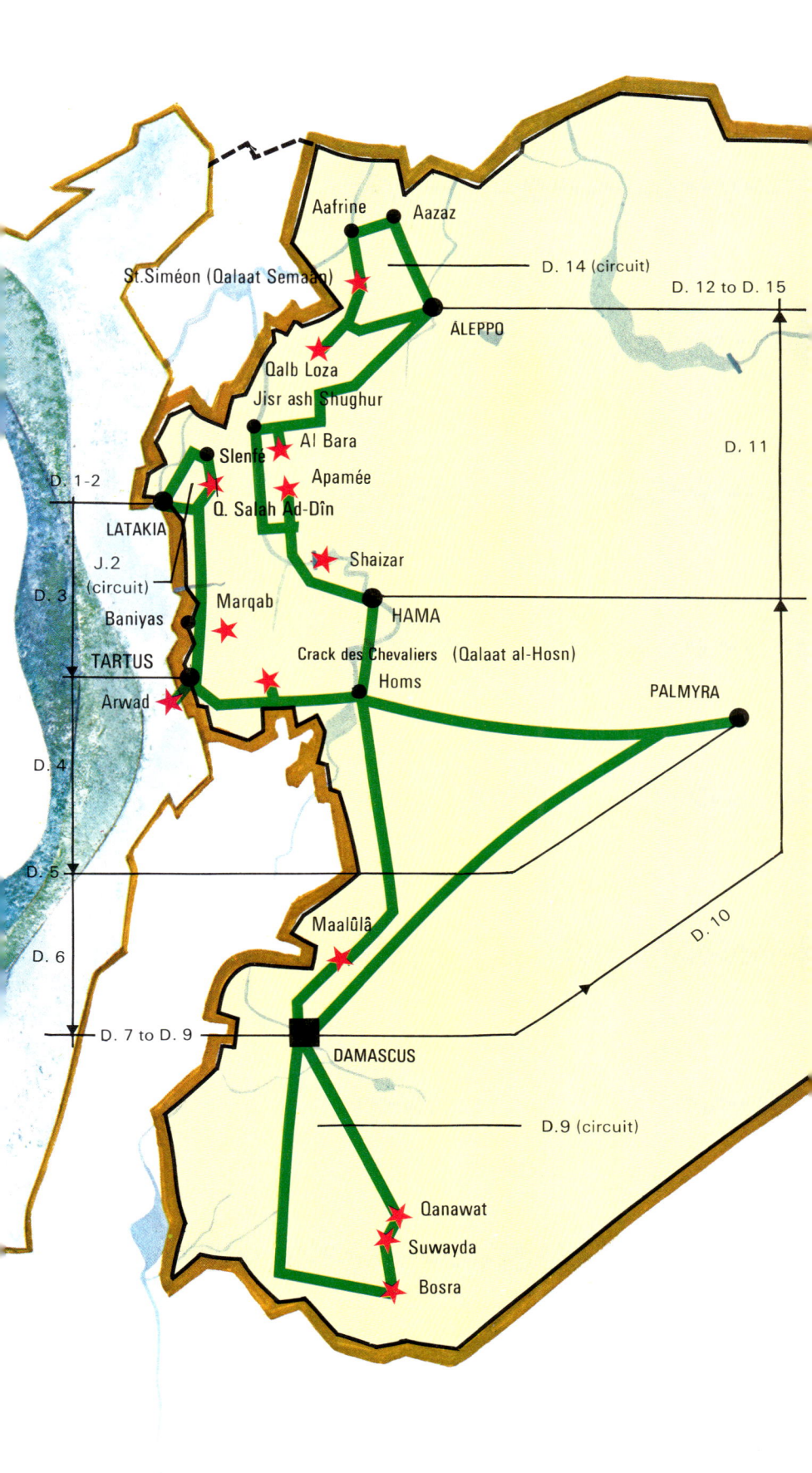

SYRIAN JOURNEY 235

SYRIA IN 30 DAYS FROM ALEPPO TO ALEPPO

236 SYRIAN JOURNEY

SYRIAN JOURNEY 237

PLAN OF THE ANTIQUITIES OF PALMYRA

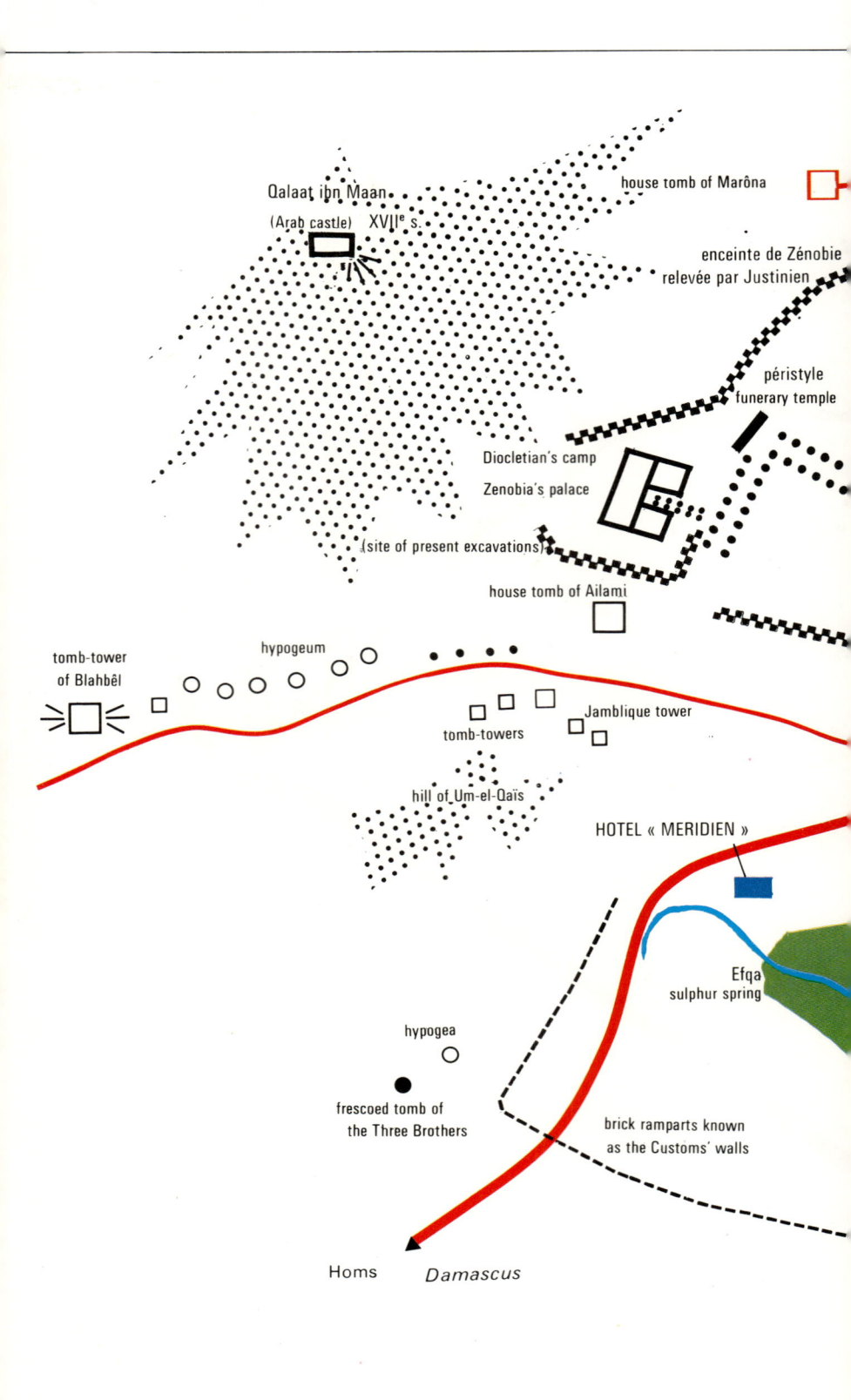

Palmyra Map

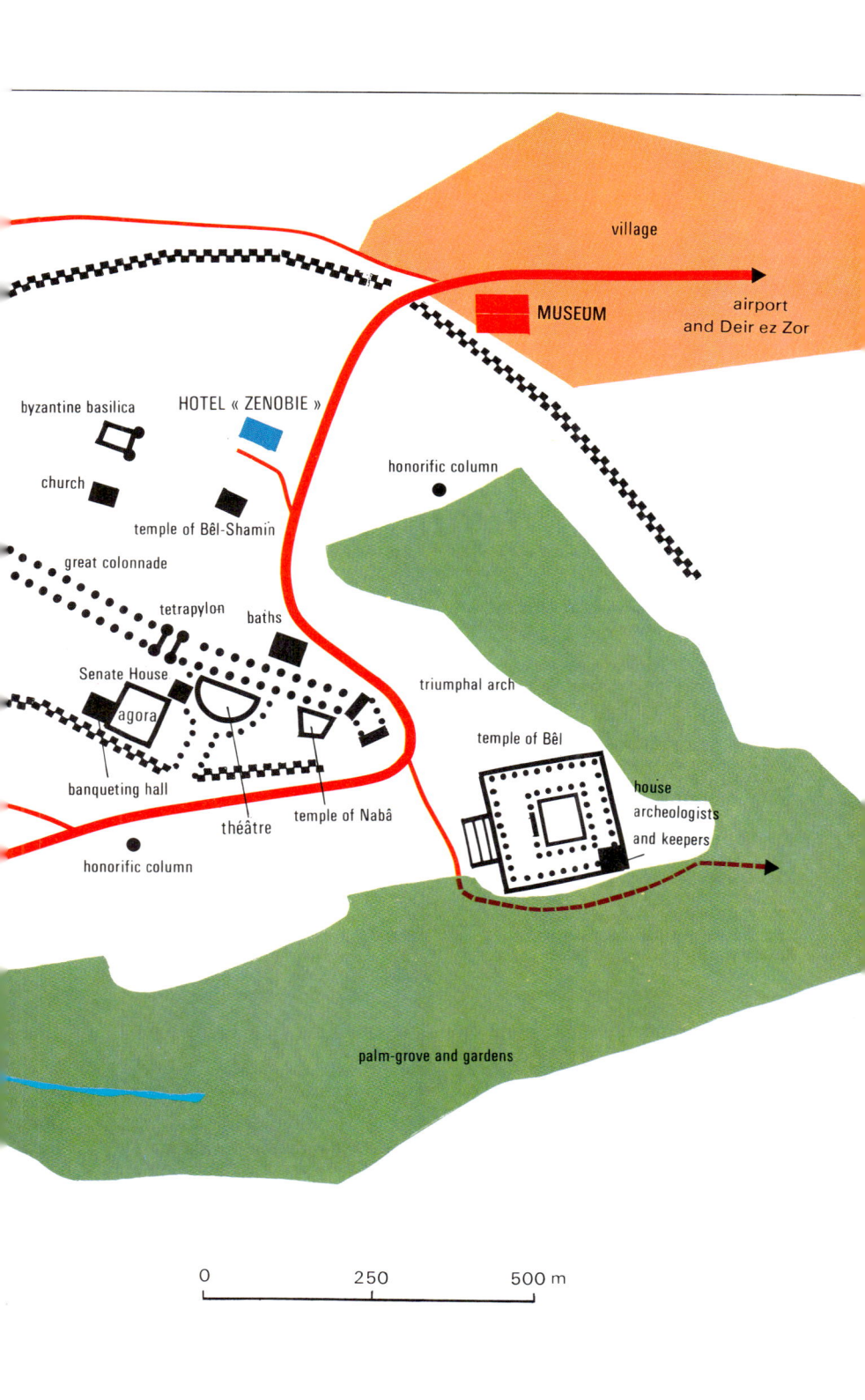

- village
- MUSEUM
- airport and Deir ez Zor
- byzantine basilica
- HOTEL « ZENOBIE »
- church
- honorific column
- temple of Bêl-Shamin
- great colonnade
- tetrapylon
- baths
- Senate House
- agora
- triumphal arch
- temple of Bêl
- banqueting hall
- théâtre
- temple of Nabâ
- house archeologists and keepers
- honorific column
- palm-grove and gardens

0   250   500 m

PLAN OF DAMASCUS

- ▭ main road
- ▭ road under construction
- ▭ secondary road
- — souk or road unsuitable for motor vehicles
- *Salhieh* name of quarter
- ⋙ view point
- ★ building, monument, building not open to the public
- ▪ luxury hotel

Nouvelle rocade

Jabal Qassioun

Bahjat — Al-Halaby — *Abû Jarach* — Assad al-Dyn

Madaress (29)

(28)

bd. Al-Hiyeh

Afif

rue Ibn Al-Amid

rue Rachyd

rue Beirouni

Al-Mouhajerine

rue Nazem Bacha

(27)

rue Mansour (25) (24)

Al-Charkassyeh

rue Masr Hijaz

bd. al-Malek al-Aad

(26)

rue Mouhammad Kourdali

rue Abd Al-Malek

ben-Marwan

← Zabadani, Beirut

(23)

av. Al-Mahdy-Al-Valaa

bd Barakah

bd Majless Al-Nyaby

av. Choukry Koutwatly

place des Omayyades

MERIDIEN (22)

(13)

(11)

SHERATON

(21)

(1) (17)

(16)

av. Choukry Koutwatly

(15) (12)

bd. Palestine

bd. Palestine

(14)

nouveau Damas (Al Mazzah)

(20)

motorway Faez Mansour

★ (19)

Olympic Centre

(18)

Al Qanawa

Al-Mazzah

▼ new Damascus (Al Mazzah), old airport Qnaytra

la Ghouta (gardens and orchards)

Kafar Sousseh

gardens and Ghouta swimming pool

Daraiya

242 SYRIAN JOURNEY

Map of Damascus

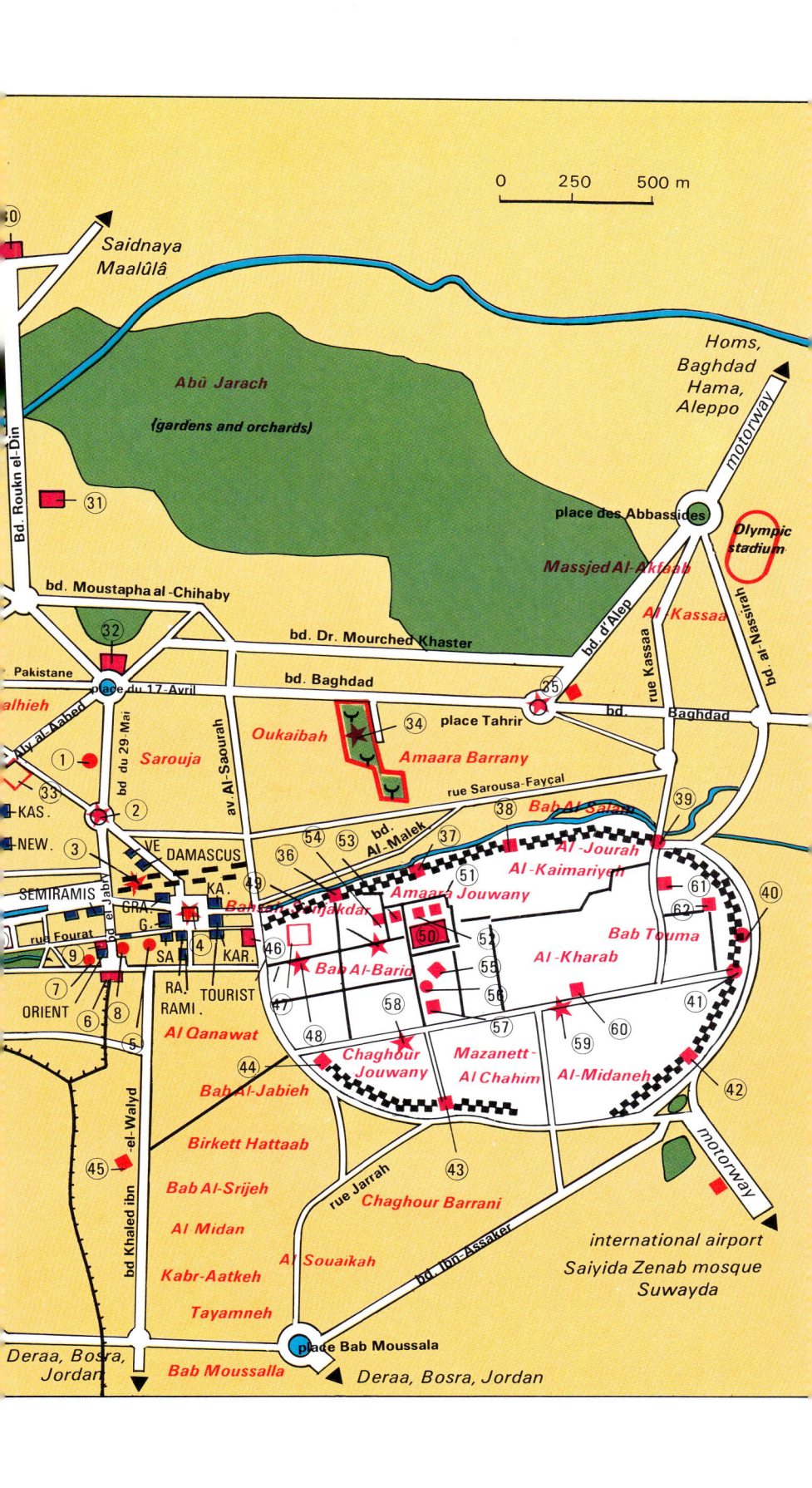

Scale: 0 – 250 – 500 m

Labels and Locations

- Saidnaya, Maalûlâ
- Homs, Baghdad, Hama, Aleppo → motorway
- Abû Jarach (gardens and orchards)
- Bd. Roukn el-Din
- (31)
- bd. Moustapha al-Chihaby
- (32)
- Pakistane
- place du 17-Avril
- bd. Dr. Mourched Khaster
- bd. Baghdad
- bd. d'Alep
- place des Abbassides
- Massjed Al-Aktaab
- Olympic stadium
- Al Kassaa
- rue Kassaa
- bd. al-Nassirah
- (35)
- bd. Baghdad
- Oukaibah
- (34) place Tahrir
- Amaara Barrany
- rue Sarousa-Fayçal
- Av. al-Aabed
- (1)
- Sarouja
- bd. du 29-Mai
- av. Al-Saourah
- (2)
- (33)
- KAS.
- NEW.
- (3)
- AVE DAMASCUS
- KA.
- bd. Al-Malek
- (36) (54) (53) (37) (38) Bab Al-Salam
- (39)
- Al-Jourah
- Al-Kaimariyeh
- (61)
- (40)
- SEMIRAMIS
- GRA.
- G.
- (4)
- Bahsat Sinjakdar
- (49)
- (51) Amaara Jouwany
- (62)
- rue Fourat
- KAR.
- (46)
- (50)
- (52)
- Bab Touma
- (9)
- SA
- Bab Al-Barid
- Al-Kharab
- (7)
- ORIENT
- (6) (8)
- RA. RAMI.
- TOURIST
- (47)
- (55)
- (56)
- (41)
- (5)
- Al Qanawat
- (48)
- (58)
- (57)
- (59) (60)
- (44) Bab Al-Jabieh
- Chaghour Jouwany
- Mazanett-Al Chahim
- Al-Midaneh
- (42)
- Birkett Hattaab
- Bab Al-Srijeh
- rue Jarrah
- Al Midan
- (43) Chaghour Barrani
- (45)
- bd. Khaled ibn -el-Walyd
- Kabr-Aatkeh
- Al Souaikah
- bd. Ibn-Assaker
- motorway
- Tayamneh
- international airport
- Saiyida Zenab mosque
- Suwayda
- Deraa, Bosra, Jordan
- Bab Moussalla
- place Bab Moussala
- Deraa, Bosra, Jordan

SYRIAN JOURNEY 243

damascus (cont'd.)

42. *Bab-Kassane: the Chapel of St. Paul, built on the site of the house from which St. Paul escaped.*
43. *Bab-al Saghir: la Petite Porte: the Little Gate.*
44. *Sinaan Pacha Mosque.*
45. *New Zaïd ibn-Thabet Mosque.*
46. *Citadel (temporarily closed to visitors).*
47. *Great al-Hamidiyeh Souk.*
48. *Roman remains: Propylaea of the Temple of Jupiter.*
49. *Omayyad Mosque: Jaameh al-Oumanawy.*
50. *Museum of Arabic Epigraphy, in a former madrassa.*
51. *Byzantine Colonnade and Saladin's Tomb.*
52. *National Library, in the former al-Zahiriyé madrassa.*
53. *Azem Palace: the Museum of Popular Arts and Traditions.*
54. *The 12th-century Hammam al-Bzourieh and the el-Goumrok Khân.*
55. *Assad Pacha Caravanserai (Khân).*
56. *"The Street called Straight", a main road dating from Roman times.*
57. *Roman remains, monumental arch.*
58. *Kanissat al-Mariamyeh: église de Marie: Church of Mary.*
59. *Kanissat al-Aazariyeh: church.*
60. *Kanissat Hananya: church and house of Hanani; association with St. Paul.*

syrian national museum

Guide-plan of the Syrian National Museum in Damascus

Oriental Antiquities

1. *Ras Shamra, Ugarit: first alphabet (14th cent. B.C.), written cylindrical tablets, gold, silver and ivory figures.*
2. *Antiquities from inland Syria: Raffiqa, two—and four-wheeled carts, figurines and miniature animals.*
3. *Antiquities from coastal areas (Amrit, Tell Kazel, Tell Soukas): cylinders, seals, amulets, weapons, statuettes.*
4. *Mari (Tell Hariri) 3rd-2nd millen. B.C.: statue of the god Itur-Shamagan, statuette of "the great singer Ur-Nina", figurines with bulging eyes, royal cylinders, ivory pictures, model of the round house, the Ur Treasure (a present from the King of Ur to the King of Mari: jewelry, precious stones...).*
5. *(first floor): The Homs Treasure: gold masks, jewelry, weapons, etc.*

Classical Antiquities

6. *5th-3rd cent. B.C.: marble and terracotta statuettes, bronze animals, 3rd.cent. Venus.*
7. *Palmyra: mosaics, funerary busts, triclinium groups, fragments of fresco.*
8. *(basement): Reconstruction of a hypogeum from the Valley of the Tombs at Palmyra.*
9. *Doura Europos: larges frescoes, Syriac stelae.*
10. *(building across small courtyard): Reconstruction of the Synagogue at Doura Europos: frescoes dating from 235 A.D.*
11. *Byzantine period; Christian art 1st-7th cents. Chinese silks from Palmyra.*
12. *Howran: Bosra and environs; basalt sculptures (also in museum gardens).*
13. *Jebel al-Druze: large mosaics, basalt sculptures (Chahba, Suweida, Qanawat and other sites in the jebel al-Arab).*

Arabo-Islamic

14. *Rooms under re-arrangement. On walls, painted designs characteristic of the interior decoration of houses in the Howran.*
15. *Qsar al-Hir al-Gharbi: model of the desert fort, mosaics, sculptured designs in stucco and wood, monumental inscriptions. First floor, stucco work. Outside, reconstruction of the fortified postern gate from Qsar.*
16. *Raqqa: models of fortified towns on the Euphrates. Famous Chinese porcelain horseman. Polychrome dishes. Vessels in the shapes of animals.*
17. *Metalwork; "damascened" weapons; scientific instruments, astrolabes, etc.*
18. *Glass: Phoenecian glass (13th cent. B.C.), blue and gold flasks.*
19. *Terracotta, painted and decorated pottery, various periods and origins.*
20. *Ceramics; flambé earthenware.*
21. *Architecture and decoration.*
22. *Numismatic collection: Umayyad, Abbasid, Ayubid, Fatimid, and other coins.*
23. *Hama.*
24. *Manuscripts: illuminated Korans, Syriac inscriptions.*
25. *Woodwork.*
26. *(first floor): Modern Art (under re-arrangment).*

GUIDE-PLAN OF THE SYRIAN NATIONAL MUSEUM IN DAMASCUS

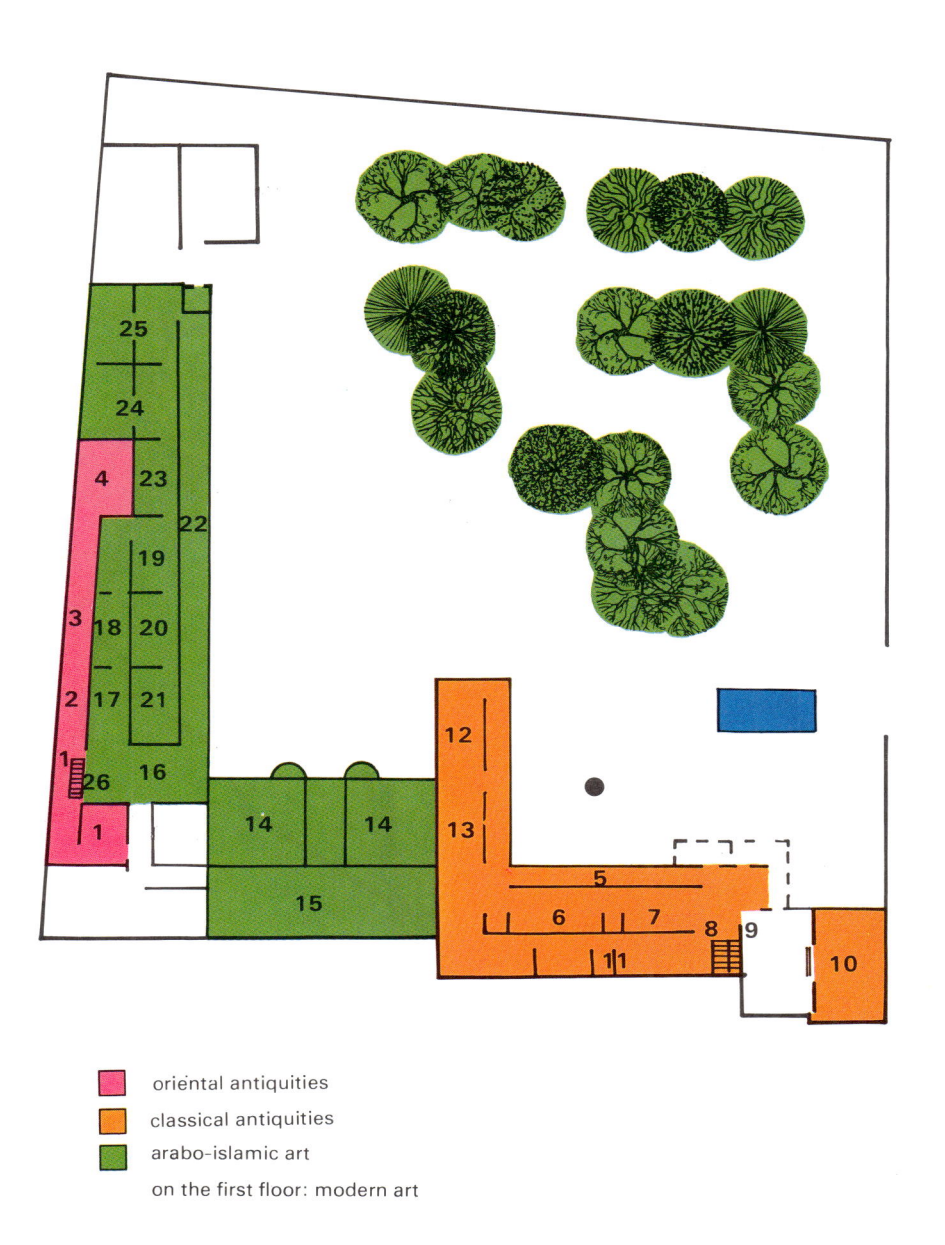

- oriental antiquities
- classical antiquities
- arabo-islamic art
- on the first floor: modern art

SYRIAN JOURNEY 245

PLAN OF ALEPPO

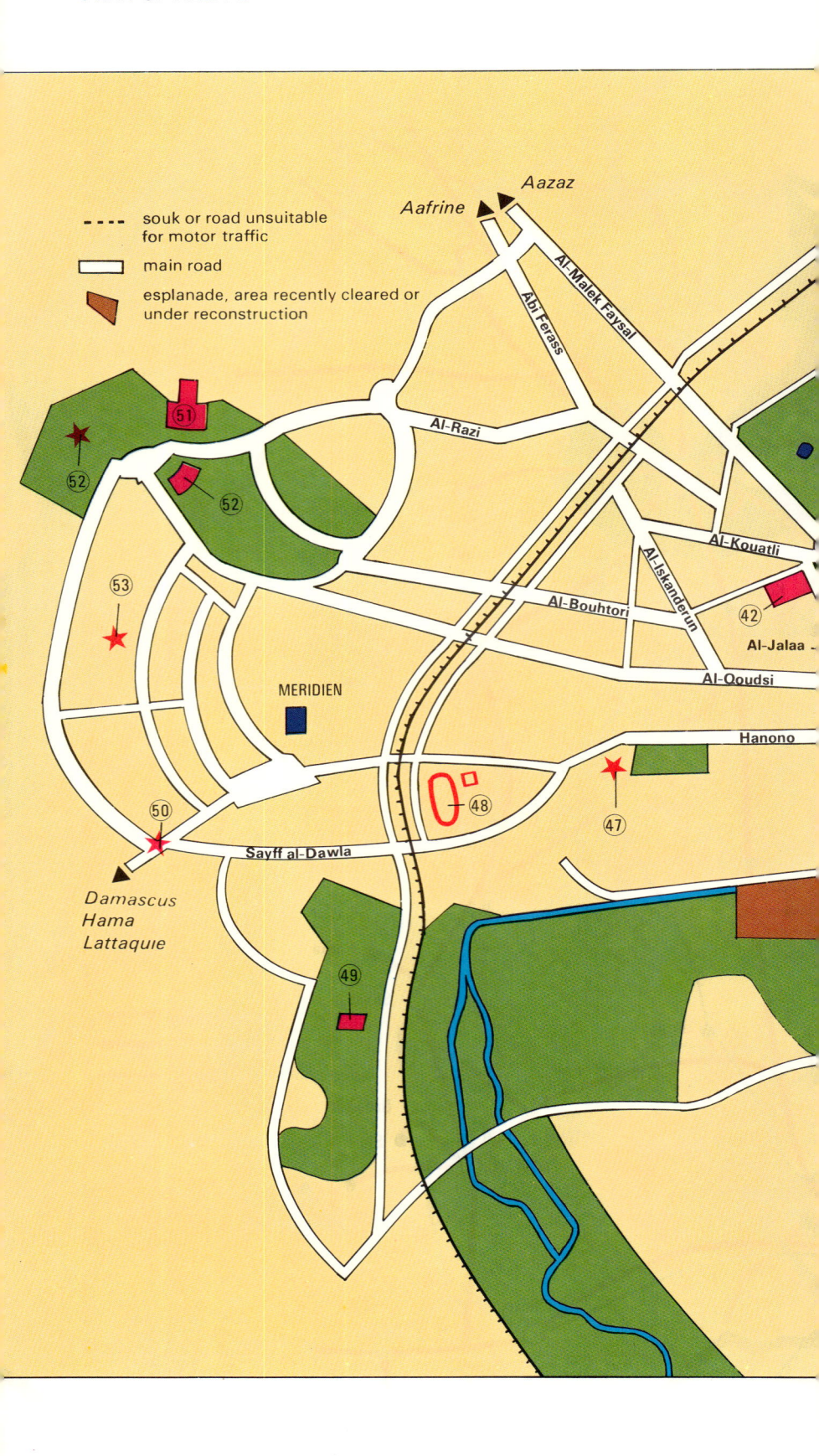

- - - - souk or road unsuitable for motor traffic
▢ main road
◢ esplanade, area recently cleared or under reconstruction

Aafrine Aazaz
Al-Malek Faysal
Abi Terass
Al-Razi
Al-Kouatli
Al-Iskanderun
Al-Bouhtori
Al-Jalaa
Al-Qoudsi
Hanono
MERIDIEN
Sayff al-Dawla

Damascus
Hama
Lattaquie

248 SYRIAN JOURNEY

SYRIAN JOURNEY 249

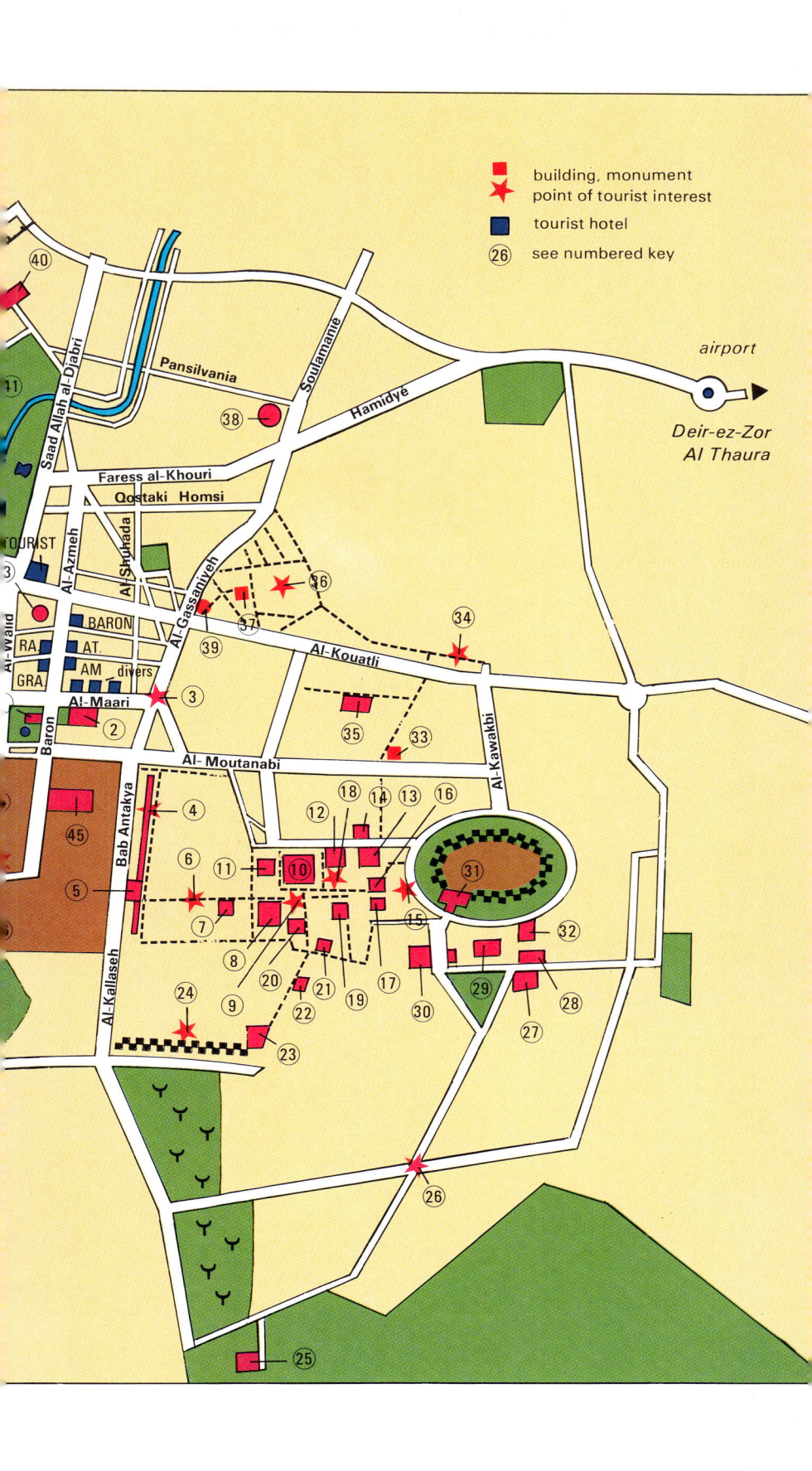

key to plan of aleppo (p. 248-249)

1. Tourist Information Bureau.
2. Archaeological Museum.
3. Clock Tower.
4. Former rampart, raised street.
5. Fortified gate: Bab Antakiah and small Amayad Mosque; entrance to the covered souks.
6. Central axis of the covered souks: Bab Antakiah, Al-Sabbaghin, Al-Bahramiah, Al-Sakatiah souks. Mainly food shops.
7. Al Bahramyah Mosque.
8. Al-Joumrok Khân (caravanserai).
9. Central part of the covered souks; specializing in different trades: Al-Itakiah souk (leather), Al-Hibal souk (ropes and cordage), Al-Hiddadin souk (blacksmiths, tinsmiths, fresh fruit), Al-Chah souk (footware), etc.
10. Omayyad Mosque (Great Mosque).
11. Al-Halawyah madrassa (former Koran school).
12. Al-Sabouf Khân (caravanserai).
13. Al-Wazir Khân (caravanserai).
14. Museum of Popular Art and Traditions in former 12th-cent. palace.
15. East entrance to the covered souks: Al-Zarb souk (hairdressers, kafieh, textiles), Al-Ibi souk (textiles), Al-Attarin (perfumers, household goods), etc.
16. Khayer Bey Khân (caravanserai).
17. Al-Chazbakhiyah madrassa (former Koran school).
18. Istamboul, al-Siyagh and others nearby, goldsmiths' and jewellers' quarter.
19. Cotton quarter, khân and souks.
20. Al-Nahasine khân (leather, footwear); former Belgian Consulate.
21. Ad-Adelia Mosque.
22. Arghon-al Kamily Birmastan (former asylum).
23. Bab Kennisrin: fortified gate, south entrance to the old city.
24. Ramparts with 12th-15th cent. towers.
25. Al Fardos madrassa (former Koran school).
26. Bab Al-Makkan: former gateway, open-air market.
27. Al-Atroush Mosque.
28. Law Courts (modern building).
29. Bank of Syria (modern building).
30. Al-Khousrawia Mosque and Zahiriya madrassa (tomb of Emir al Zaher Ghazi, son of Saladin).
31. Citadel.
32. Former Al Nasri Hammam ("Turkish bath").
33. Al Mahmandar Mosque; fluted minaret.
34. Copper souk.
35. Jumblatt House, decorated 17th century house.
36. "Old Houses" quarter—17th and 18th—century houses with decorated windows and patios; antique shops; Armenian shops.
37. Cathedral of St. Gregory (Orthodox).
38. New Maryam Maronite Church.
39. Central Police Station (tel. 93).
40. Railway Station.
41. Park and Zoo.
42. General Post Office.
43. Syrian Air Lines' City office; other airline offices nearby.
44. Fountain.
45. Bus station.
46. Open-air market.
47. Mausoleum of Ibrahim Hanano's.
48. Municipal stadium and swimming pool.
49. Mach-had Al-Hussein: Shi'ite Centre for Advance Islamic Studies. View over Aleppo.
50. New Hospital.
51. New University.
52. New quarters.

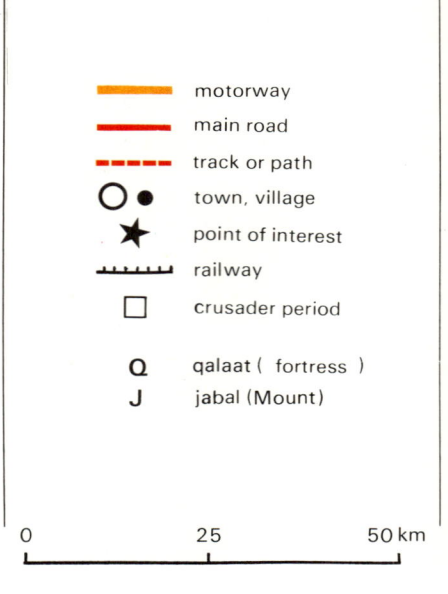

- motorway
- main road
- track or path
- town, village
- point of interest
- railway
- crusader period
- Q qalaat (fortress)
- J jabal (Mount)

0   25   50 km

250 SYRIAN JOURNEY

THE COAST AND THE ORONTES VALLEY

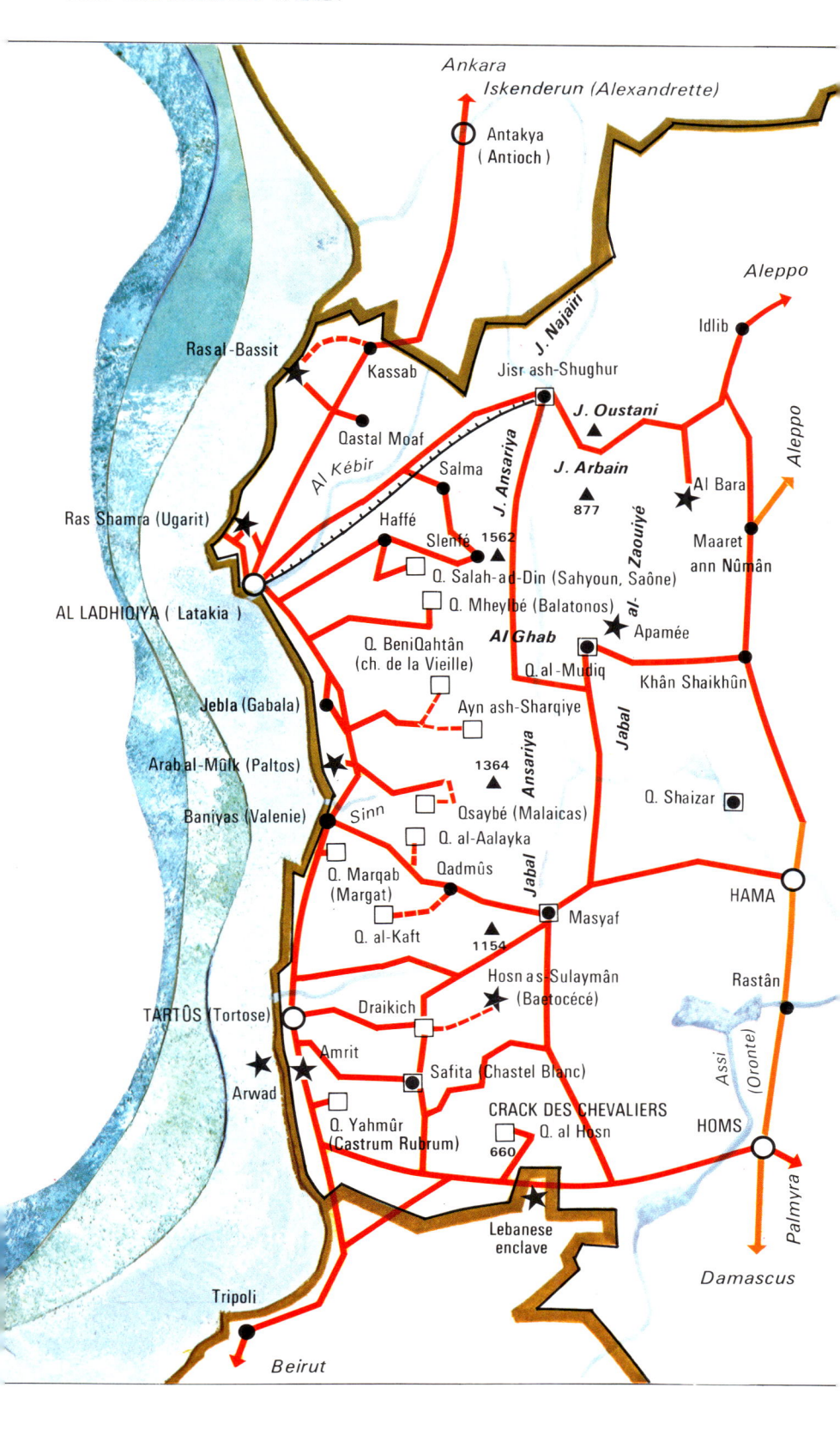

index

This index includes sites, places and water courses described in this book. Those having a special section devoted to them are printed in bold characters.

■
Aafrin, see Qalaat Samaân
Aalayqa, s. Lattaquié
Aagaz, s. Qalaat Samaâ
Abel (tomb of), s. Zabadani
Abû Hûrayra, s. Thaura (al)
Adriana Palmyra, s. Palmyra
Afqa (Ephka) (spring), s. Palmyra
Aïn al-Zarqua, s. Idlib
Akkar, s. Crac des Chevaliers
Akrad, s. Crac des Chevaliers
Al-Assad (lake), s. Thaura (al)
Al-Bab, s. Qalaat Najm
Aleppo (Halab), p. 84
Al-Faouar al-Ajib, s. Crac des Chevaliers
Al-Maabad, s. Tartûs
Al-Rafiqa, s. Raqqa
Amrit, s. Tartûs
Anastasiopolis, s. Rasafa
Anderin (al) (Androna), s. Hama
Ansariya (range), s. Latakia
Antaradus, s. Tartûs
Antoninoupolis, s. Apamea
Apamea, p. 96
Apum, s. Damascus
Arab (jabal al-), s. Sûwayda
Aradus, s. Tartûs
Aram, s. Damascus
Arima, s. Safitâ
Armanaz, s. Idlib
Isle of Arwad, s. Tartûs
Arra, s. Maarat ann-Nûmân
Ar-Riha, s. Idlib
Ashâra, s. Deir er-Zor
Auzara, s. Deir ez-Zor
Ayn Dara, s. Qalaat Samaân
Ayn Diwar, s. Qamishli
Ayn el-Fijeh, s. Zabadani
Azaz, s. Qalaat Samaân

■
Bab (Al), s. Qalaat Najm
Balanea, s. Baniyas
Bani Qahtân, s. Latakia
Baniyas, p. 101
Bara (Al), p. 102
Barada (river), s. Zabadani, Damascus
Basit (cape), s. Ras al-Bassit
Bervia, s. Aleppo
Biza, s. Qalb Loza
Blûdân, s. Zabadani
Bokkein (spring), s. Zabadani
Boquée (La), s. Crac des Chevaliers
Bosra, p. 104
Bossora, s. Bosra
Brak (Tall), s. Qamishli
Bûlbûl, s. Qalaat Samaân
Bûsayra, s. Deir ez-Zor

■
Callinicos, s. Raqqa
Canatha, s. Qanawât
Cassius (Mount), s. Ras al-Bassit

Chahba, s. Shahba
Chaîne côtière, s. Latakia
Chastel Rouge, s. Safitâ
Château Blanc, s. Safitâ
Cheikh (Mount), s. Qnaytra
Cheizar, s. Shaizar
Constantia, s. Tartûs
Crac des Chevaliers, p. 108
Croix (La) (Monastery), s. Hama
Cyrrhus, s. Qalaat Samaân

■
Damascus (Dimashq), p. 115
Dâna (al), s. Qalaat Samaân
Maarat ann Nûmân
Darkhush, s. Jisr ash-Shûgheir
Deir ez-Zor, p. 130
Deir Samaân, s. Qalaat Samaân
Delloza, s. Bara (Al)
Dimashq, s. Damascus
Dionysias, s. Sûwayda
Djeblé, s. Jablé
Djeradé, s. Maarat ann-Numan
Doummar, s. Damascus, Zabadani
Doura Europos, p. 132
Draykich, s. Safitâ

■
Ebla, s. Idlib
El-Bara, s. Bara (Al)
El-Inat (Inachos), s. Sûwayda
El-Kefr, s. Bara (Al)'
El-Maghara, s. Bara (Al)
El-Thaura (Tabqa), s. Thaura (Al)
Emesa, s. Homs
Epiphania, s. Hama
Esh Sham, s. Damas
Ezrâa (Zorova), p. 133

■
Fémié, s. Apamea
Fereiloq, s. Ras al-Bassit
Fûrqlos, s. Homs

■
Gabala, s. Jablé
Ghab (region), s. Apamea Jisr ash-Shûghûr, Shaizar

■
Haffé, s. Latakia
Halab, s. Aleppo
Halabiyé, s. Deir ez-Zor
Halaf (Tall), s. Qamishli
Hama (Hamaa), p. 134
Hamman Sheykh Issa, s. Jisr ash Shûghûr
Hamrat (al), s. Hama
Harim, s. Idlib, Jisr ash-Shûghûr, Qalb Loza
Hariri (tall), s. Mari
Hass, s. Bara (Al)
Hassaké, s. Qamishli

Hermon (Mount), s. Qnaytra
Hidleb, s. Idlib
Hiérapolis, s. Qalaat Najm
Homs, p. 142
Hosn (al), s. Crac des Chevaliers
Hosn al Akrad, s. Crac des Chevaliers
Hosn as Sath, s. Crac des Chevaliers
Hosn es Soleiman (Baetocécé), s. Safitâ
Houmayra (al), s. Crac des Chevaliers

■
Idlib, p. 145
Imtane (Mathana), s. Sûwayda
Inat (al), s. Sûwayda

■
Jabar (Qallat), s. Thaura (al)
Jablé, p. 147
Jisr ash-Shûghûr, p. 148

■
Kafra n'Barta, s. Bara (al)
Kafr al-Bara, s. Bara (AL0
Kahf, s. Latakia
Kahf (al), s. Masyaf
Kâmishliye, s. Qâmishli
Kanawât, s. Qanawât
Karropéra, s. Bara (al)
Kassab, s. Latakia, Râs al-Bassit
Kebir (al) (river), s. Crac des Chevaliers
Kefr (al), s. Bara (al)
Kfar Rûma, s. Bara (al)
Khabûr (river), s. Qamishli
Khébir (river), s. Latakia
Khirbet Hass, s. Bara (al)
Kirk Biza, s. Qalb Loza
Krak des Chevaliers, s. Crac
Kuneitra, s. Qnaytra

■
Laodicée, s. Latakia
Latakia (al Ladhiqiya), p. 150
Leuke Akté, s. Latakia
Leucas, s. Baniyas
Liche (La), s. Latakia

■
Maabed (al), s. Tartûs
Maalûlâ, p. 153
Maarat ann-Nûman, p. 156
Maghazel, s. Tartûs
Manbij, s. Qalaat Najm
Marathos, s. Tartûs
Mardikh (tell), s. Idlib, Maarat ann-Nûmân
Margat, s. Marqab
Mari (tall Hariri), p. 157
Marqab (qalaat Marqab), p. 158
Marre, s. Maarat ann-Nûmân
Maskanâ, s. Thaura (al)

Masyaf, p. 160
Mayadin, s. Deir ez-Zor
Meghara (al), s. Bara (al)
Meriane, s. Bara (al)
Mhardé, s. Shaizar
Mheylbé, s. Latakia
Mushrifé, s. Homs

■
Nabheim, s. Latakia, Ras al-Bassit
Nea Trajana Bostra, s. Bosra
Nabi Mend (tell), s. Homs
Nejm, s. Qalaat Najm
Nicephorion, s. Raqqa
Nikertai, s. Apamée
Nobah, s. Qanawât

■
Ollaiqa, s. Masyaf
Oronte (river), s. Hama

■
Palmyra (Tadmor), p. 162
Pella, s. Apamea
Pharnaké, s. Apamea
Philippopolis, s. Shahba

■
Qadash, s. Homs
Qadmûs, s. Masyaf
Qalaat Abou Sofian, s. Bara (al)
Qalaat al Arayma (Arima), s. Safitâ
Qalaat ash Shamamis, s. Hama
Qalaat al Hosn, s. Crac des Chevaliers
Qalaat al-Mudiq, s. Apamea
Qalaat Najm, p. 173
Qalaat Rabâh, s. Deir ez-Zor
Qalaat Salah ad-Din (Saône), p. 175
Qalaat Samaân St. Simon), p. 177
Qalaat Seidjar, s. Shaizar
Qalaat Yahmûr, s. Safitâ

Qalb Loza, p. 180
Qamishli, p. 182
Qanawât, p. 183
Qaratchok, s. Qamishli
Qasr al-Hi al-Gharbi, s. Palmyra
Qasr al-Hir ash-Sharqi, s. Palmyra
Qastal Moâf, s. Latakia, Ras al-Bassit
Qatna, s. Homs
Qattina (lake), s. Homs
Qatura, s. Qalaat Samaân
Qnaytra, p. 184
Qnayé, s. Jisr ash-Shûghûr
Qsar ibn Wardân, s. Hama
Qsaybé, s. Latakia
Qunaïtra, s. Qnaytra
Qûsayr, s. Homs

■
Rabâh (qalaat), s. Deir ez-Zor
Rafiqa (al), s. Raqqa
Rakka, s. Raqqa
Raqqa, p. 185
Rasafa, p. 189
Ras al-Ayn, s. Qamishli
Ras al-Bassit, p. 188
Ras Shamra, s. Ugarit
Rastân, s. Hama
Rebeia, s. Bara (al)
Refadé, s. Qalaat Samaân
Riha (ar), s. Idlib
Rouad (isle), s. Tartûs
Rueyha, s. Maarat ann-Numan

■
Safitâ (Castel Blanc), p. 191
Sahyoun, s. Qalaat Salah ad-Din
Saint-Georges (Monastery), s. Crac des Chevaliers
St. Simon, s. Qalaat Samaân
Salamiyé, s. Hama
Salklard (Salka), s. Sûwayda
Salma, s. Latakia

Salqin, s. Idlib, Qalb Loza, Jisr ash Shûghûr
Samaân, s. Qalaat Samaân
Saône, s. Qalaat Salah ad-Din
Saydnâ ŷa, s. Maalûlâ
Kanotha, s. Qanawât
Serjilla, s. Bara (al)
Sergiopolis, s. Rasafa
Shahba, p. 192
Shaizar, p. 193
Shaka, s. Shahba
Shakar Bazar, s. Qamishli
Shamamis, s. Hama
Shamra (cape), s. Latakia
Sheykh Obed, s. Qalb Loza, Idlib
Sinn (river), s. Baniyas
Slenfé, s. Latakia
Soada, s. Sûwayda
Soukas (tell), s. Jablé
Stalb Antar, s. Hama
Sûwayda, p. 194

■
Tabqa, s. Thaura (al)
Tadmor, s. Palmyra
Takiyé, s. Zabadani
Tartûs, p. 196
Taybet att Turki, s. Hama
Thaura (al), p. 201
Tortosa, s. Tartûs

■
Ugarit (Ras Shamra), p. 202
Upi, s. Damascus

■
Valénie, s. Baniyas

■
Yahmûr, s. Latakia
Yalda, s. Damascus

■
Zabadani, p. 208
Zalabiyé, s. Deir ez-Zor
Zenobia, s. Deir ez-Zor
Zibel, s. Jablé

INDEX 255

syria today

series editor jean hureau
translated by philip parks
photographs by the author
except when otherwise credited

© 1977
éditions j.a.
51, avenue des ternes - 75017 paris
all rights reserved

printed in belgium
printing completed 2nd quarter 1977
legal copy deposited 2nd quarter 1977
publisher's n° 1154/1
ISBN 2-85258-061-6

in the same series

by jean hureau	■	iran today *2nd edition*
	■	tunisia today
	■	egypt today
	■	corsica today
by raymond morineau	■	lebanon today
by mylène rémy	■	senegal today
	■	ivory coast today
	■	ghana today
by jacques-louis delpal	■	paris today
	■	the valley of the loire today
by jacques legros	■	scandinavia today
by siradiou diallo	■	zaire today
by george oor	■	yugoslavia today
by louis doucet	■	the caribbean today
in preparation	■	morocco today